"A thoughtful exploration of the ethics of contemporary education, that provides, on the way, a great deal of fascinating information about the state of education in a range of English-speaking countries around the world today."

Kwame Anthony Appiah

Education and Elitism

Education and Elitism discusses polemical debates around privilege, private schools, elitist universities, equal access to education and underlying notions of fairness. The overarching question that runs through the book is about the future of education worldwide: how can schools and universities tread the tightrope between access and quality?

This book investigates the philosophical positions that characterize elitism and anti-elitism to establish three types: meritocratic, plutocratic and cultural. These types of elitism (and their counterpositions) are used as reference points throughout the book's analysis of successive educational themes. The conclusion leads to suggestions that bridge the worlds of elitism and egalitarianism worldwide. The book covers critical questions related to the sociology and philosophy of education with a particular focus on contemporary disruptors to education such as the COVID-19 pandemic and protest movements for social justice.

With an attempt to offer readers an objective overview, this book will be an excellent compendium for students, academics and researchers of the sociology of education, education policy and comparative education. It will also be of interest to school leaders, university provosts and professionals working in curriculum design.

Conrad Hughes is Campus and Secondary Principal at the International School of Geneva, La Grande Boissière, Switzerland. He is also a member of the advisory board for the University of the People and Research Assistant at the University of Geneva's department of psychology and education.

Education and Elitism

Challenges and Opportunities

Conrad Hughes

Routledge
Taylor & Francis Group

LONDON AND NEW YORK

First published 2021
by Routledge
2 Park Square, Milton Park, Abingdon, Oxon OX14 4RN

and by Routledge
52 Vanderbilt Avenue, New York, NY 10017

Routledge is an imprint of the Taylor & Francis Group, an informa business

© 2021 Conrad Hughes

British Library Cataloguing-in-Publication Data
A catalogue record for this book is available from the British Library

Library of Congress Cataloging-in-Publication Data
A catalog record has been requested for this book

ISBN: 978-0-367-52786-0 (hbk)
ISBN: 978-0-367-52788-4 (pbk)
ISBN: 978-1-003-05837-3 (ebk)

Typeset in Bembo
by Taylor & Francis Books

This book is dedicated to my brother Octavius Colquhoun

Contents

Preface

Educational structures were created across the globe to provide instruction to a minority. For centuries this infrastructure remained intact, keeping the majority of human beings illiterate and ignorant of the powerful knowledge that remained in the hands of the clerisy.

With successive historical reforms from the Renaissance through to the 20th century, formal education became compulsory: it was now a right for everyone. Over time, universities became massified and pressure was put on institutions to function fully despite unwieldy numbers. Developments in technology have made information more accessible to the masses too, steadily changing the dynamics and purpose of schools and universities.

The goal of an education is to create individual, collective and public good through the transmission of knowledge, the nurturing of competences and the shaping of dispositions. In the best of all worlds, an education of quality should be available to all.

However, massifying education so that everyone has access to it makes it more difficult to ensure that quality is sustained. This leads to heated debates on what sort of educational model is best. Should schools and universities be selective or open access, and upon what criteria should entry be based?

This study explores the debate by investigating several themes across the globe, outlining the arguments for and against meritocratic, plutocratic and cultural elitism. It culminates in six principles that should be reinforced to find a balanced solution.

I would like to thank the following people for their help with proofing the text of this book: Anders Elf, Jeff Thompson, Paul Ellis, Veronica Newington, Alejandro Rodriguez-Giovo, Laura Italici, Maura Wernz, Michael Kewley, Sanjukta Sharma, Nick Hannell, Angie Kretzmeier and Alison Murray.

Part I

The historical background

Chapter 1

Introduction to education and elitism

Zach and Anthony

The sound of the cock crowing is a strangled, painful call. The sky is a mottled grey, a smoky whisper of the powerful heat that will pound down on the earth in the next 30 minutes. Zach gets to his feet quickly and scrubs his lean body with a bucket of water fetched from the well. For breakfast, a tapioca gruel. He slings his school satchel containing an exercise book over his back and makes his way out of the compound on to the red earth of the path he will follow for seven kilometres to get to school. His shoes are too small by now, scuffed and marked with holes, but his gait is quick and lively. The sun begins to reach out its rosy fingers beyond the palm fronds up into the vast expanse and the earth heats up quickly. Zach lives in Burkina Faso, he is 13 years old. Millions of children like him walk to school every day and they are the lucky ones, for roughly a quarter of a billion children like Zach still do not attend school at all. For them, each day is dedicated to sweeping, washing, ploughing the earth or, if living in the sprawling cities, making ends meet by any means possible, including scouring rubbish heaps for sustenance. Going to school is a risk in many parts of the country: extremist groups have threatened those who attend school with terrible punishments including death.

Two hours later, Zach arrives at his school. He rushes to the classroom where 80 children wait patiently for their teacher, Mama Estelle. When she arrives, they all stand up and greet her in unison: "good morning Mrs Estelle". "Good morning children", their teacher chirps. Zach is squeezed between his classmates on a bench. He pulls out his pen and copies the date off the board.

Around the same time, Anthony's android phone wakes him up to his favourite song. He stretches lazily in the warmth of his eiderdown, slowly gets out of bed and makes his way to a hot shower. He shampoos his hair peacefully and lathers his body with sweetly scented shower gel. He packs his MacBook in his bag and goes downstairs to breakfast, a buffet of exotic fruits including papaya flown to Switzerland from a farm not far from Zach's compound, scrambled eggs and bacon, and freshly baked pastries. Anthony, who is 13, washes this down with a cup of delicious hot chocolate. A portion of the

150,000 Swiss francs per annum school fees paid by his father, a Russian oil merchant, is dedicated to an award-winning menu devised by a French chef who used to hold a Michelin star. Classes are held in a chalet a few minutes from the dining hall. As Anthony walks to class he gazes at the spectacular mountain range in the distance and takes the opportunity to send a selfie of himself to his cousin, who is at an expensive independent school in London.

When he gets to his classroom, the teacher, Angie, is playing some soft pop music in the background. She smiles warmly at her class of 15 students and asks them all to sit comfortably, to close their eyes. She turns off the music and asks them to slowly breathe in with their noses, out with their mouths, in with their noses, out with their mouths. "Concentrate on each sound you can hear, concentrate on what you are feeling right here and now. When you are ready, come back". The children slowly open their eyes and when everyone is ready, Angie asks them to get into pairs and come up with "headlines" on what they learnt yesterday.

A divided world

We are living through a period of history where the division between rich and poor has never been greater (Picketty, 2013). The world's nine richest billionaires own more combined wealth than the four billion poorest people on the planet (Jacobs, 2017). The situation is not merely one of wealth inequality but more specifically, as Picketty has shown, one where the return on capital exceeds the rate of economic growth. In other words, individuals and groups owning major assets are becoming richer and richer. As this happens, the gap between capital wealth, that is to say asset ownership, and wealth gained through income, increases. This situation, which resembles that of the 1700s, is causing a dramatic gulf between the extremely rich and the increasingly pauperised middle and working classes throughout the world.

Access to opportunities, fair and open rules of the game, and basic principles of equal opportunity are waning every day as the world becomes more divided, favouring inherited wealth, those who have the means to trade stocks, to take risks and enjoy yield. Those wishing to become wealthy from a zero base, by climbing up the social ladder through education, hard work and performance, stand less of a chance than they did in the interwar period or just after the Second World War, which were periods of comparative economic growth. On average, Generation Z and probably their children too will earn less than their parents and will find it more difficult to access wealth than their parents ever did.

The COVID-19 pandemic has exacerbated this gulf, leaving many further behind while pushing many further ahead.

As this situation of widening financial inequality becomes more and more exacerbated, the world of the financial elite becomes more and more difficult to enter, starting with education: elite private schools are becoming less accessible while top-ranking universities are more and more expensive and difficult to enter.

It is true that there are opportunities to break out of this gridlock: some of the most expensive US colleges offer full scholarships. In fact, Harvard has made a sustained effort over recent years to diversify its student body ethnically and socioeconomically to the point where some might argue that it is more difficult to get in with privileged credentials than without (Harvard, 2020), whereas 2020 statistics showed that, for the first time, "more than 69% of undergraduate offers to study at Oxford University have been made to pupils attending state schools" (Oxford, 2020). However, what appears as accelerated access that will bring students to new and transformative socioeconomic heights is still not the overall tendency. In general, the poorest students still struggle to receive the support they need to complete university without incurring huge debts (Mansfield, 2019; Kurzweil & Wyner, 2020). Often, aid recipients come from educated, middle-class backgrounds.

There is a sprinkling of countries where, according to the World Economic Forum, the inclusive development index shows that access to high-quality education and subsequent employment opportunities is still high (Norway, Iceland, Denmark and Finland, for example) (Brezis, 2018); in other words, the pathway of national education is a near guarantee to access to a decent living for the quasi-totality of the citizens of these countries. However, Nordic countries boasting high development indices are already wealthy and therefore benefit from a virtuous cycle: wealth begets wealth. Furthermore, these are the exceptions, not the rule.

In just about every other country in the world, the reality is a dual carriageway system with expensive private schooling leading to top-ranking (often private) universities and high-ranking jobs on the one hand while, on the other, an increasingly dysfunctional, saturated, and over-populated national education system leads to state universities with high attrition rates and, eventually, little opportunity of access to wealth.

As divisions deepen, increasingly heated and polarised debates are taking place about private schools in the UK, universities in South Africa and top-tier colleges in the United States. Those promoting access criticise the selective ivory tower: some public figures are pulling the alarm bell on what they consider to be unfair privilege. For example, in the UK, the Labour Party has made polemical statements about banning private schools, scandals have erupted over corruption and privileged access to top-tier colleges in the United States, and in a number of countries, notably South Africa, students are up in arms about the decolonising of university curricula and leadership. These idealistic voices singing social justice wish to see a flattened playing field.

On the other side of the fence, pragmatists and scholars bemoan a coarsening and dumbing down of public discussion, pointing out that populism and irresponsible short-sightedness might destroy some of the most precious and fragile cultural assets belonging to humanity—the vanguards of sacred principles such as quality, meritocracy and intellectual freedom. As tends to happen in heated debate, neither position is totally free of self-interest, ideology, over-generalisation of the opposing field's position and general hyperbole.

This study aims to investigate the theme of education and elitism with as much objectivity as possible, always evoking the extremes, always pointing out their biases and assumptions but also seeking common ground and solutions.

What is elitism?

At the broadest level, elitism refers to the sociological practice whereby a group considers itself and/or is considered by others as separate from the mainstream and, in some way, superior.

This notion can be traced back to numerous societal structures such as aristocracy, oligarchy, meritocracy, plutocracy and countless variations of social hierarchy that are listed in this chapter's lexical field of elitism.

The etymology of elite is the Latin *éligere*, to elect, which is at the root of the word eligible. The *Collins English Dictionary* defines the word elite as "the most powerful, rich, gifted or educated members of a group", whereas elitism is "the belief that society should be governed" by such a group (Butterfield, 2003, p. 533).

Differences between "elitism" and "elite"

Technically speaking, "elite" merely describes the group considered to be superior to others. "Elitist" or "elitism", on the other hand, suggest a social programme that aims to uphold an elite or venerates the notion of the elite. One might describe a social configuration as elite without being elitist.

The term "elite" is fairly strong and suggests an ideological positioning either for or against the notion: it is unlikely that someone describing the "best" test scores or top performers in a domain will describe that group as "elite" without critical or supportive undertones.

In 2010, the academic James Joyner attempted to differentiate between elite and elitist by suggesting, in a blog entitled "Elites and Elitists: One Can Be an Elite and Not Be Elitist and Vice Versa", that the former is "a group or class of persons or a member of such a group or class, enjoying superior intellectual, social, or economic status", whereas the latter is "[t]he belief that certain persons or members of certain classes or groups deserve favored treatment by virtue of their perceived superiority, as in intellect, social status, or financial resources". In other words, "the elite" is a select, often ruling class of individuals, whereas "elitism" is the belief that certain individuals or groups deserve higher ranking than others. Trying to dissociate the two is not altogether straightforward as is made clear by Joyner when he goes on to state:

> I'm situationally elitist. I don't believe in aristocracy or inherited status, nor do I believe that those lucky enough to be born smarter or even those

who have become more wealthy through dint of their own achievement are better than those less fortunate. But I do think that people with superior intellect and achievement ought to, say, sit on the Supreme Court or occupy the vice presidency.

(Joyner, 2010)

From a strictly egalitarianist viewpoint, as soon as one starts to describe groups as "elite", one is in an elitist mode of thinking. Social and educational discourses centred on equity and equality are unlikely to use the term because it is loaded.

Pro-elitism

Given the nature of elitism as a sociological construct and the fact that it can be considered as anti-egalitarian and therefore politically incorrect, it is not altogether straightforward to find overt proponents of it. Many will speak of "elite" institutions and "the elite" of any given field but few will say "I am an elitist". Those who do will fall into a number of categories: political elitists, in the vein of the Italian pragmatist school who favour strong, executive leadership; cultural elitists, who believe in "high culture" that is superior to "mass culture"; and meritocratic educational elitists who are against multiple intelligence theory (perceived as a dumbing down) and tend to favour a simplified theory of intelligence that places some above others in a mean distribution curve. One might include in this category defenders of gifted education programmes such as James Delisle who says, somewhat provocatively:

> [I]f being an elitist means that I still believe in a distinct quality of giftedness that is the domain of the few, not the many; and if being an elitist means that I believe gifted individuals need to be understood as the complex intellectual and emotional beings that they are; and if being an elitist means that I will advocate for a small percentage of children to receive a level of academic rigor and emotional understanding that transcends the typical, then an elitist I shall be. It is a badge I will wear proudly.
>
> (Delisle, 2001)

Plutocratic elitism, built on preserving access to wealth for privileged in-groups, and the rights and privileges of the wealthy, can be associated with neoliberal political views such as those espoused in the current politico-economic model in the United States.

Strongly pro-elitist books that have been published in recent years include the anti-populist treatises *In Defence of Elitism* (Henry, 1995) and *In Defense of Elitism: Why I'm Better Than You and You are Better Than Someone Who Didn't Buy This Book* (Stein, 2019), which both make philosophical arguments for general hierarchical elitism in social spheres. The increasingly popular psychologist and University of Toronto professor Jordan Peterson argues that social hierarchy runs deep into the animal kingdom and he offers a deterministic, scientific defence of elitism in his 2018 book *12 Rules for Life: An Antidote for Chaos* in which he opposes a just world hypothesis with what he describes as neo-Marxist postmodernism.

Other, less strident pleas for elitism include *Critical Elitism: Deliberation, Democracy, and the Problem of Expertise* (Moore, 2017), a text that argues that society's need for technical skills requires a type of elitism and Nicholas Tate's *The Conservative Case for Education: Against the Current* (2017), which explores cultural elitism through the lens of thinkers such as TS Eliot, Michael Oakshott, Hannah Arendt, and ED Hirsh.

What pro-elitists have in common runs back to Platonic thought and can be situated, roughly speaking, in two streams: on the one hand, the notion that society should be run in a hierarchical manner and on the other, the notion that a fair and honest society should reward talent, gifts, and excellence.

Chapter 2 of this study investigates schools of elitist thinking in much more detail so as to categorise three fundamental schools of thought: meritocratic, plutocratic and cultural.

Anti-elitism

Anti-elitist positions tend to be far more vocal and easier to identify. There is a moral certitude in the voice that speaks for equality over exclusivity that makes the anti-elitist position fairly proud and strident. Post-Enlightenment doctrines of egalitarianism and subsequent reforms to social, political and educational structures to make them more inclusive have all been anti-elitist in some way, shape or form.

It is possible to group in the anti-elitist category as associated with mainstream schools of democracy and universalism, more radical schools of feminism and anti-racism and philosophies dedicated to social transformation such as socialism and, at the summit of anti-elitism, at least in theory, Marxism, with its call for a classless society.

Holbrook (1995) suggests that from the 1990s, in American academia, elitism was subsumed by postmodernism, political correctness, and popular culture: three relativistic and egalitarianist forces that have turned the tide of previously unabashed elitist thinking quite forcibly.

The work done by French poststructuralists from the end of the Second World War, deconstructing social institutions, making visible covert systems of power and control, and relativising rational discourses as culturally specific positions, opened the pathway for much contemporary thought about elitism, namely that it is a self-interested, self-protecting and largely political construct that can be subverted.

Books that look at elitist educational systems and institutions specifically, and most critically, include *Cracks in the Ivory Tower: The Moral Mess of Higher Education* (Brennan & Magness, 2019), *In the Basement of the Ivory Tower: The Truth About*

College (Professor X, 2012) and *Inside the Ivory Tower: Narratives of Women of Colour Surviving and Thriving in British Academia* (Gabriel & Tate, 2017). Books that are highly critical of public schools in Britain include *Stiff Upper Lip: Secrets, Crimes and the Schooling of a Ruling Class* (Renton, 2017) and *Engines of Privilege* (Green & Kynaston, 2019).

There are numerous articles in the press on quarrels about independent schools in the UK, Ivy League colleges in the USA, and what the future of these should be. Many of them will inform the book. More scholarly examples tend to be in the field of sociology, for example: "Élitisme et éducation: lecture critique des thèses de Bourdieu à l'aide de la pensée de Jürgen Habermas" (Robichaud & Crevier, 2016) and "Cultural Complicities: Elitism, Heteronormativity and Violence in the Education Marketplace" (Saltmarsh, 2007).

Essentially, anti-elitists reproach elitism with what is perceived to be privilege, unfairness, and social stratification.

Chapter 2 of this study looks at anti-elitist schools historically to identify three counterpoints to elitism, namely egalitarianism, Marxism and critical theory including postcolonialism.

Essential terms

It may be useful to give brief working definitions for a number of terms that will be operational throughout the book. These terms, which are highly charged, politicised and constantly used for different purposes, are often used in educational discourses, so working definitions will be useful as the book's argument unfolds.

Access: this is a commonly used term, with positive connotations, that is used to describe the extent to which areas of human development such as education, employment, wealth and wellbeing are made available to all. Access can be restricted or open and is commonly used in phrases such as "access to education", "open-access" or, when something is out of reach, "inaccessible". The idea of access is useful for the core focus of this book as any discussion around education and elitism describes levels of access to course offerings and qualifications.

Egalitarianism: this is the belief that all human beings are of equal value and, therefore, should somehow be subject to equal standards. There are different types of egalitarianism: for example, the English philosopher John Locke, who greatly influenced the English Bill of Rights (and the subsequent American Declaration of Independence), a foundation for what would become hundreds of years later the 1948 United Nations Universal Declaration of Human Rights, believed that human beings should hold equal "natural moral rights" (Locke, 1690; Scanlon, 1998). This idea has influenced much contemporary thinking on the right to happiness, the right to an education, the right to freedom of expression, and so on. A different type of egalitarianism is the notion of "equal opportunity", meaning that employment opportunities and loans for investment purposes should be open to all candidates and not just a select few. For more on the theory of equal opportunity, see Rawls, 2001. The notion of egalitarianism, like access, is helpful for this book as it discusses United Nations-related prerogatives such as Sustainable Development Goal 4 (quality education for all) that drive much contemporary education policy and highlight some of the complexities of elitism in education which, at least at first view, stand in contradiction to the idea of egalitarianism.

Equality and *equity*: these terms are often used to describe different approaches to social justice. An important distinction needs to be made between them. Equality implies the same conditions for everybody, which will not necessarily allow for equal chances, whereas equity means adapted conditions are deliberately adapted to address handicaps and to ensure that all constituents have chances that are as equal as possible. Equity implies what is sometimes called positive discrimination or affirmative action, which is contested as it is complex and can be perceived as unfair (McCartney, 2008).

Exclusivity: the term "exclusive", which has positive connotations, is more likely to be used by pro-elitists to describe selective or privileged environments with strict admissions criteria such as special clubs and societies. Although the terms literally means to exclude rather than to include and plays on lack of access, it is used as a synonym of quality and excellence. Another term that is used to denote this idea is "prestige", meaning excellent and of high status (from the Latin *praestigiae*, meaning complex tricks such as juggling, the idea being that an exclusive few can do it).

Ivory tower: this term originates from the Bible (for example, Song of Solomon, 7:4) to describe religious sanctity. However, in contemporary usage it is a negative image used to describe highly selective institutions that are seen, essentially by anti-elitists, as disconnected from reality, standing high above the grassroots ("tower") and composed of precious, scarce material ("ivory"). The term is used to describe universities and has been developed in the critical writings of Brennan and Magness (2019), who look at top-ranking universities in the United States, the anonymous Professor X (2012) and Gabriel and Tate (2017) who critique UK universities. These positions on the so-called ivory tower point out abuse of power, inner circles of power, lack of transparency, and unfairness and will be evoked in the book's analysis of elitism and universities in Chapter 7.

Meritocracy: this term describes selective systems where achievers (usually in the academic domain), such as gifted individuals and those who distinguish themselves on merit, are rewarded with placement in an institution or by gaining access to a station in life. Meritocracy has positive connotations and will be used to describe procedures that are generally seen as virtuous and fair. Examples of meritocratic systems are bursaries and scholarships.

Plutocracy: this describes the rule (*kratos* = power) of the wealthy (*Ploutos* = wealthy) and can be opposed to other systems of leadership such as timocracy (rule of the property owners), aristocracy (rule by the naturally endowed), democracy, (rule of the people) and autocracy (rule of the one—in the sense of a single-party state). Plato famously organised these different leadership paradigms in a chronology that essentially leads from aristocracy to tyranny (Plato, 2000). Plutocracy is a word with negative connotations and is more likely to be used by anti-elitists than pro-elitists. It is useful for an analysis of education and elitism since, as the book will show, on the one hand, the power of wealth and wealthy individuals (and groups) has an effect on school composition and quality and, on the other, top-ranking universities, particularly in the United States, tend to be extremely expensive and symbolise, therefore, a plutocratic system. As earlier sections of this chapter have shown, a number of scholars in elite theory who have described social organisation, even in countries advocating equal opportunity, are actually plutocratic (Chomsky, 2016, p. 61).

Populism: this term experiences a mixed reception as its associations are complex but on the whole it has come to take on negative connotations and is more likely to be used by pro-elitists to describe politics involved with the galvanising of popular, grassroots or (to view the phenomenon disparagingly), vulgar and groupthink dominated strands of society. Contemporary pro-elitist discourses in the United States (Frank, 2020) often relate populism to a political movement whereby the masses are easily manipulated by cynical leaders who play on unrealistic promises, exaggerated xenophobic fears and dumbed-down sound bites. This has been the criticism of Donald Trump's leadership and the rise of the far right in Europe. Although the term is not often used in discussions on education, it will be useful for this book's purpose since much elitist discourse, which infiltrates and affects educational policy decisions, relies on anti-populism, while some of the more refined objectives of an education, such as discernment and critical thinking, are often opposed to populist thinking, which is seen as oversimplified (Venizelos, 2019).

Privilege: this term denotes an advantage that a person or group is given over others. Associated with the term "entitlement", privilege has come to take on negative connotations, suggesting that these advantages, often social or economic, are unfair and are experienced as givens on an uneven playing field. It is a word that will be used by anti-elitists more than by pro-elitists to describe individuals and groups accessing fast-track social opportunity, often through schooling and employment. Privilege has gained strong currency in the popular form of "white privilege" to describe the accelerated opportunities and access to wealth that white people have enjoyed over non-white people from the colonial period through to the present day. The term has been appropriated to a large extent by critical race theorists such as McIntosh (1998, 2009); Carr (2017) and Oluo (2018). In this book, I will use the term "privilege" in its more general meaning of "advantage", be that economic, social, racial or other.

Scarcity principle: this is a term commonly used in the social sciences, particularly psychology and economics, to explain how humans tend to place value on commodities that are, or are perceived to be, rare. When something is rare or scarce, its value goes up because there is less of it and the need to possess it becomes more acute. When a commodity is exhausted (for example, if a school is full or there are no more places at a university), its value tends to accrue significantly. This particular dimension of scarcity is called "social proof" (Cialdini, 1993). Scarcity is an example of cognitive bias. Although scarcity is less referenced today than it was in the 1980s and 1990s, it is a useful concept to use when analysing the education market, which plays on the psychology of human perception very strongly. A major reference in studies on the scarcity principle is Mittone and Savadori (2005).

Selectivity: this is an important term in education as it describes the admissions policy of schools or educational institutions that accept certain students based on established criteria. Most selective schools admit students on the criterion of academic strength, based on results in admissions tests. "Selective" schools can be opposed to "non-selective" schools (such as comprehensive schools) which admit students irrespective of academic performance. Interestingly, a number of "non-selective" schools are private and although they describe themselves as open access, their school fees mean that, de facto, they are financially selective. Theory on selective schools can be found in work by Marsh and Hau (2003), Clark (2010) and Smith-Woolley et al. (2018).

Social mobility: this term describes a process whereby a "socially mobile" class is able to access wealth and opportunity and to climb the so-called social ladder. Social mobility was a popular term in the 1980s and 1990s to describe recently formed middle-class groups that were forming across the United States and other parts of the world with the creation of wealth and opportunity. The idea in this construct is that groups should be able to "move" from one station to the other and, essentially, gain capital. The term is useful for a discussion on education and elitism as one of the first expressions of a socially mobile group is to enrol children in a "good" school (which, in some countries and circumstances, means an expensive, selective, private school, although a highly disruptive social climate like the one created by the COVID-19 pandemic is blurring that dynamic).

Stratification: this is a Marxist idea that essentially describes the process whereby different classes are separated from one another in layers or strata, therefore the opposite of social mobility. Class stratification occurs when those at the bottom of the social pyramid are unable to integrate the next income bracket and the lower-middle class is unable to join the ranks, experiences, and privileges of the upper class, and so on. Barriers to social mobility that intensify stratification include the specialisation of labour (for example, certain qualifications or technical skills are needed to access a certain income bracket) and less formal phenomena such as favouritism, prejudice, and cronyism. Picketty's analysis of wealth disparity (Picketty, 2013) suggests that class stratification is a factor of the 21st-century's economic landscape. This notion is important in a discussion on education and elitism since, as subsequent chapters will show, some of the world's most elite educational establishments charge admission fees that make them inaccessible to substantial sections of society, keeping the value added of an elite education confined to the class that can afford entry or that already has enough social capital to access this higher, self-perpetuating circle.

Top-tier: a term that refers to the top-ranking universities according to internationally recognised ranking schemes such as QS World University Rankings. Top-tier is most often used with respect to US universities and is the American equivalent of "Oxbridge", referring to the Universities of Oxford and Cambridge.

A comprehensive analysis

It is not possible to discuss the construct of elitism and even less its relationship with education without intertwining into that analysis some reflection on economics and technology.

Economic superstructures determine degrees and styles of elitism: countries with high taxation, low unemployment and strong social support systems, such as the Nordic and Swiss models, tend to have relatively flat social and educative hierarchies: there is less social judgement of the rank and station of schools or universities attended. Countries operating in neoliberal economies with little social support, such as the United States and India, on the other hand, tend to have steep social and educative hierarchies: much importance is attached to the college one attended and the degree obtained.

This has been coloured by developments in technology through time: as different skills become necessary in the workplace, higher status school courses, universities and degrees reflect this. As such, STEM subjects are often seen as higher status in schools (Billimoria, 2020), whereas STEM university courses that lead to high remuneration, such as engineering and medicine, tend to be oversubscribed and rank in the top tier. Paradoxically, the correlation between technology and elitism is not always positive but can be negative, as shown in the penetrating analysis of Basil Bernstein who pointed out that one of the functions of a socially elitist education is to distance itself from practical, technical skills and create an ingroup tied by references to esoteric and codified knowledge which exists for its own sake and not for any practical purpose (see Chapter 7).

The English model, which came into force in the 19th century as industrial magnates started to compete with landed aristocrats in a show of wealth and power, created a highly stratified system running through schools (state, grammar, public) and universities (polytechnics, "red brick", Oxbridge). Due to the sphere of influence the United Kingdom created through colonisation, this stratified model has remained a strong influence on school and university systems in the United States, Australia, India, and South Africa. As this model, based on social judgement of the school, university, course and even college or house one attended, becomes globalised and is opened to millions of learners across the globe, it becomes difficult to decelerate or modify. With increased instability caused by highly disruptive forces such as pandemics and environmental disasters, reforming such a system seems difficult to envisage.

Today, globalisation, industry 4.0 (the internet of things and the overhaul of many systems by high-performing algorithms), the extreme and increasing wealth gap, and increasing social tensions across the world, all mean that it is important to understand not only the putative aims of education as isolated normative ethics (education for a more sustainable world, less poverty, greater individual, collective and public good) but to grapple with the actual sociopolitical mechanics of education in the light of the pressures of context (the effects of highly selective versus open admissions schooling, the cost of education, the perception of education and its status, and the practical utility of an education).

Above all, it is the focus and aim of this study to examine the extent to which education plays a socially conservative or transformative role; in other words, the ways in which schooling and university reinforce class structure and politico-economic power dynamics, or change such structures and dynamics. To discuss education and elitism is to discuss the way that the population of the world has structured itself and what direction it is taking.

References

Billimoria, J. (2020). Is STEM education all it's cracked up to be? *World Economic Forum.* www.weforum.org/agenda/2017/05/is-stem-education-all-it-s-cracked-up-to-be/.

Brennan, J., & Magness, P. (2019). *Cracks in the Ivory Tower: The Moral Mess of Higher Education.* Oxford: Oxford University Press.

Brezis, S. (2018). Elitism in higher education and inequality: Why are the Nordic countries so special? *Intereconomics,* August.

Butterfield, J. (ed.) (2003). *Collins English Dictionary.* Glasgow: HarperCollins.

Carr, P.R. (2017). Whiteness and White Privilege: Problematizing Race and Racism in a "Color-blind" World and in Education. In K. Fereidooni & M. El (eds.) *Rassismuskritik und Widerstandsformen.* Wiesbaden: Springer. https://doi.org/10.1007/978-3-658-14721-1_52.

Chomsky, N. (2016). *Who Rules the World?* New York: Henry Holt & Company.

Cialdini, R. (1993). *Influence.* 3rd ed. New York: HarperCollins.

Clark, D. (2010). Selective schools and academic achievement. *The B.E. Journal of Economic Analysis & Policy,* 10(1), 1–40.

Delisle, J. (2001). In praise of elitism. *Gifted Child Today,* 24(1), 14–15. www.davidsongifted.org/search-database/entry/a10137.

Frank, T. (2020). *The People, No: A Brief History of Anti-Populism.* New York: Metropolitan Books.

Gabriel, D., & Tate, S.A. (2017). *Inside the Ivory Tower: Narratives of Women of Colour Surviving and Thriving in British Academia.* London: UCL Institute of Education Press.

Green, F., & Kynaston, D. (2019). *Engines of Privilege: Britain's Private School Problem.* London: Bloomsbury.

Harvard University (2020). *Admissions Statistics.* https://college.harvard.edu/admissions/admissions-statistics.

Henry, W.A., III (1995). *In Defence of Elitism.* New York: Anchor Books.

Holbrook, M.B. (1995). The three faces of elitism: Postmodernism, political correctness, and popular culture. *Journal of Macromarketing*, 15(2), 128–165. https://doi.org/10.1177/027614679501500209.

Jacobs, S. (2017). Just nine of the world's richest people have more combined wealth than the poorest four billion. *The Independent.* www.independent.co.uk/news/world/richestbillionairescombinedwealthjeffbezosbillgateswarrenbuffettmarkzuckerbergcarlos slimwealth-a8163621.html.

Joyner, J. (2010). Elites and elitists: One can be an elite and not be elitist and vice versa. *Outside the Beltway.* www.outsidethebeltway.com/elites-and-elitists/.

Kurzweil, M., & Wyner, J. (2020). Rich kids are eating up the financial aid pot. *New York Times.* www.nytimes.com/2020/06/16/opinion/coronavirus-college-rich-kids.html.

Locke, J. (1690/1980). *Second Treatise of Government*, ed. C.B. MacPherson. Indianapolis: Hackett.

McCartney, J. (2008). It's not positive, it's just discrimination. *The Telegraph.* www.telegraph.co.uk/comment/columnists/jennymccartney/3559968/Its-not-positive-its-just-di scrimination.html.

McIntosh, P. (1998). White Privilege, Color and Crime: A Personal Account. In C.R. Mann, & M. Zatz (eds.) *Images of Color, Images of Crime.* Los Angeles: Roxbury Publishing Company, pp. 207–216.

McIntosh, P. (2009). *White Privilege: An Account to Spend.* Saint Paul, MN: Saint Paul Foundation.

Mansfield, S. (2019). Oxford scholarships should be for the poorest, not just the brightest. *The Guardian.* www.theguardian.com/education/2019/jan/22/oxford-scholarships-should-be-for-the-poorest-not-just-the-brightest.

Marsh, H.W., & Hau, K.-T. (2003). Big-fish-little-pond effect on academic self-concept: A cross-cultural (26-country) test of the negative effects of academically selective schools. *American Psychologist*, 58(5), 364–376. https://doi.org/10.1037/0003-066X.58.5.364.

Mittone, L., & Savadori, L. (2005). "The Scarcity Bias", CEEL Working Papers 0505, Cognitive and Experimental Economics Laboratory, Department of Economics, University of Trento, Italy.

Moore, A. (2017). *Critical Elitism: Deliberation, Democracy, and the Problem of Expertise.* Cambridge: Cambridge University Press.

Oluo, I. (2018). *So You Want to Talk About Race.* New York: Seal Press.

Oxford University (2020). *Oxford student offers show significant state school increase.* www.ox.ac.uk/news/2020-01-15-oxford-student-offers-show-significant-state-school-increase.

Peterson, J. (2018). *12 Rules for Life: An Antidote to Chaos.* New York: Random House.

Picketty, T. (2013). *Capital in the 21st Century.* Cambridge, MA: Harvard University Press.

Plato (2000). *The Republic*, trans T. Griffith. Cambridge: Cambridge University Press.

Professor X (2012). *In the Basement of the Ivory Tower: The Truth About College.* London: Penguin Books.

Rawls, J. (2001). *Justice as Fairness: A Restatement.* Cambridge, MA: Harvard University Press.

Renton, A. (2017). *Stiff Upper Lip: Secrets, Crimes and the Schooling of a Ruling Class.* London: Hachette.

Robichaud, A., & Crevier, J. (2016). Élitisme et éducation: lecture critique des thèses de Bourdieu à l'aide de la pensée de Jürgen Habermas. *Le philosophoire*, 46(2), 37–58. www.cairn.info/revue-le-philosophoire-2016-2-page-37.htm.

Saltmarsh, S. (2007). Cultural complicities: Elitism, heteronormativity and violence in the education marketplace, *International Journal of Qualitative Studies in Education*, 20(3), 335–354. doi:doi:10.1080/09518390701281934.

Scanlon, T.M. (1998). *What Do We Owe to One Another?*Cambridge, MA: Harvard University Press.

Smith-Woolley E., Pingault J.B., Selzam, S., et al. (2018). Differences in exam performance between pupils attending selective and non-selective schools mirror the genetic differences between them. *NPJ Sci Learn*, 3(3). doi:doi:10.1038/s41539-018-0019-8.

Stein, J. (2019). *In Defense of Elitism: Why I'm Better Than You and You Are Better Than Someone Who Didn't Buy This Book*. New York: Grand Central Books.

Tate, N. (2017). *The Conservative Case for Education: Against the Current*. Oxford: Routledge.

Venizelos, G. (2019). The elitism of the "anti-populists". *Jacobin*. https://jacobinmag.com/2019/09/the-elitism-of-the-anti-populists.

Chapter 2

Philosophies of elitism and anti-elitism

Zach and Anthony

Zach's classroom is dark, the neon light works one time out of ten, the blackboard is badly damaged and it is difficult to read Mama Estelle's handwriting. There is nothing on the brick walls. Outside the open window, men are offloading a truck, slamming sacks and pieces of corrugated iron onto the ground, making a deafening noise that interjects the sound of the children chanting in unison "two times two is four, two times three is six, two times four is eight". The corrugated iron is to fix the roof of the classroom that has several holes in it. During the rainy season, the rain drums against the roof in a powerful roar that drowns out Mama Estelle's strident voice totally.

Anthony's classroom is decorated with furniture that gives it a natural, earthy feel. "We are a sustainable community", it says on a collective artwork. On one wall there hangs a framed poster depicting each of the United Nations Sustainable Development Goals, on another there are 15 small framed paintings, each one chosen by a student to represent a core concept. They have chosen sophisticated works by Picasso, Renoir, Basquiat and Keith Haring. Angie explains: "The kids chose a different painting for each unit of inquiry. It anchors their thinking and allows them to transfer some of their learning to works of art, and it teaches them some art history, which is kind of cool!" The classroom is laid out in such a way that children are sitting in small groups. Many classes take place elsewhere: in the co-lab enjoying robotics, virtual reality, 3D printing and laser cutting with their young dashing IT coordinator Chad, or in the arts centre where the students spend time doing drama and music. The headmaster, Dr Tristan Jackson, explains that the arts are important: "We are looking to stimulate creativity, divergent thinking, confidence and all those marvellous transferrable skills that children will need in an unknown, exciting future".

Mama Estelle loses her temper with the children. They are off-task and are giggling among themselves. She makes the guilty culprits, about ten children sitting crammed together on half a bench, stand up and she tells them off: "You must be disciplined! You must listen to your teacher!" "Yes, Mama

Estelle, we are sorry", the children chant in unison. "Discipline is everybody's business", Estelle says, "it's important for our children to understand the value of respect and hard work. Some of these children come from very poor households and education is a chance they have to break out of that situation that is holding them back. Education can lead them to a different future to the one that their parents have as small-scale subsistence farmers or migrant work-ers". Estelle has been teaching for 25 years; she earns a salary of US $250 per month. Most of that money goes towards paying five of her eight children's uni-versity education. Once she has got through the month, there is not much left and there's no real prospect of a pension scheme either. Estelle has state qualifications. She holds a Master's degree in Education from the University of Dakar where she lived as a young woman. She wrote her thesis on the importance of civil education in teaching and learning. That was during the honeymoon of independence, when there was a dream of education transforming future generations for the future of Africa. Estelle has leadership qualities but in order to become a director in this school, you need to be able to pay.

Anthony's class is doing physical education. They play dodge ball in a state of the art gym. Angie can see into the gym from the stylish glass walls above it where she sits. "Most of our classes use constructivist pedagogy", Angie says, smiling over a cup of coffee, "and inquiry-based learning. We believe that learning happens in a social space and that a child can deepen curiosity through exploration. Above all", she continues, "we want our learners to be confident and happy in their learning, to take risks and know that the classroom is a safe space". Angie uses Apple TV, Google Classroom and an interactive white-board, and she has been teaching for ten years now. She holds a Bachelor's degree from Columbia Teacher's College and a Master's degree in Education from the Institute of Education at Imperial College London where she met her boyfriend, Peter, who teaches history to senior students. Angie wrote her dis-sertation on the effects of technology on learning. She earns a comfortable salary—well over 100,000 Swiss francs per annum—and she owns a house in the mountains and belongs to an excellent pension scheme. She has leadership aspirations and would like to climb up the corporate ladder in the next few years, possibly assuming her first headship in about five years from now. Angie enjoys excellent ongoing professional development: she has been sent to workshops and training sessions all over Europe. She is a big fan of the Reggio Emilia system: children have a language of 1,000 voices, she says. We need to listen to them and believe in them.

The bell is rung in the courtyard, school is over and it's time for Zach to make his way along the rugged seven kilometres that lead him back to his compound. He took some notes in his tired workbook but no one has checked them and he is not sure if his spelling is correct. Zach is not entirely clear about why he learns what he does. Today the students were told about the tem-perature at which water boils and what happens when you put salt in the water. When Zach gets home, he will bathe his little brother, help his aunt cook, sweep the compound and wash his only shirt that he wears to school. It will already be late by then and time for some rest. Zach's father died some years ago of chronic, ongoing malaria. His mother works in town as a housekeeper. His aunt looks after the household of six children but, in reality, Zach holds the reins because his aunt suffers from gout and is partly blind. As he dozes off under the palm frond eaves with the sounds of the bush resonating in his ears, a thin film of sweat covering his neck from the humidity, Zach allows himself to be projected into his dream: he sees himself as a famous footballer, proudly wearing the colours of Burkina Faso. Zach is a gifted footballer and no one can overtake him in a race. They call him "the cheetah". One day, if I make it as a great footballer, he tells himself, I'll build a school right here in my village and make sure all the children in my commune get a good education, because education is important. The thought sends him to sleep.

Anthony's day ends with a 'philosophy for children' styled discussion with his peers on whether the ends justify the means. Angie roams between discussion groups, nodding her head in approval. The discussion observer, Yuga, feeds back to the group, commenting that on the whole the students were respectful and showed active listening. Anthony has swimming in 30 minutes, so there's a bit of time to relax in his boarding chalet with his chalet mates Dmitri, Youssef and Chi-Wha. Anthony will probably go to an already targeted top US university. His father went there as did his two older brothers. He will be what is known as a "legacy" student, meaning that he will follow in the established legacy of his family at the university, including the funding of an entire sports building. The future is bright for Anthony. His father, who has remarried twice and has a fortune of US $70 million, tells his son not to worry about the future but to just enjoy childhood. And that's precisely what Anthony is doing.

Historical perspectives on the development of theories on elitism and anti-elitism

Robichaud and Crevier (2016), when discussing political theory, describe elite theory as a broad school of thought in sociology that has brought together heterogeneous, even opposing voices, both for and against elitism. This does not include the philosophies of culture that I have added to the discussion.

In order to grapple with the constructs of elitism and anti-elitism, it is necessary to describe the way in which both fields have developed in recent history. This allows the reader to appreciate the sociopolitical, ideological, economic and historical frames that have shaped the discourses. Furthermore, since elitism and anti-elitism are not only philosophical positions but political ones, it is helpful to describe, when necessary and useful, the lives of the academics and theoreticians behind the ideas so as better to understand and appreciate the epistemological contexts, personal convictions and stories behind the notions in question. Western academia, built on the principles of scientific objectivity, tend to leave the details of authors out of any academic exegesis of their ideas. When looking at elitism and anti-elitism, however, understanding is better informed when there is some reckoning with the political and institutional affiliations of the authors of theories for a richer overall analysis.

The following sections of this analysis group elitist thinkers (mainly political and cultural) and anti-elitist thinkers (critics of economic, political and cultural elitism) before turning to some of the foundational positions on elitism in the specific realm of education.

Pro-elitism

The Italian pragmatist school: in defence of political elitism

The late 1800s and early 1900s witnessed the emergence of a number of positions on elitism in Italy. This was a time in European history when different political experiments based on the idea of the "new man" of the future were being implemented, these being communism, fascism and modern capitalism.

Vilfredo Pareto (1848–1923) was chair of political economy at the University of Lausanne. He had a chequered political career: defeated twice when standing for parliament in Italy, he died only two years after a personal political breakthrough when he was invited by Mussolini to join the League of Nations Disarmament Commission in 1921 (Hawthorn, 1980). An early advocate of proportional representation, following Mill's famous liberal essay "On liberty" and keen not to allow tyranny to take over leadership unchecked, his views morphed over time and became less and less tolerant of democratic and egalitarian notions. His main work was *The Mind and Society* (1916), a pragmatic argument for the inevitability of elitist rule. In it he talks of power passing from the "foxes" to the "lions" and back again, using Machiavelli's famous description of leaders in *The Prince* (1513). By the end of his career, embittered by what he saw as corrupt Italian politics, living in debt and solitude in the small Swiss village of Céligny, he argued that a natural intellectual superiority of the few was the answer to society's ills. Pareto's endorsement of elitist leadership, by force if necessary, led him to support Fascism. One of Pareto's most famous dictums, highlighting the omnipresence and strong tradition of elitism in the past, was that "history is a graveyard of aristocracies" (1966, p. 249).

The political scientist Gaetano Mosca (1858–1941) was chairman of Constitutional Law at the University of Turin and Chair of Public Law at the University of Rome. He had been undersecretary for the colonies earlier in his career (shortly after Italy's occupation of Libya) and was elected to parliament in 1909 (Parisi, 2011). Mosca's seminal works were his *Theory of Governments* (1884) and *The Ruling Class* (1896). He observed what he viewed as the inevitability of minority rule by a political class. For Mosca, this was a universal, transcendent and timeless principle. He described the political and organisational culture of elitist groups as being superior to that of a disorganised mass and argued that elites are essentially more prepared than those they govern. Mosca did not see elitist traits as hereditary but as socially developed and he noticed that elitist groups tend to be engaged in battles for leadership, one group taking over from the other through time in what he called a "circulation of elites". Unlike Pareto, Mosca openly disagreed with fascism. A 20th-century analysis of Mosca's worldview might evoke the contradiction of him being an active part of Italy's colonial administration while arguing against fascism.

Robert Michels (1876–1936), born in Germany but an Italian sociologist, was a professor of politics and economics at the University of Turin and, later, a professor of economics at the University of Basel. He had a rich professional life involving a close collaboration with Max Weber and directing the Italian Socialist Party's newsletter *Avanti!* Michels believed that there is a natural need for an elite and in his best-known work, *Political Parties: A Sociological Study of the Oligarchical Tendencies of Modern Democracies* (1911) described their behaviour as a necessary "iron law of oligarchy". Michels was a fascist and was attracted to the model of the highly charismatic working-class leader that he saw in Mussolini, believing that a political elite could be achieved through a strong visionary individual.

These positions on elitism all point to the belief that the world is ordered in a necessarily hierarchical manner and that this is a positive and healthy phenomenon. Such ideas can be traced back to Plato's vision of a vertically organised political structure in his work *The Republic*. For Plato, rulers should come from a select stock of philosophers (known as "philosophers kings"). Plato, like Socrates, was deeply anti-democratic, believing that the demos could never rule itself successfully and needed to be led by an elite. Plato's student Aristotle was not far from the belief that an aristocratic class should rule. Other prominent philosophers who defended elitism and influenced the Italian school of thought include Thomas Hobbes, whose *Leviathan* (1651) promulgated strong leadership in the form of a Cromwellian-styled protector and Hegel, whose arguments for historical dialecticism were founded on the master-slave relationship whereby one person or party would necessarily govern another. John Stewart Mill, who possibly influenced more political science authors and theorists than many other philosophers because of the balance and moderation of his views, was still overtly elitist in a classical, Platonic sense:

> No government by a democracy or a numerous aristocracy, either in its political acts or in the opinions, qualities, and tone of mind which it fosters, ever did or could rise above mediocrity ... Many have let themselves be guided (which in their best times they always have done) by the counsels and influence of a more highly gifted and instructed One or Few.
>
> (1977, p. 269)

Indeed, as AC Grayling has shown in his lucid *Democracy and Its Crisis* (2017), despite the overall putative aims of democracy, egalitarianism, equal opportunity and fair representation, the Anglo-American incarnations of democracy with their substantial buffers and filters such as the electoral college, House of Lords and whipping system, are in reality elitist systems.

Undoubtedly, the greatest Italian sociologist was Antonio Gramsci (1891–1937). Imprisoned by the fascist government for his communist activities, his prison notebooks elaborated a Marxist theory that showed how ruling classes create a hegemony of ideas and culture that is more powerful than the strictly and uniquely materialist assertions of militaristic and economic rule. Hegemony is a system of beliefs and affiliations that the ruling class confections through cultural production and this shapes the worldview of an entire population. As such, what is believed to be "common sense" or normal is in fact cultural hegemony, created by a ruling elite. This line of thinking has influenced all subsequent sociology and much philosophy, notably the ideas of Foucault and Bourdieu.

In a probing analysis of Gramsci's approach to political elitism, Finocchiaro (1999) compares him to Mosca as advocating for a pragmatic approach to political organisation, thus implying elitism. Indeed, Gramsci was not merely critical of systems of leadership; instead, his letters make it clear that he regarded them as necessary:

> Among the many meanings of democracy, the most realistic and concrete one seems to me to be that which connects with the concept of hegemony. In an hegemonic system, there is democracy between the leading group and the groups led to the extent that (the development of the economy and thus) the legislation (that expresses this development) favors the (molecular) transition from the groups led to the leading group. In the Roman Empire there existed an imperial-territorial democracy through the granting of citizenship to conquered peoples, etc. There could not be democracy in feudalism on account of the existence of closed groups.
>
> (1975, p. 1056)

Here Gramsci joins Lenin who believed that the working class might be capable of economic revolt but needed guidance to achieve political, structured revolt. He wrote that "The history of all countries shows that the working class, exclusively by its own effort, is able to develop only trade-union consciousness" (Lenin, 1901, p. 131) and that "the only serious organization principle the active workers of our movement can accept is: strict secrecy, strict selection of members, and the training of professional revolutionists" (p. 141).

Gramsci was sensitive to what he described as the internal colonisation of Italy during the *Risorgamento* (he was from Sardinia and viewed the northern influence over Italy as a form of hegemonic intrusion). As such, he advocated a critical, questioning and even subversive approach to knowledge and politics. His political convictions cost him his life: he spent that last 11 years of his life imprisoned under Mussolini and died at the age of 46 from ailments related to Pott's disease.

It is important to situate the Italian school's view of elitism in time and place. Three essential points can be established that influence further analysis of elitism as a discourse:

1   All the theorists mentioned were in some way engaged in a discussion or in a direct political relationship with fascism and were operating at a time of imperialism and war. Thus, elitist discourses tended to view strong leadership as a necessity.
2   The Italian school viewed elitism as natural and unavoidable, drawing on a just world theory (meaning that social inegalitarianism is a natural phenomenon).
3   The Italian school theorists were specialists in economics, law and politics. This points out that elitist discourses tend to draw on a pragmatic worldview in the educational debate.

Cultural elitism

Less pragmatic and more focused on academia, canonical knowledge and so-called high culture is cultural elitism, emblematised by 19th- and 20th-century intellectuals such as Matthew Arnold (1822–1888), T.S. Eliot (1905–1965) and, more recently, Harold Bloom (1930–2019), Roger Scruton (1944–2020) and Christopher Hitchens (1949–2011).

Viewed critically by Marxists such as Adorno, Gramsci and Bourdieu as a controlling mechanism that the bourgeoisie uses to maintain power, cultural elitism focuses on aesthetics, art and humanistic traditions, seen as salvatory expressions of a higher state of being and thinking. The 19th-century French Orientalist Joseph Ernest Renan (1823–1892) saw an intrinsic link between high culture and nationalism in that the latter tends to sublimate the works of art of a culture or civilisation and turn them into icons. Hence, Western cultural elitists tend to be Eurocentric and romantically inclined to celebrate the Graeco-Roman narrative and other historical European artistic movements that depict European civilisation. This explains the natural link between cultural conservatism and cultural elitism.

Nicholas Tate's *Against the Current: The Conservative Case for Education* (2017) discusses the school of cultural elitism in some detail. In describing T.S. Eliot's position on "high culture", Tate writes:

> His [T.S. Eliot's] argument was that the maintenance of 'culture' in the normative sense – both 'high culture' and the wider culture of society – required the stability that could only come from a hierarchical social structure within which cultural transmission took place organically via classes and families.
>
> (2017, p. 50)

In other words, there is a coalescence of plutocratic and meritocratic elitism through the necessary existence of a ruling class that acts as a type of cultural "clerisy" (p. 51) in championing high culture and the institutions that preserve it. Not only should education be selective, it should aim to preserve class structure, in particular the class of "high culture" that will lead the way.

In fact, Eliot's approach, as told by Tate, was more radical than this and was somewhat against meritocratic elitism as he felt that "the products of equality and opportunity in education … would come from many different backgrounds and 'be united only by their common interests' and not by their culture or by any 'piety towards the dead'" (2017, p. 52). Cultural transmission, the lifeblood of cultural elitism, had to come from a group that had been ensconced in the traditions of fine music, poetry, food and literature from birth and inheritance. The extreme conservativism of this position is well expressed in Eliot's heavily elitist self-declarative statement: "I am an Anglo-Catholic in religion, a classicist in literature and a royalist in politics".

Cultural elitism is an important force in education as it defines much of the ethos and decision making around curriculum content in defence of "the canon". A central expression of this is Harold Bloom's *The Western Canon* (1994) in which he argues why 26 writers (all white, 22 of whom are European men) are quintessential for a Western education. The argument that the canon should be central in schooling is espoused in particular by educational theorist E.D. Hirsch (1928–).

Hirsch, who has had a long and prestigious academic career and developed the core knowledge curriculum in the United States, is an example of someone who is a political egalitarianist but a cultural elitist. He is suspicious of anti-knowledge curricular approaches based on soft skills as he points out that the effect of these programmes is often to leave students from deprived socioeconomic and cultural backgrounds even further behind, therefore augmenting inequality.

Some parallels might be made with Gramsci. Although Gramsci was a Marxist, and therefore in many respects an anti-elitist politically and culturally speaking, he believed in strong transmission and the importance of a classical education in order to empower the working class with the intellectual tools of hegemonic rule. This can be seen in his prison letters to his children in which he prescribes a strict diet of Greek and Latin literature. From a contemporary perspective, one might consider his ideas on the importance of classical content transmission to be conservative and culturally elitist.

It should be noted that there was a strong elitist strain of thought that developed in the 1980s around the publication of *The Closing of the American Mind* (1987) by Allan Bloom (1930–1992), who advocated an anti-populist, extremely elitist and conservative vision of culture and education that was espoused by the likes of Arnold and Bloom, and continues to be supported by W.A. Henry (1995) and Joel Stein (2019).

Parallels between political and cultural pro-elitism

Both political and cultural elitism espouse certain generic principles: clear, organised leadership, a hierarchical approach to knowledge and society and a system whereby the best and the brightest can rise to the top as one would expect in a meritocracy. The early political pragmatists' scorn of the lower classes and belief that they were fundamentally unable to organise themselves politically is not a view that is overtly fashionable in the 21st century and is not mirrored in any openly broadcast view of education since the overall thrust of education, especially after the Second World War, has been humanitarian and inclusive in drive and rhetoric.

Political elitism in the 21st century is a complex phenomenon since politicians in the democracies of late capitalism need to appeal to an electoral base, which might be populist, anti-establishment and, therefore, anti-elitist (in that the political elite is seen as the inner ruling caucus of power) but at the same time they need to appeal to the powerful market forces of neoliberalism, thus representing plutocratic elitism. Therefore, modern leaders like Donald Trump and Boris Johnson tend to hold contradictory discourses that espouse populist sentiments on the one hand (anti-immigrant rhetoric for example), but simultaneously elitist ones on the other hand (preserving fiscal arrangements that suit big business). To some extent, there is a mirroring of this phenomenon in education which is designed to give universal and equitable access to all at one level but also stands for quality, excellence and supporting gifted students. The political tension between populism and plutocratic elitism is somewhat reflected in the educational tension between access and meritocracy.

Another tension is created in the educational landscape between free state education and an expensive, privatised industry on the other, creating a dual carriageway moving at different speeds for different children due to financial means and background.

Anti-elitism

Post-Second World War: American political anti-elitist theory

The United States of the 1950s, a period of strong economic growth, witnessed sociological and political theories of elitism that can be considered to be part of elite theory but are much more critical of elitism than the Italian school. American democracy was meant to be a world model of inclusion and equal opportunity, therefore in many ways the polar opposite of elitism, but a number of critiques pointed out that in reality political leadership was dominated by various forms of elitism.

Elmer Eric Schattschneider (1892–1971) was president of the American Political Science Association and taught at Columbia, Rutgers and Wesleyan universities. He published widely but is best known for his work *The*

Semisovereign People: A Realist's View of Democracy in America (1960) in which he critiqued the American democratic system as "skewed, loaded and unbalanced in favor of a fraction of a minority" (p. 30). Schattschneider argued that American society and politics were pressured by high-income and well-educated interest groups, whereas the majority stand at the side-lines. He wrote that "the flaw in the pluralist heaven is that the heavenly chorus sings with a strong upper-class accent" (p. 35).

Charles Wright Mills (1916–1962), professor of sociology at Columbia, like Michels was also influenced heavily by Weber and Marxist theory in general but he was equally interested in the ideas of the American pragmatist school (Pierce, Dewey, James). Mills was known as an explosive, sometimes pugilistic character and criticised his academic colleagues openly, sometimes to the point of insulting them (Dandaneau, 2007, p. 3051). Mills visited Cuba, where he interviewed and later advised Fidel Castro. He was not afraid to critique Soviet censorship. His book *The Power Elite* (1956) deals with the question of elitism by pointing out that, at the time of its writing (and arguably up until and including the present day), elitist political groups in the United States protect their own interests, empower themselves through propaganda and express themselves primarily through military strength, thus fuelling a war economy:

> We must remember that these men of the power elite now occupy the strategic places in the structure of American Society; that they command the dominant institutions of a dominant nation; that, as a set of men, they are in a position to make decisions with terrible consequences for the underlying populations of the world.
>
> (Mills, 1956/2000, p. 276)

Mills believed that elite groups could move from one area of leadership to the next in a "horizontal" manner. This thesis was investigated and substantiated to a certain extent by Bourdieu in an analysis of French power elites (1984).

Floyd Hunter (1912–1992) was a social worker and later an academic at the University of North Carolina. He grew up during the Great Depression and was wholeheartedly engaged in questions of social justice. His major work was the publication of his doctoral thesis, *Community Power Structure: A Study of Decision Makers* (1953), which focused on his experiences in Atlanta where he worked for the Community Council (and was later fired, probably due to his populist views, which were considered controversial at the time). Hunter, analysing the subtle interplay of influence and power in the city network of Atlanta, pointed out that elitist groups could gather informally, away from legitimised and official forms. Hence, Hunter offers a new perspective to the discussion on elitism by eliciting community groups and grassroots-level initia-tives that take on leadership roles.

The post-war American contributions to elite theory are essentially anti-elitist and are all influenced by the ideas of Karl Marx. Marxist theory sees history as dialectical materialism whereby an ongoing class struggle for ownership of the means of production opposes the bourgeoisie and the proletariat. The ultimate goal of Marxism is to do away with elitism by creating a classless society based on firm principles of egalitarianism, shared production and the abolition of private property. However, one of the fundamental contradictions in Marxist theory is the question of revolution and leadership: who will lead the proletariat and how? History has shown that a political elite, made up of an inner-party intelligentsia, comes to form a new elite, confirming Mosca's thesis of an ongoing dance of power for leadership in all political and social structures.

The ideas of Schattschneider, Mills and Hunter are characterised by three foundational points that are all helpful for subsequent analysis of elitism and education:

1   Anti-elitist positions tend to be influenced by Marxist theory or at least traditional left-leaning ideology.
2   The post-war American school is highly specific and deconstructs political leadership in the United States as opposed to the Italian school's universalist philosophy. The chapters that follow will show how very often communitarian and egalitarian discourses are formulated around context-specific parameters and differ from one educational institution and/or country to the next, whereas elitist structures form a less diverse pattern across the globe, singing off a more standardised and globalised hymn sheet.
3   Anti-elitist positions point out, in their criticisms of political elitist governance, that vested interests and oblique, hidden causes and positions, drive social dynamics while disguising themselves in the appearance of need-blind, equal opportunity offerings. In other words, political leaders might claim to represent the people but in fact they represent the military or big business. To a certain extent this holds for educational elitism since this book will show how putatively agnostic structures designed for meritocratic purposes often lead to financially and socio-ethnically privileged children accessing such opportunities to a greater degree than their peers. In other words, admissions protocols might claim to be based solely on academic merit but are often tuned into candidates' social backgrounds and financial means (Marcus, 2017).

American theorists of the 1970s to the present day and the highlighting of neoliberal elitism

As neoliberalism fastened its grip on the socioeconomic structure of the United States, elitism theorists became more interested in how power groups were less defined by political or social authority and much more by financial and managerial power.

Although much of his work was composed prior to the 1970s, I will situate James Burnham (1905–1987) in this school because of the tenor of his thesis of elitism. A brilliant young scholar who gained places at Princeton and then Balliol, Oxford, where he studied under Tolkien (Kimball, 2002), Burnham had a fascinating political career that saw him initially devoted to Trotskyite ideas as he was an active party member of the American Socialist Workers Party and then, after disagreement with the orientation the Soviet Union took during the Second World War, he became an active anti-totalitarian spokesman and member of the CIA. He also taught philosophy at New York University. He was awarded the Presidential Medal of Freedom by Ronald Reagan and became a source of inspiration for American neoconservatives.

Burnham's best-known work was *The Managerial Revolution* (1941) in which he describes a future world regime made up of an elitist class of experts. The book is said to have influenced George Orwell heavily, who corresponded with Burnham about his views on power and bureaucracy (Kimball, 2002). Orwell summarised *The Managerial Revolution* thus:

> Capitalism is disappearing, but Socialism is not replacing it. What is now arising is a new kind of planned, centralised society which will be neither capitalist nor, in any accepted sense of the word, democratic. The rulers of this new society will be the people who effectively control the means of production: that is, business executives, technicians, bureaucrats and soldiers, lumped together by Burnham, under the name of 'managers'. These people will eliminate the old capitalist class, crush the working class, and so organise society that all power and economic privilege remain in their own hands ... The new 'managerial' societies will not consist of a patchwork of small, independent states, but of great super-states grouped round the main industrial centres in Europe, Asia, and America. These super-states will fight among themselves for possession of the remaining uncaptured portions of the earth, but will probably be unable to conquer one another completely. Internally, each society will be hierarchical, with an aristocracy of talent at the top and a mass of semi-slaves at the bottom.
>
> (Orwell, 1946)

It is difficult to read these lines, composed in the early 1940s, without a sense of foreboding, as if what Burnham was proposing in 1941 was prophetic since the political and economic world of 2020 could, indeed, be seen this way. One also notices how Burnham's ideas influenced Orwell's novel *1984* in which he describes three superpowers: Eastasia, Eurasia and Oceania.

The Machiavellians: Defenders of Freedom (1943) is more explicitly focused on the matter of political elitism. In this book, Burnham claims that all societies are run by self-serving elites. His career ended in relative obscurity as he took his criticism of abuse of power and totalitarianism to the nerve centre of American political life by criticising McCarthyism, the result of which was his ostracism from the circle of public opinion.

G. William Domhoff (1936–) is a professor of psychology and sociology at the University of California, Santa Cruz. Influenced by C. Wright Mills and Marx, Domhoff published the bestselling work *Who Rules America? The Triumph of the Corporate Rich* (1967), the thesis of which he has further refined and developed in subsequent works, notably a series of essays in 2016 that show how, 50 years later, economic divide and elitism are stronger than ever in the United States. Domhoff's thesis is that the American political structure is dominated by corporations and lobbies representing the interests of corporations.

Thomas Ferguson (1949–), professor of political science at the University of Massachusetts, spent a significant part of his academic career at MIT, working alongside Noam Chomsky. Ferguson's study *Golden Rule: The Investment Theory of Party Competition and the Logic of Money-Driven Political Systems* (1995), not unlike Domhoff's work, situates political elitism as lying mainly in the hands of corporations. Noam Chomsky writes how, when teaching at MIT, Ferguson was warned that he would not gain tenure in the political science department (of MIT) if he persisted in critiquing what he saw as a plutocratic elitist reign in the United States, built on a system of electoral financing by large corporations that had become extremely powerful pressure groups (2003, p. 243).

Robert David Putnam (1941–) is the Peter and Isabel Malkin professor of public policy at Harvard's John F. Kennedy School of Government. Much in the vein of Domhoff and Ferguson, Putman deplores what he views as a politically and financially elitist system governing the United States, marginalising present and future generations. More specifically, Putman points out that powerful caucuses tend to be constituted by minorities possessing rare technical skills and knowledge: a technocratic minority becomes the core of elitist leadership. This thesis is explored in his well-known book *Bowling Alone: The Collapse and Revival of American Community* (2000). Part of the book's argument is that after the 1960s, with the rise of neoliberalism, many of the social institutions that protected some degree of equality, such as civic societies and associations, disintegrated, leading to a decline in what Tocqueville once coined "social capital", in other words, the capacity for society to maintain and resuscitate its productivity through a broad base of talented individuals working in communal tandem. His more recent study *Our Kids: The American Dream in Crisis* (2015) further explores this trend that is accelerating as the United States takes on a type of hyper neoliberal approach to politics and finance.

Thomas R. Dye (1935–), emeritus professor of political science at Florida State University, is the author of *Who's Running America? The Clinton Years* (1995). In this work, which has been re-edited from its initial publication in the 1970s through successive waves of government, Dye's position on elitism, like so many in elite theory thinking, is essentially deterministic: "in all societies—primitive and advanced, totalitarian and democratic, capitalist and socialist—only a few people exercise great power" (1995, p. 8). Dye's thesis on elitism is that elitist groups stay in power by retaining specialist skills and knowledge that gives them a cutting edge and perceived superiority over the masses. He points out that the concentration of power in the United States is acute:

> Great power in America is concentrated in a handful of people. A few thousand individuals out of 250 million Americans decide about war and peace, wages and prices, consumption and investment, employment and production, law and justice, taxes and benefits, education and learning, health and welfare, advertising and communication, life and leisure.
>
> (1995, p. 8)

The most recent school of American elite theory thinkers focuses on the manner in which neoliberal, corporate and technocratic power has hijacked American political institutions. These criticisms of the structure of elitist power are influenced by or related to the theses of Noam Chomsky (2015), whose devastating social commentary critiques the United States as a totalitarian and entirely elitist superpower.

The common analysis of elitism that runs through these political scientists' and sociologists' commentaries on authority and hierarchy is that elitist groups sustain their power over the masses in a variety of different ways but always through a rarefication of means, skills or knowledge. This is significant as I will show in subsequent chapters since, when we turn to the specific issue of education and elitism, it becomes clear that educational institutions and products (degrees and qualifications) retain their specific valency (elite status) through a complex symbolic system that is multifaceted, drawing on economic and technical sources of value and constantly morphing to represent knowledge that is seen as lifeworthy and future-proof.

Contemporary schools of political anti-elitism from around the world

Ralph Dahrendorf (1929–2009) was a German-British philosopher and sociologist who was a member of both the German parliament and the British House of Lords. Throughout his prestigious career he investigated class conflict from a Marxist viewpoint to point out that an intricate political system is at work in power structures that essentially elects elites into positions based on the promise of providing the masses with the competences necessary for good governance. Therefore, elitist groups empower themselves further through alliances with technocratic specialists that become, in essence, service providers. Dahrendorf, although influenced by Marx, sees the power struggle that transcends history as one between those in authority and those who are not rather than as a pure class struggle per se or a struggle over the ownership of the means of production as purports traditional Marxism. His major contribution to the field was *Class Conflict in Industrial Society* (1959).

John Peter Scott (1949–) is a British sociologist who, using social network analysis as a method (which is a way of mapping relationships between people and establishing nodes of knowledge, meaning and intent), has produced a discourse on elitism that moves away from the recent reliance on economic power structures and "managerialism" to inform the field by suggesting, rather in the vein of Foucault, that elitist structures are created by power yielding that is not uniquely technocratic or political but can be social, communal, ideological and cultural. A useful overview of elite theory can be read in his 2008 article "Modes of Power and the Re-Conceptualization of Elites". In this work, Scott points out that elitist groups are not set in stone: they are defined by "counteraction" (2008, p. 37) and express themselves not only through the exercise of power but the holding of power too. In essence, Scott has nuanced and specified the school of elite theory to state that:

> the word "elite" should be used only in relation to those groups that have a degree of power … people with high IQ, for example, do not constitute an elite in any sociologically meaningful sense. They may be very significant in many walks of life and it may be very important to study them, but they are not a category to which the word "elite" should be applied. Similarly, highly paid occupational groups should not be described as elites simply because of their high pay, however privileged or advantaged they may be. Such groups become elites only if their intelligence or high pay becomes a basis for significant power.
>
> (2008, p. 28)

In other words, the defining characteristic of elitism, for Scott, is the extent to which a group yields power.

Other contemporary well-known political anti-elitists include the Indian author Arundhati Roy (1961–), who writes against the centralisation of power and "power companies" (Wolfword, 2002); the Canadian anti-neoliberal journalist Naomi Klein (1970–); British journalist and Labour Party activist Owen Jones (1984–); American political activist Angela Davis (1944–), who militates against neoliberalism and the prison industry in the United States; and the American anti-Establishment film-maker Michael Moore (1951–), who has directed documentaries against political and economic elitism.

Cultural anti-elitism

Although it is not entirely straightforward to oppose the school of cultural elitism with one coherent group of voices, it is not unreasonable to group them into two positions we could call, loosely, that of critical theory and postcolonialism.

Since cultural elitism tends to be aristocratic or royalist in nature, insisting on the importance of what Eliot called the "clerisy" as agents of cultural transmission, a historical counter-voice has been the celebration and defence of grassroots culture, away from the stuffiness and bookishness of academia and fine art. Such a counter-approach works against the class-related element of cultural elitism. Proponents of this proletariat culture of "the people" would include intellectual or cultural leaders championing a working-class ethic such as literature centred on the working class, for example, some of the work of the English authors William Blake, Charles Dickens, the American novelist John Steinbeck or the Italian dramatist Dario Fo. The English essayist and novelist George Orwell's corpus has been consistently focused and critical of questions of class, elitism and power.

From a more contemporary perspective, the French populist philosopher Michel Onfray, whose popular University of Caen attempted to democratise higher education, could be considered a cultural anti-elitist and the socialist British film directors Mike Leigh, Ken Loach and the French realist director Stéphane Brizé all use their art to attack the injustices of neoliberalism while making visible the working-class ethic.

The corpus of the American historian Howard Zinn (1922–2010), including the Zinn project, a set of teaching resources, is very much in this line of thinking. One might include critics of class structure such as Orwell. A more militant, active position would follow classical Marxism, in the vein of Maoist and Leninist principles of anti-elitism, engaging in active anti-elitist class struggle, an example being the Swiss radical Marxist political writer Jean Ziegler. This type of anti-cultural elitism thought can span a broad spectrum of political thought from Marxism to anarchy and populism to fascism. In essence, it fights against plutocratic elitism or the class dimension of cultural elitism.

Critical theory

The sociological school of critical theory, associated with the Frankfurt School and earlier thinkers such as Georg Lukács and Antonio Gramsci, deconstructs the power relationships that are latent in assumptions about identity and institutional knowledge, pointing out that a legacy of historical and cultural elitism lies hidden in many of the actions and social institutions that characterise Western society. It is helpful to look to critical theory as a clear anti-elitist movement in that it underpins most of the sociopolitical and philosophical reasoning against institutions of power based on class and cultural hegemony. However, critical theory tends to look at mass culture as a source of political manipulation and, ironically, it has been accused by some of being elitist in that it is often expressed in torrid philosophical language that is inaccessible to a broad-based readership.

Postcolonialism

Since cultural elitism tends to use classical, canonical European culture as its main example of high culture, opposition to this can also fall into the school of postcolonialism. This school of thought is focused on deconstructing imperialistic European narratives that "other" outgroups and normalise the cultural hegemony of colonialist or former colonial powers. In other words, when cultural elitists insist on a canon of Graeco-Latin, Christian art and literature, they are excluding multiple voices and perspectives, those that were colonised by Europe and have been historically sidelined in the process. Champions of postcolonial thought (Martiniquais psychiatrist Frantz Fanon [1925–1961], Palestinian American historian Edward Said [1935–2003], Indian theoreticians Gayatri Spivak [1942–] and Homi Bhabha [1949–] for example) are often "on the side" of the subaltern proletariat too, as is the case for Frantz Fanon, whose epic *The Wretched of the Earth* (1961) speaks to the oppressed in terms of culture and economics. Postcolonial theory works against what is perceived as the inherent racism and imperialism of Western cultural imperialism and it calls for the curriculum to be decolonised.

Foundational discourses on education and elitism

Chapter 3 of this book will take the reader though a history of access to education, while Chapter 4 will provide an overview of the history of selective schools, and throughout this I will discuss theoretical positions on education and elitism. In order to lead us into these chapters, a short résumé of the major positions on education and elitism should be outlined. The positions embraced by these figures influence the subsequent analysis of education and elitism.

The three most influential figures on the question of elitism and education are Pierre Bourdieu (1930–2001), Paolo Freire (1921–1997) and E.D. Hirsch (1928–). As this short section will show, Bourdieu offers a sociological critique of educational philosophy and structuring, Paolo Freire describes a Marxist deconstruction of formal education towards a communal, distributed and informal distribution of knowledge, while Hirsh argues for the need to base education on strong knowledge that has currency in the world. It would be over-simplistic to label these minds as pro- or anti-elitist, but it is safe to say that Hirsch has a more traditional, canonical approach, Freire suggests a radical praxis for education, to break the ivory tower as it were, and Bourdieu is somewhere in the middle, pointing out the hidden ideological premises and biases that lurk in the structuring of education and the types of power structure that are encultured and reproduced by educational institutions. They all follow the ideas of Emile Durkheim on education, who saw it primarily as an act of social transmission:

> Education is the influence exercised by adult generations on those that are not yet ready for social life. Its object is to arouse and to develop in the child a certain number of physical, intellectual and moral states which are demanded of him by both the political society as a whole and the special milieu for which he is specifically destined.
>
> (1956, pp. 70–71)

Bourdieu: social elitism as the hidden curriculum of schooling

Bourdieu, a hugely influential French sociologist who studied under Louis Althusser and who was a high school teacher before eventually becoming chair of sociology at the Collège de France, published mainly during the structuralist and post-structuralist philosophical movement at a time when French education was heavily criticised as a vehicle of institutionalised bourgeois ideology. The May 1968 student uprising was a symbol of a general critique of education as ideological inculcation.

Bourdieu's most influential texts on education (1966, 1970, 1971) point out that most curricula, certainly those prominent in the French educational system at the time, were reproducing power structures, relationships to authority, capitalist values and social hierarchy in ways that were not only hidden to learners but often invisible to teachers too (Bourdieu & Passeron, 1970, p. 84). For Bourdieu, education was not just cultural transmission, but, importantly and tacitly, social reproduction too. This is what creates what we call "society" (1971, p. 47).

This notion can be found in the ideas of Michel Foucault (1926–1984), whose work on *The Archaeology of Knowledge* (1969), *The History of the Clinic* (1963) and systems of social coercion (in *Discipline and Punish* [1975]) point out that education is first and foremost a tool to mould individuals into an accepted way of being. Michael Apple's work on *Ideology and Curriculum* (1979) suggests that many curriculum decisions duplicate and normalise middle-class values, the separation of labour and capitalist notions of the accumulation of knowledge.

There are two reasons why Bourdieu's ideas are important for a discussion on education and elitism: first, many educational discourses and practices, although referenced as pedagogic and neutral, are in reality propagating elitist systems of knowledge (selecting certain historical narratives, certain literary texts, enculturing learners to accept hierarchical leadership through a system of headmasters, prefects, student councils, and so on); and, second, because the idea that an educated person has gained knowledge and skills above others who are less educated, a clearly elitist idea that is arguably at the root of the whole design of formal education, is an idea close to Bourdieu's epistemological critique. Indeed, he coined the term "homo academicus" as the educational version of Adam Smith's "homo economicus" to suggest the person who seeks to increase his/her capital of knowledge, and in so doing aspires to a higher form of being.

Freire: seeking common humanity beyond elitism

The iconic Brazilian sociologist Paolo Freire, who was influenced by Hegel, Marx, Gramsci and Fanon, aimed to eradicate illiteracy among formerly colonised people and to activate education and positive self-awareness for the formerly colonised. One might say that he took Bourdieu's ideas a step further. Not only did Freire criticise formal education as a type of banking system whereby surplus knowledge would be accumulated by an educated class (resembling, therefore, Bourdieu's idea of "homo academicus"), he believed that formal schooling should be surpassed by an informal community-based educational paradigm where indigenous knowledge, local traditions and communal values would drive educational development in "cultural circles". His best-known work is the 1968 *Pedagogy of the Oppressed*.

A Marxist, but also influenced by Dewey's model of inquiry-based learning, Freire was clearly deeply anti-elitist, seeing most formal education as a stronghold of colonial power, indoctrination and a way of alienating people from their cultural roots. In a sense, Freire wished to see Marx's idea of a classless society pervade the educational world and destroy the bourgeois bastion of formal education. As a response to elitist didactic knowledge transmission, Freire preferred an inquiry-based, social constructivist pedagogy where knowledge would be built through community and discovery with the instructor taking on a position of facilitator and equal rather than master. Thinkers who can be grouped with Freire include a number of scholars loosely grounded in the field of critical pedagogy such as Peter McLaren (2015), Henry Giroux (2020) and bell hooks (2014).

Freire is an important reference for the analysis of education and elitism since his vision influences many positions against elitism to this day. Strategies to democratise education and reduce elitism in education tend to refer to the Freirean principle that the role of the teacher is to act as cultural facilitator.

E.D. Hirsch: breaking into elite circles—core knowledge as power

In contrast to Bourdieu and Freire, Eric Donald Hirsch, professor emeritus of education and humanities at the University of Virginia, is a conservative who for years has defended the old idea of education as the transmission of knowledge, more particularly a canon of literature and humanities in the Western world, arguing that students need to understand a core of knowledge that has currency in order to become part of cultural and literary circles.

Hirsch has been critical of what he considers failed Romantic educational strategies that put the student at the centre and focus less on knowledge acquisition and more on skills development. Although Hirsch does not describe himself as an elitist and actually situates himself firmly as a Democrat, he argues that "educational traditionalism" (Moore, 2010) that espouses cultural literacy is necessary to empower young people entering the world of references and canons.

In this regard, his ideas are not unlike those of Gramsci, who, despite believing that an "organic" class of intellectuals needed to be developed in society to counter the ivory tower of institutionalised, elitist intellectuals, his prison notebooks show clearly that he believed that the path to intellectualism was through a highly canonical approach to the humanities and literature. Another educational theorist who has married left-leaning social views with a conservative (what some might call elitist) approach to knowledge, is the English sociologist Michael Young (2007), who advocates for a strong knowledge-based curriculum as a way of empowering marginalised classes.

Hirsch's position on education is useful when discussing elitism and education as he bridges cultural conservatism (and what could be seen as elitist proclivity for an overtly canonical knowledge-based education) and socioeconomic egalitarianism (the need to empower those outside cultural circles with such an education). This complex bridge between cultural conservatism and social transformation runs across my analysis of elitist constructs in education as we look at schools, universities, questions of access and quality and all the heated arguments they bring with them.

One of the nuances of the discussion on education and elitism is that meritocracy and plutocracy have a complex, intertwined relationship with one another. At times they stand in opposition to one another and at others they coalesce.

Conclusion

The thrust of established positions in elite theory are political: "the elite" carries the connotations of a political elite in most contexts. However, schools of thought for or against elitism have developed in specific historical contexts through time and they span not only political but economic, cultural and social dimensions of the human experience. Pro- and anti-elitist positions influence larger sets of belief, ideology and policy. When turning to education, the political roots of elitism and anti-elitism can always be felt. Lurking behind meritocratic, pluto-cratic or cultural elitist positions are the ideas of Plato, Hobbes, Pareto and Mosca— positions on egalitarianism, free education and decolonising the curriculum are clearly influenced by Marx.

In order to schematise a discussion about elitism and education, it is possible to group three core elements of elitism: meritocratic (based on academic and scholarly merit); plutocratic (based on wealth); and cultural (based on intellectualism and canonical references). These are opposed by egalitarianist discourses (propagating open access and inclusivity), Marxist discourses (education for the masses, need-blind and geared towards social transformation) and cultural anti-elitism (critical theory, deconstructing relations of power in curriculum and postcolonialism, deconstructing cultural imperialism in curriculum). Although it is reductive to formulate these positions in binary oppositions, for the sake of this study, it is convenient to schematise their relationship in the matrix below.

Pro-elitist	Anti-elitist
Meritocratic	Egalitarianist
Plutocratic	Marxist
Cultural	Critical theorist and postcolonialist

As this book unfolds, it discusses the pressures and contexts involving education and elitism, and these schools, or elements of these schools, will surface, often exhibiting an antagonistic relationship between them. Ultimately, what runs through pro-elitist discourses is a worldview that is conservative and seeks to preserve order and hierarchy—this notion goes back at least as far as Plato. The advantage of this worldview is that high standards of excellence are maintained by filtering entry to leading institutions so as to preserve a concentration of intellectual and social capital, be it at the level of politics, schooling or social institutions. The disadvantage is that it excludes a majority and only operates for a privileged few, even if these few are seen to deserve a position of privilege when selected through meritocratic entry criteria.

On the anti-elitist side of the fence is a broad view of society as socially unjust and in need of renewal so that selective systems of social organisation are reformed to allow as many people as possible to gain access to a high-quality education. The advantage of this worldview is that it promises universal education for all and builds on the democratic principle of a right to an education. The disadvantage is that if systems are opened to all, it becomes difficult to preserve the necessary exclusivity of leadership and quality: pockets of excellence will be subsumed in mass systems that are open access, leading to low standards.

Ultimately, what is the purpose of an educational institution such as a school or a university? Is it to provide a baseline level of education for everybody or to create corridors of excellence that few will take but which will allow them to develop beyond what they might achieve were the system designed primarily to care for the masses? Currently, the overarching design of education is base-line access for all at the primary years of instruction with steadily increasing levels of selectivity as education continues into secondary and tertiary stages.

References

Apple, M. (1979). *Ideology and Curriculum*. London: Routledge.

Arneson, R. (2013). Egalitarianism. *Stanford Encyclopedia of Philosophy*. https://plato.sta nford.edu/entries/egalitarianism/.

Bloom, A. (1987). *The Closing of the American Mind: How Higher Education Has Failed Democracy and Impoverished the Souls of Today's Students*. New York: Simon & Schuster.

Bloom, H. (1995). *The Western Canon: The Books and School of the Ages*. New York: Riverhead Books.

Bourdieu, P. (1966). L'école conservatrice: Les inégalités devant l'école et devant la culture, *Revue française de sociologie*, 7(3), 325–347.

Bourdieu, P. (1971). Reproduction culturelle et reproduction sociale, *Social Science Information*, 10(2), 45–79.

Bourdieu, P. (1984). *Distinction: A Social Critique of the Judgment of Taste*. Cambridge, MA: Harvard University Press.

Bourdieu, P. (1993). *The Field of Cultural Production*. Cambridge: Polity Press.

Bourdieu, P., & Passeron, J.-C. (1970). *La reproduction: Éléments pour une théorie du système d'enseignement*. Paris: Minuit.

Brennan, J., & Magness, P. (2019). *Cracks in the Ivory Tower: The Moral Mess of Higher Education*. Oxford: Oxford University Press.

Burnham, J. (1941). *The Managerial Revolution*. New York: The John Day Company.

Burnham, J. (1943). *The Machiavellians: Defenders of Freedom*. New York: The John Day Company.

Chomsky, N. (2003). *Understanding Power: The Indispensable Chomsky*, ed. P. Rounds Mitchell & J. Schoeffel. New York: New Press.

Chomsky, N. (2015). America is a plutocracy masquerading as a democracy. *Salon*, October. www.salon.com

Dahrendorf, R. (1959). *Class and Class Conflict in Industrial Society*. Palo Alto, CA: Stanford University Press.

Dandaneau, S.P. (2007). C. Wright Mills. *Blackwell Encyclopedia of Sociology*, ed. G. Rizter. Oxford: Blackwell, pp. 3050–3055.

Domhoff, G.W. (1967). *Who Rules America? The Triumph of the Corporate Rich*. New York: McGraw Hill.

Durkheim, E. (1956). *Education and Sociology*, trans. S.D. Fox. New York: Free Press. www.onlinethinktank.com/documents/education.pdf.

Dye, T.R. (1995). *Who's Running America? The Clinton Years*. New York: Pearson.

Ferguson, T. (1995). *Golden Rule: The Investment Theory of Party Competition and the Logic of Money-Driven Political Systems*. Chicago: University of Chicago Press.

Finocchiaro, M.A. (1999). *Beyond Right and Left: Democratic Elitism in Mosca and Gramsci*. New Haven, CT: Yale University Press.

Foucault, M. (1963). *Naissance de la clinique: une archéologie du regard médical*. Paris: Payot.

Foucault, M. (1969). *L'archéologie du savoir*. Paris: Gallimard.

Foucault, M. (1975). *Surveiller et punir*. Paris: Gallimard.

Freire, P. (1970). *Pedagogy of the Oppressed*. New York: Continuum.

Gabriel, D., & Tate, S.A. (2017). *Inside the Ivory Tower: Narratives of Women of Colour Surviving and Thriving in British Academia*. London: UCL Institute of Education Press.

Gramsci, A. (1975). *Quaderni del carcere*, ed. V. Gerratana. Turin: Einaudi.

Giroux, H. (2020). *On Critical Pedagogy*. 2nd ed. New York: Bloomsbury Academic.

Grayling, A.C. (2002). A question of discrimination. *The Guardian*. www.theguardian.com/books/2002/jul/13/arts.artsfeatures.

Grayling, A.C. (2016). *Democracy and Its Crisis*. London: Oneworld.

Hawthorn, G. (1980). Pareto and elitism. *London Review of Books*, 2(13), April.

Henry, W.A., III. (1995). *In Defence of Elitism*. New York: Anchor Books.

Hofstadter, R. (1963). *Anti-Intellectualism in American Life*. New York: Alfred A. Knopf.

hooks, b. (2014). *Teaching to Transgress: Education as the Practice of Freedom (Harvest in Translation)*. New York: Routledge.

Hunter, F. (1953). *Community Power Structure: A Study of Decision Makers*. Chapel Hill: University of North Carolina Press.

Kimball, R. (2002). The power of James Burnham. *New Criterion*. https://newcriterion.com/issues/2002/9/the-power-of-james-burnham.

Lasch, C. (1994). *The Revolt of the Elites: And the Betrayal of Democracy*. New York: Norton.

Lenin, V.I. (1901). *What Is to Be Done? Burning Questions of Our Movement*. Trans. J. Fineberg & G. Hanna. Marxists Internet Archive. www.marxists.org/archive/lenin/works/1901/witbd/.

Lipstitz, G. (1998). *The Possessive Investment in Whiteness: How White People Profit from Identity Politics*. Philadelphia: Temple University Press.

Locke, J. (1690/1980). *Second Treatise of Government*, ed. C.B. MacPherson. Indianapolis: Hackett.

Marcus, J. (2017). In an era of inequity, more and more college financial aid is going to the rich. The Hetchinger Report. https://hechingerreport.org/era-inequity-college-financial-aid-going-rich/.

McLaren, P. (2015). *Life in Schools: An Introduction to Critical Pedagogy in the Foundations of Education*. 6th ed. New York: Routledge.

Michels, R. (1911). *Political Parties: A Sociological Study of the Oligarchial Tendencies of Modern Democracy*, trans. E. & C. Paul. New York: Free Press.

Mills, C.W. (1956/2000). *The Power Elite: New Edition*. Oxford: Oxford University Press.

Mill, J.S. (1977). *On Liberty in Collected Works*, ed. J.M. Robson. London: Routledge and Kegan Paul.

Moore, T.O. (2010). The Making of an Educational Conservative: A Review of The Making of Americans: Democracy and Our Schools, by E.D. Hirsch. *Claremont Review of Books*, 10 (2), Spring. https://claremontreviewofbooks.com/the-making-of-an-educational-conservative/

Mosca, G. (1884/1982).Teorica dei governi e governo parlamentare. In G. Sola (ed.) *Scritti politici di Gaetano Mosca*, Vol. I. Turin: UTET.

Mosca, G. (1896/1982). Elementi di Scienza Politica. In G. Sola (ed.) *Scritti politici di Gaetano Mosca*, Vol. 2. Turin: UTET.

Oluo, I. (2018). *So You Want to Talk About Race*. New York: Seal Press.

Orwell, G. (1946). *Second Thoughts on James Burnham*. London: Polemic. https://orwell.ru/library/reviews/burnham/english/e_burnh.

Pareto, V.(1916). *Traité de sociologie générale*. Geneva: Droz.

Pareto,V. (1966). Mythes et ideologies. In G. Busino (ed.)*Oeuvres complètes*, vol. 9. Geneva: Droz.

Parisi, M. (2011). Gaetano Mosca. *Sicily Magazine*. www.bestofsicily.com.

Professor X (2012). *In the Basement of the Ivory Tower: The Truth About College*. London: Penguin.

Putnam, R.D. (2000). *Bowling Alone: The Collapse and Revival of American Community*. New York: Simon & Schuster.

Putnam, R.D. (2015). *Our Kids: The American Dream in Crisis*. New York: Simon & Schuster.

Rawls, J. (2001). *Justice as Fairness: A Restatement*, ed. E. Kelly. Cambridge, MA: Harvard University Press.

Robichaud, A., & Crevier, J.-P. (2016). Élitisme et éducation: lecture critique des thèses de Bourdieu à l'aide de la pensée de Jürgen Habermas, *Le Philosophoire*, 2(46), 37–58. www.cairn.info/revue-le-philosophoire-2016-2-page-37.htm.

Schattschneider, E. (1960). *The Semisovereign People: A Realist's View of Democracy in America*. Boston, MA: Wadsworth

Scott, J. (2008). Modes of Power and the Re-Conceptualization of Elites. *Sociological Review*. May. https://doi.org/10.1111/j.1467-954X.2008.00760.x.

Stein, J. (2019). *In Defense of Elitism: Why I'm Better Than You and You are Better Than Someone Who Didn't Buy This Book*. New York: Grand Central Books.

Tate, N. (2017). *Against the Current: The Conservative Case for Education*. Oxford: Routledge.

Young, M. (2008). *Bringing Knowledge Back In: From Social Constructivism to Social Realism in the Sociology of Education*. Oxford: Routledge.

Wolfwood, T. (2002). Arundhati Roy, "Power Politics". *Peace News*. https://pea cenews.info/node/5232/arundhati-roy-power-politics.

Wong, A. (2018). Private schools are becoming more elite. *The Atlantic*, July 26. www. theatlantic.com/education/archive/2018/07/why-private-schools-are-becoming-m ore-elite/566144/.

Chapter 3

A short history of access to schooling

Zach and Anthony

Before he died, Zach's father had told him about the basic education he had received in his local village. This was in the 1980s. Independence had spread through most African countries and there was a special vibrancy and magic in the air at the time, the feeling that anything was possible. In Burkina Faso, the revolutionary President Thomas Sankara had made it an imperative to improve school attendance. He increased literacy rates by more than 50% over a four-year period by developing strong educational schemes in every school (Kouraogo, 2010). There was also a strong feeling of national pride: in the mornings, students would sing the new national anthem, that the president himself had composed with his own electric guitar (Ray, 2013). Teachers were prepared to go the extra mile as they knew they were helping to shape the future of the nation. Zach's father learned the local language, Moré, at school, as well as the language of the colonisers, French. Every child had a right to this education. Sankara described every child in Burkina Faso as a president: the idea of accessing greatness seemed open and possible to everyone.

Zach's grandfather had been educated in the early 1950s under the French colonial system. Children were not taught the local language and lessons consisted in understanding the history and importance of France, the colonial power. Zach's grandfather learned by rote the facts and details of the Napoleonic Wars and France's involvement in the First World War. He was taught to refer to the Ancient Gauls as his "ancestors". Over a cup of tea beneath the tree where the villagers gathered to make decisions Zach's grandfather once told him, with a strange look in his eyes, that he could still remember standing up every morning to sing "La Marseillaise" but never understanding who he was really singing for.

Zach's great-grandfather, however, had never been to school, not to a formal bricks and mortar school in any case: this was at the turn of the 20th century when the missionaries offered instruction to children in the major cities. Those living in rural areas could not access what they had to offer. Zach's great-grandfather grew up herding cows since the local missionary school, run by Catholic priests, was too far from his homestead for him to attend. The only story Zach was ever told about his great-grandfather and missionary education was that he once travelled to the city of Koupéla with his family and saw children wearing uniforms and carrying books.

Zach's father had witnessed Thomas Sankara marrying the principle of compulsory free government education with the traditions of ancestral African education, and for a short time he was successful. But Sankara was cut down in the early 1980s, assassinated and replaced by a dictator whose vision of education was non-existent, and the content of the curriculum swayed back to that of France, literacy rates dropped, teachers' salaries were not paid and students stopped going to class.

Today, in 2020, Zach receives a free national education, a school education that is available to all. However, literacy rates in Burkina Faso are now among the lowest in the world (UNESCO, 2020), teachers are frequently absent and prospects to access the ladder of social opportunities seem further away than they were for his father. Extremists are active in preventing children from attending school too, saying it is "haram" ("forbidden"). They have not yet stopped Zach.

Anthony's father is a highly successful entrepreneur who fought his way through a late Soviet and early post-Soviet state education and, being a brilliant fencer, managed to secure a place at a top US university. Anthony's grandfather, who had been educated in the rigorous Soviet state system, was a high-ranking member of the KGB and, with the advent of perestroika, he placed a number of previously state-owned assets on the stock exchange and became a well-known billionaire in Russia. Much of his money was made at a time when Anthony's father needed a secure financial footing in order to follow his dreams. By the mid-1990s, when he graduated, money was not a problem and his father not only paid the annual fees of US $50,000 plus the expenses that were needed at the time, he invested heavily in the university, sponsoring the construction of a brand-new sports centre. This meant that a strong relationship was established between the family and the university. This could only help Anthony's application to join the university in the same way that it had helped his older brothers.

Yet quality education for all was free and available to children in both Russia and Switzerland and had been for nearly 100 years. Technically, there was no need to send Anthony to an expensive private school. Furthermore, both countries boasted outstanding state universities, also essentially free of cost. For most Soviet and Swiss children of previous decades, these were excellent options. It was only the very wealthy and globally mobile who looked beyond the state offer, to more prestigious and specialised offerings. One would have to go back to the end of the 1800s, before the Soviet revolution and the modernisation of Switzerland, when Anthony's great-grandparents, who were peasants, grew potatoes in Georgia and drew water from the local well, to find an education system that was open only to the few and not the many.

In Antony's great-grandparents' time, when the Czar was in power, most young people did not stay on at school much after the age of 11 or sometimes 14 (Brooks, 1981, p. 513) and education was not as developed nor did it last as long as it would do under the Soviets. In Anthony's great-grandparents' time, roughly 20% of the population of Russia was literate and there were only a handful of kindergartens in the country (Khaldey, 2020). It was only in the 1920s that Lenin established kindergartens in rural Russia, and by then Anthony's great-grandparents were too old to benefit from this.

But even so, Anthony's great-grandparents, like Zach's great-grandparents, had received an education. For that generation, the precepts of the Russian Orthodox church guided every step of life while ancient beliefs in spirits, such as house and water spirits, were communicated down the generations through seasonal pageants. Young people would learn wood carving, embroidery, dance and music. Although formal compulsory education had not taken a strong grip on society, children were still receiving an education that was rich and varied.

Zach and Anthony's historical lineages follow similar paths: their great-grandparents were brought up traditionally without a formal education, their grandparents and parents lived through the creation of the modern nation state and therefore benefited from a free state education. However, today, in the early 21st century, Zach and Anthony live completely different realities. To understand how the path forked, we need to go back in time to the way that access to education has been developed historically.

Understanding the complexities of tracing the history of education

What this chapter seeks to do is to examine the extent to which formal schooling, in the modern understanding of that term, has been open to societies across the globe.

It is difficult to trace the origins of formal education. This is essentially because its development from the informal generational transmission of knowledge, to the more structured, institutionalised schooling as it is practiced in the majority of formal models today, is blurred. A simplistic view would be to begin with European and American education reforms in the 19th century and to say that this is where formal schooling starts, but as this chapter will show, the situation is more complex. To view formal education as a development of, or progression from, informal education is perhaps more a question of cultural perspective than anything else. The Western teleological assumption of linearity tends to influence the overarching analysis of history in all fields, including education; as such, there is a belief in models that steadily become improved through the positivism of history.

Considering that indigenous knowledge systems, where collective transmission of knowledge, storytelling and group tutorials, inherent to hunter-gatherer culture, have been in place for thousands of years and continue to operate in numerous cultures, it is incorrect to view them as prototypes of primitive pre-educational models. Indeed, it is possible to view education in a broad, inclusive sense in order to appreciate the full diversity of its expression across cultures and periods of time. To speak of education "starting" in any given period is slightly absurd; it would be like arguing that human consciousness or communication "starts" at some point before which there is a void, for education is at the centre of what it means to be human and the transmission of knowledge is an intrinsic feature of the human condition.

There is a tendency to correlate education with literacy and therefore to see the origins of education taking place c. 3500 BCE in the Middle East, China and India with the origins of writing. Again, this disregards other forms of education that do not follow the logocentric tendencies concentrated in the Western and Eastern traditions. These legacies, which are largely undocumented, come through to the present day in the stories and myths that have been passed down about ancient and First Nations peoples such as the Indigenous peoples of Australia and the Americas:

> First Nations education systems served the same purpose as education systems today. Education was the means by which the values, beliefs, customs, lifestyle, and the accumulated knowledge and skills of First Nations peoples were passed from generation to generation. It was also the means by which individuals were prepared to take on specific tasks and roles within the family and community. The traditional education was family and community based. Education was grounded firmly in the First Nations' sense of spirituality and responded to the practical demands of day to day living within a defined traditional territory. Although there was some specialization of instruction by specific individuals, the task of education was undertaken by many people; the parents, elders, and the extended family all contributed their knowledge.
>
> (Matthew, 2001)

Therefore, before we consider the origins of formal schooling, let us not forget that such an enterprise is more a question of perspective than fact: formal schooling is not the only way of learning; it is one way among others.

The earliest records of formal schooling: Egypt, Mesopotamia, India, China, the Americas and Europe

The origins of formal education seem to appear at the time of the great agricultural revolutions that humans experienced in the fertile crescent of India and China c. 5000 BCE as migratory cultures transformed into agrarian cultures and the resultant political military and class divisions became stronger. As there was a need to protect parcels of land and agriculture, and to formalise trading systems with other sedentary hubs, an early division of labour emerged and this developed into a segregated class system that was much more complex and anchored than that which had been in existence in previous hunter–gatherer phases of human development.

Indeed, the whole idea of access to formal education cannot be dissociated from the development of superstructural economic, militaristic and political powers. The notion that education is a resource that should, or should not, be made accessible to people is a modern idea that takes root with the behaviours and belief systems of sedentary society along with its expressions of commerce, mathematics and writing within what could be called a logocentric culture.

Records of the formal literacy training of scribes under Mentuhotep II of Egypt in the Middle Kingdom (c. 3400 BCE) suggest that some form of schooling was designed for a select group of boys, whereas girls would stay at home and learn housekeeping (Thomason, 2005). Literacy rates in Ancient Egypt and, consequently, the corresponding formal education in literacy offered to apprentice scribes, was very low, in the region of 1% (Baines, 1983). In sub-Saharan Africa, records suggest that education tended to be home-based and was focused on practical skills and cultural rituals with clear gender separation (Kaschula, 1999). A reputed centre of religious instruction, offered to the select few who were engaged in spiritual studies, was known to exist in Ethiopia.

Records of education systems in other parts of the world trace first instances of formal schooling to roughly 2000 BCE onwards. In China, the Xia dynasty government offered schooling to the children of aristocrats. Throughout the Shang and Zhou dynasties, government schools grew in the cities and more and more children were given access to education. However, a two-tiered system meant that the wealthy, who studied at government schools, received higher quality instruction, whereas peasants could only access more rudimentary, practical instruction in private schools located away from the cities (Kinney, 2004).

During the Vedic period of India (starting c. 1500 BCE), a broad-based education based on Vedic literature, the sciences, grammar, logic and traditional knowledge was freely available to children, although girls followed a programme based more on dance and housekeeping (Gupta, 2007). However, through time, the caste system delineated different levels of access and quality according to the group in question: Brahmins were given access to the most intellectual education.

In Mesopotamia, by the time Babylon was a thriving city in 1770 BCE and writing had evolved into a syllabic system, there are records of fairly widespread literacy rates and schools (Veldhuis, 2004). Most students would learn cuneiform through drills in the early stages of the curriculum but few would advance to the latter stages that allowed them to master the trade of the scribe. Persia followed a similar structure: under the Achaemenians, formal education was essentially reserved for "priests, warriors, tillers of the soil, and merchants" (*Encyclopaedia Britannica*, 2020).

Ancient Incan education was selective, dedicated to the youth of nobles who learned politics, history, military techniques, religion and languages, whereas the vast majority of the population, essentially subsistence farmers, received an informal, practical education. There is some evidence that bright and outstanding children were scouted in the Incan Empire and that they received the formal schooled education of the nobles. As was the case in other parts of the world, boys received a vastly different education to girls; the latter group learned weaving, cooking and the arts, although the daughters of nobles attended specialised schools in governance for the privileged (Davies, 1995).

Ancient European societies followed a similar pattern to those of Africa, the Americas and Asia; in other words, formal educational provision in the form of schools was restricted to the children of nobility, whereas the majority of the population received an informal education based on agriculture and life skills. There is some conjecture about the system of education during the Minoan period and more confident hypotheses have been made that during the Mycenaean period, in Crete at Knossos, for example, classrooms were built and some form of artistic and calligraphic skills were transmitted to the youth (Burrage, 1920). However, who exactly had access to formal education remains unknown and there is every likelihood that it was a small elite. In Ancient Athens, c. 500 BCE, the Sophists provided paid lessons in rhetoric to the children of wealthy politicians, while Plato's famous Academy, arguably one of the first schools in Europe, was highly selective with the statement "Let no one ignorant of geometry enter" inscribed over the entrance.

Therefore, it can be stated with relative confidence that across the globe the earliest traces of formal education, as in a structured, schooled approach with an emphasis on writing, abstract and theoretical studies such as geometry and literature, were reserved for tiny elites, mainly the children of the wealthy or those groomed for a life in the priesthood. This coincides with the general epistemology of ancient sedentary civilisations, in which certain types of knowledge, giving access to power, were seen as arcane and, therefore, were not distributed widely but retained for those in positions of authority and leadership.

Interestingly, an exception to this can be found in Ancient Israel where the system of the Torah insisted in at least three of the commandments that each father provide an education to his children in literacy, involving the reading and writing of scrolls (Deuteronomy 31: 10, 11). Not only did every family therefore access abstract intellectual literacy skills through the process, but this led to reforms whereby teachers could be appointed to ensure the transmission of the Torah and, therefore, the development of schools. One of the earliest and best known of these was that of the mythic scribe Ezra, who, in the fourth century BCE along with his Synod, established a school that some 600 years later, c. 64 BCE, was reformed into several schools so as to offer a free education to every child over five years of age. This reform was enacted by the famous High Priest Joshua ben Gamla who organised for the appointment of teachers and essentially represents a precursor to free public education. It could be said, therefore, that access to free formal education started in Israel during this period[1] (Babylonian Talmud).

Access to education in Ancient Rome

The Roman Republic and early Roman Empire used a similar system to the Ancient Greek one where private tutors worked with small groups of fee-paying students, mainly the children of patricians. There is little evidence of any formal education being offered to the wider population. However, by the time of Quintilian (35 CE–c. 100 CE) single classroom schools were common, although they remained selective to those who could afford them. Higher institutes of learning began to be prominent, possibly the best known being the Pandidakterion, a centre of learning in the sciences, philosophy and rhetoric founded by Theodosius II in 425 CE (Constantelos, 1999). Education became steadily more accessible to the masses.

Although during the first Roman Empire, Roman schools remained institutions that were open only to those who could afford them, by the time that the Eastern Empire was thriving with Constantinople as its capital, there is evidence of a much more widespread offering of primary education with schools operating in most communes (Rietbergen, 1998, p. 101). During the Holy Roman Empire, educational offerings became more and more widespread. Charlemagne accelerated the growth of literacy programmes through the church with the aim of educating as many subjects as possible, albeit through the monastic structure that had become the staple organ of education. Much of this educational reform was carried out by Alcuin of York (732–804) (Pavlac & Lott, 2019, p. 14).

The Middle Ages

Schooling in Europe during the Middle Ages was essentially run by the church and it was free. Schools were attached to cathedrals and provided a liberal arts education to boys. This was effectively the origin of public schools in the United Kingdom as well as some of Europe's oldest schools. It should be noted that a major source of education throughout the Middle Ages in Europe came through the Benedictine order whose model at Cluny Abbey (founded in 910) offered a model that proliferated throughout Europe until well beyond the 12th century.

Therefore, the ongoing structure of formal education being made available to a select few and not offered freely to the many remained in place throughout the Middle Ages even if, as schools and universities became more prominent, access widened and literacy rates grew slowly but steadily.

For the vast majority, the Middle Ages in any part of the world was still feudally structured with hamlets of informal education operating at a grassroots level with pockets of prestige and access to abstract, intellectual formulations of knowledge taking place in important city centres only. These narrow access schools were mainly rhetoric and grammar schools or universities, run by the religious order. The idea that education is a paid service was strong, particularly in Europe. Exceptions to this rule can be seen in Eastern models of formal education such as the madrassa.

During the Islamic Golden Age (800–1400), madrassas across various caliphates offered religious and scientific instruction to young scholars irrespective of their social status.

Education in India during the Middle Ages, even if it was free in certain pockets, was by and large a system of private tuition since the construct of state education did not exist. Private tutors, known as "riyazi", could make considerable sums of money by teaching the children of the wealthy and nobility (Kumar, 2003, p. 680). Through time this evolved into a more organised system of schooling called "gurukuls", run by local gurus. Although these were funded by a system of public donation, they were open only to the ruling caste (Dharampal, 2000). However, by the time the British arrived in India to colonise it, madrassas were operating widely and provided free education for thousands of children (Dharampal 2000).

Over the course of thousand years during this period of history, schooling became more and more widespread and sophisticated, evolving from bone pens used on wax tablets to quills and parchment. In some ways this education was not elitist as it was open access and, as is the case in the UK's earliest charity schools, designed specifically to educate the poor. However, girls were not admitted and had to learn from home.

The medieval period saw the development of education unlike any age before—and while it is true that education for women was severely limited, the booming trade and economic success of society during the Middle Ages shows that education was beginning to be commonly accessible in society.

The Renaissance and Enlightenment in Europe

This system of a structured, formal education offered to the wealthy only continued throughout the Renaissance in Western Europe: most boys were educated at home while a small elite worked with paid tutors, as had been the case during the majority of the Ancient Greek, Roman and Medieval periods. Girls, for the most part, received a different and essentially inferior education to boys.

Following the invention of the printing press, there was a greater necessity to know how to read and, therefore, literacy rates increased as did the establishment of formal institutions of learning that could help with this process. The Renaissance accelerated the growth of educational institutions in Europe, in particular through the design of universities, art and research centres. Not entirely unlike the information revolution that the age of the internet created in the 1990s and the 2democratisation of knowledge that this implied, the printing press changed the dynamic relationship between instructor and student:

> Previous relations between masters and disciples were altered. Students who took full advantage of technical texts which served as silent instructors …

Young minds provided with updated editions, especially of mathematical texts, began to surpass not only their own elders but the wisdom of ancients as well.

(Eisenstein, 1979/1997, p. 689)

Although education was still largely reserved for a minority, what we could term an elite—at least demographically, geographically and socio-economically—literacy became increasingly accessible outside of the hallowed and restricted monasteries and studios that historically had been open to the privileged few only. It was now possible to access theoretical, intellectual formations from home, and home schooling started to become characterised by literacy education.

This is a fundamental point that recurs throughout the history of access to education: technological reforms, in general, allow greater access to learning.

The particular case of the translation of the Bible into German under Martin Luther in 1534 is worthy of some focus. Luther's desire to have the Bible translated was part of his worldview that espoused a democratisation of religious knowledge. Importantly, the Bible could be read at home in the vernacular, opening access to the text and abstract ideas beyond the significant thresholds of Ancient Greek and Latin—the languages of the clergy and the minority.

Luther not only argued for universal access to education, open to all stations of society, he made considerable efforts to ensure that schools were opened for boys and girls (Williams, 2017). One of his earliest reforms was to convert churches into schools in order to ensure that a maximum number of young people, including the very poor, could be educated. Some theories of why there are such high standards of education and literacy in Nordic countries can be traced back to Lutheran reformism, most specifically concerning reforms in schools. Becker and Woessmann (2009) have argued that Max Weber's well-established theory that capitalism was accelerated in Anglo-Saxon nations because of a Protestant ethic could be misguided as the real driver of economic prosperity in Protestant nations came from the early development of literacy and its comparatively equal distribution, something Luther believed in and fought for throughout his life. Education in Northern European countries developed quickly throughout the Renaissance, and by the time of the Enlightenment it had become a highly structured, albeit selective, system. The kindergarten and gymnasium, still in operation today, are remnants of this.

This Protestant vision of education as a right rather than a paid privilege affected initiatives across many European countries to open schools to the masses. For example, in Scotland, the 1633 Education Act ordered the establishment of a church-run school in every parish (Brown, 2011).

England started to open schools to the masses, notably the Sunday School system, institutionalised by the likes of Thomas Wilson on the Isle of Man in 1703, William King in 1751, Hannah Ball in 1769 and Robert Raikes from the

1780s. By 1785, a quarter of a million children in England attended free Sunday Schools (Towns, 1993). Although these were denominational schools and, therefore, not strictly open to all but to those who attended the church, over time they became cross-denominational. The offering remained fairly rudimentary with courses in basic literacy and Bible studies open to children, adolescents and adults. In time Sunday Schools were opened to girls too.

In Ireland, the first Sunday School, opened in 1777 by Catholic priest Daniel Delaney, operated at a fairly complex level and developed modern school practices such as publishing timetables, levelling classes according to ability and even publishing teacher schemes of work (Brennan, 1935). In the United States, Sunday Schools started in textile mill communities in the 1790s under the leadership of the wealthy entrepreneur Samuel Slater. The tradition of offering some sort of educational provision to the poor became reinforced in England with the official recognition and appellation of Charity Schools, stemming from the work done by the Society for the Propagation of Christian Knowledge (founded in 1699).[2] The work of this organisation grew and by the 1700s aimed to provide education to poor children aged between seven and 11 as much as possible. The Society was also involved in the development of teacher training programmes (UK Parliament, 2020).

However, it was not only on the Protestant side of Christianity that education became increasingly democratised: the Jesuit Order was responsible for the establishment of schools throughout Europe and beyond, into the so-called New World and colonial Empire. Indeed, throughout the Renaissance, some of France's most prominent thinkers were educated at Jesuit schools, a famous example being Descartes, who was educated at the French Jesuit college in La Flèche. Voltaire was also educated at the Jesuit school Louis-le-Grand in the early 1700s and Diderot was schooled at a Jesuit college in Langres. The first Jesuit school was opened in Messina, Italy, in 1548 and by the end of the 1500s Jesuit colleges had been opened in Macau and Japan. By 1773, there were roughly 800 Jesuit educational institutions in the world (O'Malley, 2000). Jesuit schools were part of a religious effort to provide education to all. In the words of St Ignatius, the aim of these institutions was to provide an education "to rich and poor alike, without distinction" (O'Malley, 1989, p. 3). However, this vision was short-lived as today Jesuit private schools tend to be selective and expensive.

The Renaissance gave way to the Enlightenment in Europe, and educational institutions flourished as the systems of patronage and royal societies gathered funds for research institutions and their corresponding instructional units. The opening of the Royal Society (founded in 1660) and the Royal Academy of Arts (founded in 1768) in the UK signified this increase in scholarship and general access to education.

The important social upheaval caused by the American and French revolutions created a wave of reform throughout the Western world whereby education finally began to be seen as something that should be offered to all. The egalitarian discourses of major philosophers of the time, such as those of Jean-Jacques

Rousseau (1755/1975) influenced the origins of modern state education. At the heart of this Romantic discourse was the belief that the role of government was to support and enable populations to enjoy intellectual and moral freedoms, and that government had a social contract with its citizens to provide them with unalienable rights. The idea that education was one of those rights had not been formalised yet, but it was a latent influence in the reforms that were to come in the following century.

This vision struggled to materialise in France. During the time of the French Revolution, Catholic schools might not have been accessible to all, but most students were given bursaries and they managed to provide an education for roughly 50,000 boys throughout the country. The revolutionaries confiscated church land and institutions and aimed to redistribute these resources to the population through the organ of the state, but the management of this was not successful and by the end of the 1700s the government was obliged to sell these assets in order to generate income for foreign wars (Palmer, 1986). Reforms under Condorcet and Napoleon tried to open access to education, but it was not until the late 19th century that the modern model of free, compulsory state education was finally erected.

Of course, it is possible to view compulsory state education more cynically, not only as a disseminator of intellectual capital but alternatively as a vehicle that would standardise thought and attitudes in a programme of propaganda. Benedict Anderson's work on the origins of the nation state makes it clear how the standardisation of language and education is inseparably linked to the ideological formatting of minds necessary to create a feeling of nationhood and acceptance of national authority (Anderson, 1991). As Cubberly points out, while a "new individualistic theory for a secular school was created [and the] original purpose in the establishment of schools by the State was everywhere to promote literacy and citizenship", a strong aim in France and the United States was to "serve national ends" (Cubberly, 1920, p. 787).

The 19th century

The 19th century is the era of the introduction of mass education, made free and compulsory for all by the state. One of the initial drivers was child labour. The Industrial Revolution in Britain had brought terrible working conditions with it and child labour was rife.

The Elementary Education Act of 1870 in England and Wales

In 1876, the Royal Commission on the Factory Acts was passed in Britain to stop child labour. This rapidly evolved into the Elementary Education Act of 1870, otherwise known as the Forster Act, which was reformed several times, making education compulsory for children aged between five to 13 in England and Wales. It stated that parents were to pay for their children's education, but if they could not, tuition fees would be exempted. This was because schools were to be publicly funded. Attendance at school was compulsory. State schools were to be secular and, therefore, "religious teaching should be non-denominational, and … parents could withdraw their children from religious education" (Dalgleish, 1870).

Subsequent reforms to the Act made education even more inclusive. In 1893, the Act "extended the age of compulsory attendance to 11, and in 1899 to 12". Further to this,

> Compulsory education was also extended to blind and deaf children under the Elementary Education (Blind and Deaf Children) Act of 1893, which established special schools. Similar provision was made for physically impaired children in the Elementary Education (Defective and Epileptic Children) Act of 1899.
>
> (UK Parliament, 2020)

The Act caused substantial anxiety since it represented a new way of considering education, divesting the church of its key role as the institution that had provided schooling for centuries and, of course, the moral message of religious instruction that came with it. With educational provision came power over minds and attitudes, and this would be transferred from the church to the state.

On the other hand, the Act committed to subsidising the education of poor children, even if they were to choose denominational schools. Therefore, non-conformists felt that taxes were being used to fund the Church of England, which caused some anger. By 1891, education was free and compulsory for all children up to the age of ten.

While the waves of British educational reform of the 19th century opened access to learning, girls were only partially included in these developments:

> The Education Act of 1870 set the framework for the elementary education of children, but secondary education was largely unavailable to working class girls. The 1918 Education Act raised the compulsory school leaving age to 14, but it was not until the 1944 Education Act that secondary education became free and the compulsory leaving age rose to 15. The majority of secondary schools were single-sex until the comprehensive reform of the 1960s and 1970s.
>
> (UCL, 2019)

The Jules Ferry laws in France

Jules Ferry (1832–1893), republican philosopher and politician, who became minister of public instruction, put in place a series of laws from 1881 to 1882 that would make primary education free and compulsory to all those living in the French nation. French was to be the language of instruction (which led to the demise of a number of other languages or so-called dialects in France since the necessity to speak a nationally standardised French washed out the growth of smaller languages).

Ferry was determined to promulgate a secular state philosophy through education and insisted that schools be non-denominational, something that has remained core to national education to this day, causing various polemics around the wearing of religious icons in schools. Ferry also worked to reform tertiary education by moving university teaching out of the church. Under his ministries, the number of university professors grew substantially.

State education in the United States

Education in the United States, provided mainly in an informal manner within European settler communities and, in a diminished form, for slaves, followed the Enlightenment movement's thrust for universal access to education. President John Adams said in 1795 that "there should not be a district of one mile square, without a school in it, not founded by a charitable individual, but maintained at the public expense of the people themselves" (Adams, 1854, p. 540).

The first American public schools were established in the 1820s. A number of faith-based community schools were set up too but they were not funded by the government. From 1852 to 1917, a series of laws in different states made schooling compulsory (Bandiera et al., 2018). This had an impact on literacy rates which were, according to some scholars, among the highest in the world (Goldin, 2005). An icon of universal access to education in the United Sates was Horace Mann (1796–1859), a Massachusetts statesman who pioneered for the cause in the 1830s, leading to the expansion and standardisation of so-called common schools, which were essentially religious secondary schools that were inclusive and free of charge. It should be noted that black Americans struggled to enjoy the same kind of access to these institutions as their white counterparts (Moss, 2007).

Colonisation

While European nations were steadily implementing Enlightenment philosophies of egalitarianism and free access to education on the continent, many were also colonising nations around the globe in order to exploit natural and human resources so as to fuel their economies. This was made abundantly clear when colonised nations became decolonised and it was revealed just how high illiteracy rates were after decades of a void of any real educational structure for the masses (Banya, 1993).

In general, 18th- and 19th-century French, British, Portuguese and Spanish colonisation in Asia, Latin America and Africa did not open access to formal schooling to local children as the imperative was essentially imperialistic and exploitative. Early mission schools operated mainly in the major cities and offered a formal education to small numbers with the goal of proselytisation, but once the more institutionalised and organised process of colonisation started, very little was provided for indigenous populations.

India and Africa

Efforts were put in place to provide free schooling to certain population groups for entirely strategic reasons. In India, for example, the English Education Act of 1835 ensured that the language of instruction was no longer Sanskrit or Persian but English. Thomas Macaulay, the colonial engineer of British-styled education in India, famously said that

> we must at present do our best to form a class who may be interpreters between us and the millions whom we govern; a class of persons, Indian in blood and colour, but English in taste, in opinions, in morals, and in intellect.
> (Macaulay, 1835)

Thus, the prerogative to offer a standardised education was to form the minds of future colonial clerks.

In French colonial West Africa, the approach was one of assimilation, whereby through the apparatus of a national education, which initially was only offered to the elite but gradually became widespread, the language, culture and history of France would displace local culture. In Mali and Senegal, the so-called hostage school entailed the children of local dignitaries being forced into French schools so as to impose a French system of language and values onto them.

Latin America

In Latin America, historians point out that little was done to educate subjects (Burkholder & Johnson, 2014): formal schooling was provided for the elite and children of interracial encounters between Europeans and Incas but not for indigenous populations. Any formal education prior to systematic colonisation was carried out by Jesuit friars, but once formal colonisation began the Spanish Crown stopped that work and did not replace it adequately, which led to fewer schools being in operation, and those that did run being concentrated in cities only.

The hero of Latin American independence, Venezuelan Simón Bolívar (1783–1830), exhorted countries to enable universal access to education in 1819 although this did not materialise as he might have hoped and it was not until deep into the 20th century that free compulsory education began to be common across most Latin American countries. Slow adoption was mainly due to political turmoil and difficulties dissociating the church from education in order to secularise and nationalise it in the same way that Ferry had done in France.

China

Throughout the provinces of China during the 19th-century Qing dynasty, selective academies offered high-quality education for free. There were different types of academy: those offering an educational pathway that led to governance; and those inducting students to an appreciation of literature and the arts (Hsu, 1964). However, it would only be 100 years later, in 1986, that the National People's Congress brought into force the "Compulsory Education Law of the People's Republic of China".

Essentially, the colonial period, concentrated around the Opium Wars and the occupation of China by Britain in 1839 following the ceding of Hong Kong, was marked by poor educational standards, formal structures offered to elites only with a pragmatic design. It was less about giving citizens access to literacy and more about shaping mindsets and political docility through language instruction (Evans, 2006). Educational systems slowly began to resemble European ones during the 20th-century era of colonisation, but it was still a poor and fragmented shadow of what universal access to education might be.

The 20th century to the present day

The last waves of reforms that took place in educational systems across the globe were rooted in Enlightenment beliefs but unfolded on the ground about 100 years later. One of these beliefs, recognised by Thomas Jefferson and others, was that in order for a democracy to function well, citizens had to be educated, otherwise essentially they would be manipulated and would not know who to vote for. This is a simple idea but one that is a profound cornerstone of democracy.

The idea that education is not just necessary for society but is also a human right became prominent in the 20th century. Article 26 of the Universal Declaration of Human Rights, drafted in 1948, states that:

1   Everyone has the right to education. Education shall be free, at least in the elementary and fundamental stages. Elementary education shall be compulsory. Technical and professional education shall be made generally available and higher education shall be equally accessible to all on the basis of merit.
2   Education shall be directed to the full development of the human personality and to the strengthening of respect for human rights and fundamental freedoms. It shall promote understanding, tolerance and friendship among all nations, racial or religious groups, and shall further the activities of the United Nations for the maintenance of peace.
3   Parents have a prior right to choose the kind of education that shall be given to their children.

(United Nations, 2020a)

These ideas have been operationalised by organisations affiliated with the United Nations, such as UNICEF and UNESCO. The latter devised the following six Education For All goals at the World Education Forum held in 2000 in Dakar, Senegal:

Goal 1: Expand early childhood care and education
Goal 2: Provide free and compulsory primary education for all
Goal 3: Promote learning and life skills for young people and adults
Goal 4: Increase adult literacy by 50 percent
Goal 5: Achieve gender parity by 2005, gender equality by 2015
Goal 6: Improve the quality of education

(Suter, Smith & Denman, 2019)

In 2017, UNESCO reported that none of these goals had yet to be completely met and that globally roughly 264 million young people were not in school (Bleiker, 2017). At the time of writing, it was estimated that approximately 268 million young people were not in school (UNESCO Institute of Statistics, 2020). This shows that thus far free compulsory education remains an objective more than a reality enjoyed by all.

There are complex politico-economic reasons why not all children are in school. Furthermore, many classroom environments are substandard: learning takes place under very difficult circumstances compounded by absent teachers, broken infrastructures and a lack of resources.

Despite the fact that children in many countries are still not in school and that much of the groundwork needed on numeracy and literacy to ensure that quality education can thrive is not yet in place, the United Nations' 2030 Sustainable Development Goal (SDG) 4, Quality Education for All, looks to "Ensure inclusive and equitable quality education and promote lifelong learning opportunities for all" (United Nations, 2020b). However, roughly 750 million of the global population is illiterate, the majority of them concentrated in sub-Saharan Africa and South Asia and in 2015 roughly half of the world's primary and lower secondary school students were not achieving basic literacy levels, despite many of them being in school (United Nations, 2020b).

Standards of state education

One of the problems is that even though we are closer to universal access to education for every child than ever before in history, the quality of the education accessed is extremely variable.

Progress in International Reading Literacy Study (PIRLS) scores in literacy make this quite clear. The overall reading average scale scores of fourth-grade students, by education system, saw Norway, Finland, Ireland, Hong Kong, Singapore and the Russian Federation score well over 550 points (with a centre point of 500 points), whereas Morocco, Egypt and South Africa all fell below 400 points (IEA, 2016). Results were roughly similar for mathematics (Mullis et al., 2016).

Gender discrimination

It has been shown how, historically, educational provision has either been exclusively for boys or differentiated in such a way that more intellectual, abstract knowledge would be offered to boys, whereas girls would be educated to remain active in households and to attain basic practical competences. This situation is of course better today than it has been historically, but we are still very far from equality or equity. UNICEF reported in 2020 that one in three adolescent girls from the poorest households had never been to school (UNICEF, 2020). This came from a study on 42 countries that showed how:

> Ten countries across Africa account for the highest disparities in education spending, with four times as much funding allocated to the richest children compared with the poorest. In Guinea and the Central African Republic – countries with some of the world's highest rates of out-of-school children – the richest children benefit from nine and six times, respectively, the amount of public education funds than the poorest children.
>
> Barbados, Denmark, Ireland, Norway and Sweden are the only countries included in the analysis that distribute education funding equally between the richest and poorest quintiles.
>
> (UNICEF, 2020)

Disability discrimination

Children with disabilities have not been given real access to quality education historically and while the situation has improved, there are still many parts of the world where it is not the case. The Convention on the Rights of the Child has issued statements that children with disabilities should be able to access education, but a 2016 UNICEF report argued, shockingly, that an estimated "90% of children with disabilities in the developing world do not go to school" (GPE, 2020).

For example, a Human Rights Watch article showed that in Iran "during the 2018–2019 school year, only 150,000 out of an estimated 1.5 million children with disabilities of school age were enrolled in school" (Human Rights Watch, 2019).

The impact of the internet

An argument might be made that the most recent surge in technology, the World Wide Web, has widened access to education to a previously unimaginable extent. Few could argue that the availability of Massive Online Open Courses (MOOCs), MasterClasses, free webinars and general information on the web has not changed the morphology of access to knowledge dramatically.

However, the extent to which the availability of information online can be seen as a serious proxy to formal education with its tutoring, scaffolding, interactive feedback, marking, correction, coaching and human-to-human inspiration, begs many questions.

The recent COVID-19 crisis has demonstrated the effects of a digital divide too: some schools, mostly private, were able to continue lessons fairly well through the use of videoconferencing, enjoying the luxury of strong bandwidth connections on all sides, high-performing computerised devices and teaching expertise in the field of online learning. Those in other environments, however, had to carry on teaching and learning through mobile phones, through work being sent to families once a week and many of these activities were disrupted by poor connectivity, lack of sufficient competence and training in online learning. This could be termed, broadly speaking, the digital divide.

In 2012 the Pew Research Center's Internet & American Life Project showed that in the USA access to the internet is varied and tends to echo socioeconomic insertion patterns. Thus, according to the study:

- "young adults, minorities, those with no college experience, and those with lower household income levels" are more likely to access the internet primarily through their phones;
- 49% of African Americans and 51% of Hispanics have high-speed internet at home, as compared with 66% of Caucasians. (Soltan, 2019)

Thus, access to online learning, which is restricted, might broaden the educational experience to a certain degree, but is still not enough to provide the universal access to quality education that is the imperative of the United Nations SDGs. Chapter 8 discusses online learning in the light of the COVID-19 pandemic in detail.

Conclusion

This chapter has shown how a rapid overview of the history of access to education paints a clear picture. For the overwhelmingly large part of the last 5,000 years, human beings have restricted access to education for the wealthy and noble. In short, it has been an elitist education.

Historically, the role of religious institutions in the promulgation of education and the opening of education to the poor has been significant. Some cultural institutions such as madrassas in ancient India and the church in Europe managed to open opportunities to a fairly wide constituency early on in historical development. However, even in these cases, it was still only for a minority.

Enlightenment ideas, ensconced in Romantic ideals about human nature and human rights, leading to modern discourses on access to education, have opened schools to billions of children throughout the world and there is little doubt that humanity lives in a far more egalitarian world today, concerning education, than in many previous periods of history. The chapter has shown how successive spikes in technology have created different and often increased levels of access to education: with the agricultural revolution came writing and the need to build academies; with the invention of the printing press came widespread literacy programmes and heightened access to knowledge; with the development of the nation state came the need to standardise education and create a common historical narrative; and with the information revolution through the development of the internet access to knowledge has become individualised and, in some ways, almost unfettered.

However, access is still not completely open, despite the increased distribution of knowledge through technology. Many children are not in school and many children receive a substandard education when in school. To be clear, this is not the case everywhere: the child educated in the state system in Finland, Singapore or Switzerland does not experience anything like the child learning in state schools in rural Mexico and South Africa or Morocco. What can be done to improve access to quality education for all learners?

This is part of the problem in the debate on elitism and education: the universal access to education that has been won for children through the hard work of reformers and idealists over time is not enough. What is needed is access to high-quality, impactful education, something that is currently only available in extremely wealthy countries or in countries that have invested heavily in education.

This chapter has indicated some of the tensions that arise with universal access to education, because it begs the question of which education? Whose history? Which knowledge and why? Some philosophers have seen state education primarily as a vehicle for the programming of minds rather than an access to literacy. This is one of the arguments for the privatisation of education—the fact that it allows for more independence and healthy intellectual multiplicities in approach.

Finally, it should not be forgotten that the rich tapestry of informal education that has characterised human activity from the earliest traces has had an important role to play in the development of society. This too is part of the history of access to education.

Indeed, rather than to view the development of formal schooling as something that came from nowhere, it would be more appropriate to see it as a phenomenon of displacement. This is because formal classroom education clearly takes up the space that was occupied by traditional education. As a result, fewer non-standardised languages will be learnt, and there will be less transmission of highly localised culture and mythology. Indeed, rather than adopt a naïve positivist understanding of formal education as nothing but a linear trajectory that represents force for good, it is important to see it alongside informal education as an alternative route.

Notes

1 See Babylonian Talmud (n.d.) Tractate Baba Bathra, Folio 21a. https://halakhah. com/bababathra/bababathra_21.html.
2 Fascinatingly, as this book shows in Chapter 4, in the 19th century, charity schools morphed into public schools and became extremely expensive and selective.

References

Adams, J. (1854). *The Works of John Adams, Second President of the United States: With a Life of the Author, Notes and Illustrations*, Vol. 9. Boston: Little, Brown and Company, p. 540.

Anderson, B. (1991). *Imagined Communities: Reflections on the Origin and Spread of Nationalism*. London: Verso.

Baines, J. (1983). Literacy and ancient Egyptian society. *Man* (New Series), 18(3), 572–599.

Bandiera, O., Mohnen, M., Rasul, I., & Viarengo, M. (2018). Nation-building through compulsory schooling during the age of mass migration. *Economic Journal*, 129(617), 62–109.

Banya, K. (1993). Illiteracy, Colonial Legacy and Education: The Case of Modern Sierra Leone. *Comparative Education*, 29(2), 159–170. www.jstor.org/stable/3099274 (accessed August 6, 2020).

Brennan, M. (1935). *Schools of Kildare and Leighlin, A.D. 1775–1835*. Dublin: M.H. Gill and Son Ltd.

Becker, S., & Woessmann, L. (2009). Was Weber wrong? A human capital theory of protestant economic history. *Quarterly Journal of Economics*, 124(2), 531–596. https:// EconPapers.repec.org/RePEc:oup:qjecon:v:124:y:2009:i:2:p:531-596.

Bleiker, C. (2017). UNESCO: 264 million children don't go to school. *DW*. www.dw. com/en/unesco-264-million-children-dont-go-to-school/a-41084932.

Burrage, D. (1920). *Educational Progress in Greece during the Minoan, Mycenaean and Lyric periods*. Doctoral thesis. University of Nebraska. www.archive.org/stream/educationa lprogr00burrrich/educationalprogr00burrrich_djvu.txt.

Brooks, J. (1981). Education in pre-revolutionary Russia. *History of Education Quarterly*, 21(4), 509–515. doi:doi:10.2307/367931.

Brown, K.M. (2011). *Noble Power in Scotland from the Reformation to the Revolution*. Edinburgh: Edinburgh University Press, pp.155–166.

Burkholder, M.A., & Johnson, L.L. (2014). *Colonial Latin America*. 9th edn. Oxford: Oxford University Press.

Constantelos, D.J. (1999). *Christian Hellenism. Essays and Studies in Continuity and Change*. New York: Aristide D. Karatzis.

Cubberly, E.P. (1920). *The History of Education: Educational Practice and Progress Considered as a Phase of the Development and Spread of Western Civilization*. Boston, MA: Houghton Mifflin Company.

Dalgleish, W. (1870). *A Plain Reading of the Elementary Education Act*. London: John Marshall & Co. www.bl.uk/collection-items/synopsis-of-the-forster-education-act-1870.

Davies, N. (1995). *The Incas*. Boulder: University Press of Colorado.

Dharampal (2000). *The Beautiful Tree: Indigenous Indian Education in the Eighteenth Century*. New Delhi: Biblia Impex.

Eisenstein, E.L. (1979/1997). *The Printing Press as an Agent of Change*. Cambridge: Cambridge University Press.

Encyclopaedia Britannica (2020). *Aims and Purposes of Muslim Education*. www.britannica. com/topic/education/Aims-and-purposes-of-Muslim-education.

Evans, S. (2006) Language policy in British Colonial Education: Evidence from nineteenth-century Hong Kong. *Journal of Educational Administration and History*, 38(3), 293–312, doi:doi:10.1080/00220620600984214.

Goldin, C. (2005). A Brief History of Education in the United States. *Historical Statistics of the United States*. New York: Cambridge University Press.

Global Partnership of Education (GPE) (2016). *Children with Disabilities Face the Longest Road to Education*. www.globalpartnership.org/blog/children-disabilities-face-longest-road-education.

Gupta, A. (2007). *Going to School in South Asia*. Westport, CT: Greenwood Publishing Group, 73–76.

Hardaker, G., & Sabki, A.A. (2019). *Pedagogy in Islamic Education: The Madrasah Context*. Bingley: Emerald Group Publishing. pp. 8–9.

Hsu, I. (1964). The Reorganisation of Higher Education in Communist China, 1949–1961. *China Quarterly*, 19, 128–160.

Human Rights Watch (2019). *"Just Like Other Kids". Lack of Access to Inclusive Quality Education for Children with Disabilities in Iran*. www.hrw.org/report/2019/10/02/just-other-kids/lack-access-inclusive-quality-education-children-disabilities-iran.

International Association for the Evaluation of Educational Achievement (IEA) (2016). *Progress in International Reading Literacy Study (PIRLS)*. https://nces.ed.gov/surveys/pirls/pirls2016/tables/pirls2016_Table01.Asp.

Kaschula, R.H. (1999). Imbongi and Griot: Toward a comparitive analysis of oral poetics in Southern and West Africa. *Journal of African Cultural Studies*, 12: 55–76. doi: doi:10.1080/13696819908717840.

Kinney, A.B. (2004). *Representations of Childhood and Youth in Early China*. Stanford, CA: Stanford University Press, pp. 14–15.

Kouraogo, P. (2010). *Policy Measures to Improve the Quality of Education in Burkina Faso*. University of Ouagadougou. https://home.hiroshima-u.ac.jp/cice/wp-content/uploads/2014/03/4-1-21.pdf.

Kumar, D. (2003). India. In *The Cambridge History of Science*, Vol. 4: *Eighteenth-Century Science*, ed. Roy Porter. Cambridge: Cambridge University Press, pp. 669–687.

Lines, D.A. (2017). The University and the City: Cultural Interactions. In Sarah Rubin Blanshei (ed.) *A Companion to Medieval and Renaissance Bologna*. Leiden: Brill.

Macaulay, T. (1835). *Macaulay's Minute on Indian Education*. Comp. R. Daley. Santa Barbara: University of California. http://oldsite.english.ucsb.edu/faculty/rraley/research/english/macaulay.html.

Matthew, N. (2001). *Stolen Lives: The Indigenous Peoples of Canada and the Indian Residential Schools*. Brookline, MA: Facing History and Ourselves. https://www.facinghistory.org/stolen-lives-indigenous-peoples-canada-and-indian-residential-schools/historical-background/traditional-education.

Moss, H.J. (2007). The tarring and feathering of Thomas Paul Smith: Common Schools, revolutionary memory, and the crisis of black citizenship in antebellum Boston. *New England Quarterly*, 80(2), 218–241.

Mullis, I.V.S., Martin, M.O., Foy, P., & Hooper, M. (2016). *TIMSS 2015 International Results in Mathematics*. Chestnut Hill, MA: Boston College, TIMSS & PIRLS International Study Center. http://timssandpirls.bc.edu/timss2015/international-results/.

O'Malley, J.W. (1989). Early Jesuit Spirituality: Spain and Italy. In L. Dupre & D.E. Saliers *(eds.) Christian Spirituality: Post-Reformation and Modern*, Vol. 18, *World Spirituality: An Encyclopedic History of the Religious Quest*. New York: Crossroad, pp. 3–27.

O'Malley, J.W. (2000). How the First Jesuits Became Involved in Education. In V.J. Duminuco (ed.) *The Jesuit Ratio Studiorum: 400th Anniversary Perspectives*. New York: Fordham University Press, pp. 56–74. www.bc.edu/content/dam/files/top/church21/p df/HowtheFirstJesuitsBecameInvolvedinEducation.pdf.

Palmer, R.R. (1986). How five centuries of educational philanthropy disappeared in the French Revolution. *History of Education Quarterly*, 26(2), 181–197.

Pavlac, B.A., & Lott, E.S. (2019). *The Holy Roman Empire: A Historical Encyclopaedia*. Santa Barbara, CA: ABC CLIO.

Ray, C. (2013). Thomas Sankara, President of Burkina Faso, *Encyclopaedia Britannica*. www.britannica.com/biography/Thomas-Sankara.

Rietbergen, P. (1998). *Europe: A Cultural History*. London: Routledge, p. 101.

Rousseau, J.J. (1755/1975). Discourse on the Origin and Basis of Inequality Among Men. In L. Bair (trans.) *The Essential Rousseau*. New York: Penguin, pp. 125–201.

Soltan, L. (2019). *Digital Divide: The Technology Gap between the Rich and Poor*. www.digitalresponsibility.org/digital-divide-the-technology-gap-between-rich-and-poor.

Sorbonne University (2020). *The Sorbonne in the Middle Ages*. www.sorbonne.fr/en/the-sorbonne/history-of-the-sorbonne/la-fondation-de-la-sorbonne-au-moyen-age-par-le-theologien-robert-de-sorbon/.

Suter, L.E., Smith, E., & Denman, B. (2019). *The SAGE Handbook of Comparative Studies in Education*. London: SAGE.

Thomason, A. K. (2005). *Luxury and Legitimation: Royal Collecting in Ancient Mesopotamia*. Farnham: Ashgate.

Timofeychev, A. (2018). Here's why education in the USSR was among the best in the world. *Russia Beyond*. www.rbth.com/history/328721-education-in-ussr-the-best.

Towns, E.L. (1993). History of Sunday School. *Town's Sunday School Encyclopaedia*. Liberty University. https://www.scribd.com/document/104367044/Towns-Sunda y-School-Encyclopedia.

UK Parliament (2020). *The 1870 Education Act*. www.parliament.uk/about/living-herita ge/transformingsociety/livinglearning/school/overview/1870educationact/.

United Nations (2020a). *Universal Declaration of Human Rights*. https://www.un.org/en/ universal-declaration-human-rights/.

United Nations (2020b). *Sustainable Development Goal 4*. https://sustainabledevelopment. un.org/sdg4.

United Nations Children's Fund (UNICEF) (2020). *1 in 3 Adolescent Girls from the Poorest Households Has Never Been to School*. www.unicef.org/press-releases/1-3-a dolescent-girls-poorest-households-has-never-been-school.

United Nations Educational, Scientific and Cultural Organization (UNESCO) Institute of Statistics (2020). *Burkina Faso: Education and Literacy*. http://uis.unesco.org/en/country/bf.

United Nations Educational, Scientific and Cultural Organization (UNESCO) Institute of Statistics (2020). *Out-of-School Children and Youth*. http://uis.unesco.org/en/topic/ out-school-children-and-youth.

University College London (UCL) (2019) *Women and Education: Context*. London: Institute of Education LibGuides. https://libguides.ioe.ac.uk/c.php?g=482254&p=3298244.

Veldhuis, N. (2004). *Religion, Literature and Scholarship: The Sumerian Composition of Nanše and the Birds*. Cuneiform Monographs 42. Brill: Leiden and Boston, MA.

Williams, A. (2017). How Martin Luther Invented Modern Education. *Handesblatt Today.* www.handelsblatt.com/today/from-our-magazine-how-martin-luther-invented-moder n-education/23567636.html?ticket=ST-2760360-a2zfVuhFKngYn4uHaRJs-ap1.

World Economic Forum (WEF) (2016). *Human Capital Report.* http://reports.weforum. org/human-capital-report-2016/rankings/.

Zamora, Margarita (2016). *Inca Garcilaso and Contemporary World-Making.* Pittsburgh, PA: University of Pittsburgh Press.

Chapter 4

A history of selective schools

Zach and Anthony

There are some expensive private schools in Burkina Faso but there was never any real question that Zach would attend them. Once, one of his cousins showed him photographs on his mobile phone of a lavish-looking school in Ouagadougou complete with a swimming pool and an athletics track that was attended by expatriate children from the United States. The boys laughed at the images in wonder. Zach pretended he wanted to be there like his friend who was clearly envious, but deep down inside he knew he would not want to be at a place like that. People would laugh at the state of his shoes and he would feel left out.

Zach follows the national education structure, which is highly selective. At the age of seven, children have to sit an examination that will determine whether they can carry on with an academic curriculum or whether they should move into the "technical" system. From there, if he survives in the academic stream, he will have to pass more examinations in order to be awarded the right diplomas and perhaps even bursaries that might lead to success (Moumoula, 2006). This system comes from France and has been in place in Burkina Faso for decades.

Not many students at Zach's village school manage to pass these examinations and most drop out of school before they get to the end of the path. Zach has told himself that he will stick it out and study hard. "I must survive", he tells himself often. But without enough textbooks, with only a few notes that he tries to look after but struggles to manage properly, and no one to help him with his studies other than Elias, his older brother, Zach is not sure if he will make it.

Elias went to the Lycée Professionelle (Vocational Lycée) and earned a professional baccalaureate, allowing him to work as a plumber. In order to get work he had to move to the city. Elias understands the maths and science that Zach struggles with and can explain the subjects to him easily, but he is not often there to help.

Zach has a secret that he keeps to himself, and that is his three-part plan: plan A, plan B and plan C. Plan A is this: if it all works out, one day a talent scout from Manchester United or Barcelona will see Zach dribbling the ball through the legs of his opponents on the red earth of the village clearing and he will be flown to Europe where he will become one of the greatest footballers of all time. If that does not work then there is plan B. Plan B is that Zach is not recruited by an international football club but manages to pass all his examinations. Then he will become a teacher and start a school in his village. And if that does not work then there is plan C, which involves Zach going to the Lycée Professionelle and becoming a plumber like his brother.

Zach keeps this three-pronged plan secret as he feels that if people find out it might not work. And he would not want his brother to find out that what he has become is only the third wish that Zach has for his own future.

Anthony's parents had an extraordinarily wide range of private schools to choose from in Switzerland. One could go down the British-style boarding school route, with its pathway to the top UK universities, or down the private Swiss school route, with its traditions, family enrolment and networking opportunities. There were community schools, American schools and specialised schools. Then there were over 20 international schools to choose from.

Most of these schools were selective, meaning that students would be admitted according to their academic ability. Some were not. However, given the costs involved, all of these schools were selective economically. Few local families could afford the hefty fees.

Despite the fact that the Swiss national education system is one of the best in the world, the number of private schools is extremely high. In the end Anthony's family chose a prominent international boarding school that followed the International Baccalaureate (IB) programme. According to colleagues of Anthony's father, the IB is commonly recognised as the gold standard in international education and opens many doors. One of the criteria for choosing a private school was the fact that there was quasi-automatic progression to the terminal examinations, whereas in the state system, Anthony would have to pass the middle school examinations in order to be eligible for the prestigious "maturité" matriculation. At his current international school students generally progress from one year to the next unless their results are dire. Therefore, although there was a price to pay, thus making the school financially selective, access to the best school leaving certificate was actually open, and this fact rendered it academically non-selective.

Anthony struggles in science but has a paid private tutor who Skypes him every week. And although the school has three different university guidance counsellors, Anthony's parents prefer to work with a private company that claims to have a special relationship with the university he is aiming for and could help to design a powerful personal statement for Anthony. Once, during a moment of mild exasperation, as the family was out sailing together on a bright Sunday morning on one of Switzerland's spectacular lakes, his father had referred to Anthony's education as a "damned shopping market" given that everything was for sale. Everyone had found the joke funny. It was worth the price, there was no question about that in his mind. After all, surely this is what all good parents do—they provide the very best for their children no matter what the cost.

On one occasion, Anthony had got into trouble with the school after he was accused of cyberbullying by another student. The school had asked the parents to come together to engage in what it described as "mindful collaboration and active listening time". Anthony's father was forced to pull out of an important meeting in order to attend this meeting and he did so in good faith, expecting something concise and sensible. However, he was disappointed by the process, which went on for over an hour and involved a softly spoken, slightly dotty-looking teacher letting everybody speak until they had nothing left to say. Anthony's father calculated that he had lost about US $5,000 in earnings because of the meeting and at the end of it, in private, while gritting his teeth, he let the teacher know how frustrated he was. She looked somewhat taken aback and spoke about the importance of parents and schools working together in part-nership. Anthony's father lost his temper and snapped at her, "just remember who is paying the fees here and, therefore, your salary". That put paid to any future conversation between the two of them.

Anthony's life would be thoroughly private: private schooling, private tutors, private university, work in the private sector. The state system neither provided the quality of education, nor the opportunities that were needed to get ahead. As a survivor of the Soviet state system, Anthony's father knew that only too well.

Selective education

Most countries in the world offer a free primary education to children, some offer a secondary education for free, and even rarer, a university education for free, in any case at a nominal cost. Some of the countries where students are lucky enough to make their way through the entire educational process without paying fees, or in any case, paying fees that are so low that they are tantamount to being free, include Sweden, Finland, France, Spain and Switzerland.

When it comes to secondary schools, there are fundamentally two types of selective school: schools that are academically selective and those that are finan-cially selective. Of course, there are variations within this dichotomy: state schools can be academically selective, whereas private schools that are financially selective may be academically non-selective. There are financially selective primary schools too meaning that they are private.

This chapter gives a historical overview of selective systems and the private school systems in the United Kingdom, India, Australia, South Africa, the United States and Switzerland. International schools, a parallel expression of this notion of selectivity, will be looked at in Chapter 6.

The argument running through the chapter is, fundamentally, that when we enter the realm of selectivity, and the educational offer in question is no longer a right but something that must be earned, there are two types of elitism at work. The first is meritocratic elitism, meaning that groups of students are selected above others on the basis of their performance in academic entrance tests. The meritocratic premise nods to Plato and the early Italian elitists (Pareto, Mosca, Michels), who saw a natural hierarchy in human activity and argued, therefore, for selective processes to separate the more naturally endowed from the less so. When examined carefully, we see how such filtering mechanisms often reinforce Bourdieu's social elitism with its echoes of social fragmentation in the hierarchy of ability, access and credentials it creates. For Gorard and Siddiqui:

> [I]t is quite clear that the extent to which pupils are clustered together with others like them socially and ethnically as well as in terms of ability is much higher in countries with selective systems ... Such 'segregation' tends to be low in developed countries with little or no diversity of schooling such as those in Scandinavia, linked to low achievement gaps, higher average attainment and also a high percentage of very skilled students ... Segregation tends to be high in countries with tracking or selection at a young age such as Germany, Austria, Belgium and Hungary.
>
> (2018, p. 912)

The second is plutocratic elitism, meaning that students are eligible to enter certain schools based on their capacity to pay fees. The private sector of schooling can be looked at from two perspectives. From a classical economic liberal perspective, by privatising education and making it fees-based, a healthy competition will be created between schools that will increase productivity and heighten academic results as schools fight to dominate the market. Classical capitalist economists such as Smith and Ricardo would argue that private schools bolster competition, regulate cost and increase quality. However, from a Marxist perspective, much in the vein of post-1970s elite theory, private schooling allows dominant classes to increase their dominance ever more by buying privileged places. Quality teachers are sucked up by the private market and state education is ghettoised.

There is a confluence of both types of elitism in schools that are both expensive and academically selective, meaning that they cater for the wealthy and the academically able. This creates a type of mega elitism. Efforts will be made throughout the chapter to show that the situation is not completely black and white: many private schools have bursary programmes and many national selective schools create quota systems, guaranteeing places to poverty-stricken students.

The United Kingdom

The secondary school system in the UK is extremely complex and divides schools into several categories: comprehensive schools (non-selective); community schools (academically selective and non-selective); foundation schools (academically selective and non-selective); voluntary controlled schools (academically selective and non-selective); multi-academy trusts (academically selective and non-selective); grammar schools (academically selective); public schools (academically and financially selective); partially selective schools; private schools; and independent schools (financially selective and often academically selective too). Some primary schools are selective either because they are independent or because they are so-called preparatory schools (meaning they prepare children for examinations to enter public schools).

It is important to investigate the UK model carefully since its broad brush strokes, dividing schools into comprehensive, grammar and public, have influenced numerous school systems around the world, essentially because of Britain's global colonial legacy. Understanding the essential elements of the English and Welsh school system explains school systems in Australia, South Africa and India, to mention just a few countries.

Comprehensive schools

Comprehensive schools are non-selective secondary schools that are funded by the state. The term "comprehensive" came into force in the 1940s and was developed for the next 35 years, mainly under the Labour government, to become the main secondary school provision in the country. The overwhelming majority of children in England study at comprehensive schools: the UK government published statistics in June 2019 that showed that out of 8.82 million pupils in the country over 8 million were in state-funded schools (Department for Education, 2019).

Comprehensive schools became particularly prominent during the 1970s when a number of grammar schools became comprehensives and some towns decided to convert all of their schools to comprehensives. Although this system of free schooling is still the most prominent in the UK, its success as a system was somewhat dented in 1988 with the Education Reform Act, which made it possible for parents to choose if they wanted their children to attend a comprehensive school or another type of state-funded education including home-schooling, faith schools and specialised education.

Grant-maintained schools (1988–1998)

Following the passage of the Education Act of 1902, schools were to be run by district or county authorities, known as Local Education Authorities (LEAs). However, this decentralisation led many education reformers to criticise the lack of a nationwide common curriculum and to point out that some LEAs were unable to fund the successful operation of the schools well. One of the efforts of the 1988 Education Reform Act was to make an allowance for schools to apply for state grants that would make them fall under government and not local authority jurisdiction and funding (Levinson et al., 2002).

The criteria for running grant-maintained schools were different to those established by LEAs and some of these schools became partially selective or even fully selective grammar schools. This situation caused understandable friction between local and government authorities and saw the ideal of universal access to education suffer a blow. Arguments raged in the Labour Party during Tony Blair's time in office since their support of grant-maintained schools was seen by many as flying in the face of the egalitarian rhetoric that characterised the party's ethos (Wintour, 1995).

In 1998, grant-maintained schools were disbanded altogether under the Schools Standards and Frameworks Act. Previously, grant-maintained schools either became voluntary aided or voluntary controlled meaning that they were run partly by the state, partly by a foundation or trust. Foundation schools are those which would be run by a board despite falling under government jurisdiction and not charging fees, and might include faith schools or community schools (previously known as county schools), which are state-funded but run by LEAs. Yet another category of school to consider is the academy, which is exempt from LEA control and is financed by the Department for Education, very often with part-funding by sponsors. Academies can be academically selective and are run by multi-academy trusts that work in partnership with the government. Many of these schools are academically selective.

In essence, the plethora of different types of government school in the UK and the historical trajectory it has followed, is marked by a tension between centralised and independent jurisdiction. This mirrors to a certain extent the economic debate between socialism and free-market capitalism: should schools be run centrally by the state or privately by independent boards? The degree of complexity that is sustained on the heavily politicised UK education scene with its hybrid models suggests that there is no clear-cut solution.

What this has meant is that comprehensive schools are the only type of school in the UK that are free of charge and operate an open enrolment policy, meaning that they are universally accessible. However, the splintering off from the comprehensive system into several hybrid models indicates that it has not been entirely successful and is under threat. Bernard Barker of Leicester University said that

> we have a deeply unequal, selfish and less trusting society. People wanted greater equality of opportunity and social mobility in the 1960s and 70s when comprehensives were established. They still want it now ... but only for themselves. The invention of all these new types of school in England has allowed parents to achieve some kind of market-place differentiation so they feel they are protecting their interests.
>
> (Cited in Northern, 2011)

Part of this "market-place differentiation" comes about when certain comprehensive schools outperform the others and, because of their reputation, affect the housing market as parents move closer to such schools in order to be eligible for places. For Gorard, the "comprehensive ideal is not simply worth retaining … its implementation could be seen as the clear ethical duty of any secretary of state" (2015, p. 257).

Some have pointed out that the splintering of the comprehensive model in the UK has eroded its initial idealistic premise (Haydn, 2004), while others argue that conditions such as class size and pedagogic provision are substandard in comprehensive schools (Murray, 2012). According to Green and Kynaston (2019), comprehensive schools in the UK had an average teacher-to-student ratio of 1:17 (p. 100). Some studies, such as that complied by Gorard and Siddiqui (2018), suggest that grammar schools are no better or worse than non-selective state schools in terms of attainment (Durham University, 2018). The division is one between state-level idealism versus parent-level pragmatism.

League tables

The Education Reform Act also meant that children no longer had to attend their local council school and could, therefore, choose between comprehensive schools (although admissions preference is given to those who live closest to the school). From 1992, parents could compare schools by referring to league tables that are published every year and rank schools according to performance (Leckie & Goldstein, 2016, p. 3). Primary schools are ranked on national curriculum tests (known as Standard Assessment Tests—SATs) and secondary schools on examination results (GCSEs and A-levels). School league tables in the UK have clearly exacerbated a culture of competition between schools.

At this point, it is useful to draw out the essentials of a philosophical discussion about the relationship between ranking systems and elitism: one argument is that educational quality should be tracked openly and that institutions should be compared according to their results. This creates transparency, gives parents essential knowledge and, therefore, meaningful agency. Indeed, if schools know that they will be inspected and ranked and that this could affect their status and enrolment, it will be in their interests to improve quality, which must be a good thing. This is not necessarily an elitist way of thinking, but instead offers a capitalistic, free market approach. In defence of this argument, when league tables were dropped in Wales in 2001, a study run by the University of Bristol showed that it led to a drop of 1.92 GCSE grades per student per year (Bevan & Wilson, 2013).

On the other hand, a more egalitarian, socialist approach would say that it is unhealthy to rank schools because it will invariably create a ghettoising effect at the bottom of the table and a scarcity principle at the top: parents will try to gain admission at the highest-ranking schools and do what they can not to send their children to those that rank the lowest. This can damage the self-esteem of those who find themselves in low-scoring schools and concentrate families in councils with low-ranking schools who are not able to travel to better-performing schools located in other councils. King's College researcher Nuala Burgess claims that ranking is an "unjust system that pitches schools into needless competition with each other" (Burgess, 2019). There has also been discussion over the educational validity of ranking: Wiggins and Tymms (2002) see it as dysfunctional, mainly because the data are high-stakes and single proxy. One of the problems is that it is very difficult to control results for confounding variables concerning student demographics. Because this cannot be controlled successfully, academically selective schools tend to come out better than academically non-selective schools. However, if ranking tables place selective schools at the top and non-selective schools at the bottom, they are not describing added value but instead are merely emphasising differences in baseline entry ability.

Meritocratic elitism: entrance examinations, preparatory schools and grammar schools

The 11-plus examination

In 1944, in what was known as the Butler Education Act, the UK government created an examination for Year 6 students (roughly 11 years old) called the "11-plus". This was to allow entrance to grammar schools. Based on reasoning, mathematics and English (although different boroughs use different elements in their test batteries), test results dictate whether children must remain in comprehensive schools or progress to grammar schools. At the time there were also technical colleges—a third tier—but these have been discontinued.

The test is meant to screen for ability, the idea being that bright children who fare well in it should be allowed to progress to academically selective grammar schools. However, the test is controversial. In the 1950s and 1960s, many of the test questions revealed class bias.

The structure of the 11-plus was revised to root out class bias and make it more psychometrically objective, but despite this recent studies have shown that the majority of students who progress to academically selective grammar schools having performed well in the 11-plus are of middle-class origin (Hart et al., 2012).

The test, which is still used for grammar school selection and some other types of selective school, is seen as a passport to class ascension. Former Assistant Director-General of UNESCO, Herbert Hoggart, said that

> what happens in thousands of homes is that the eleven-plus examination is identified in the minds of parents, not with 'our Jimmy is a clever lad and he's going to have his talents trained', but 'our Jimmy is going to move into another class, he's going to get a white-collar job' or something like that.
>
> (Kynaston, 2014, p. 192)

Hence, despite an assessment aimed at meritocratic rather than plutocratic elitism, the effects of it on society have translated into a social rather than a strictly intellectual phenomenon. This is a recurring theme in educational structures that have been bolstered by a prestigious reputation, such as public schools, grammar schools, the so-called Russell Group of universities, Ivy League and top-tier colleges in the United States. Although intrinsically they might represent character, high standards, intellectual pursuits and quality research, the grassroots understanding of them is that they represent power, access to wealth and social exclusivity.

Grammar schools

Initially dedicated to the instruction of future priests and monks in Latin, the first grammar schools in the UK were in operation by the seventh century, including King's School Canterbury (England's oldest school founded in 597) and King's School Rochester (founded in 604). In 685, the Royal Grammar School Worcester was founded by Bishop Bosel. The school was separated from the Cathedral of Worcester in 1291 and is recognised as the first grammar school in England (RGSW, 2020).

These schools continued to provide a highly academic education, essentially focusing on the trivium (grammar, logic and rhetoric), while the quadrivium (arithmetic, geometry, music and astronomy) would be taught at university. By the end of the Middle Ages, grammar schools included well-known boarding schools such as Winchester College (founded in 1382) and Eton College (founded in 1440). Similar versions of the grammar school system existed in many continental European countries (such as the Gymnasium in Germany), which explains why students still follow a "Latin" route in France and Italy (The Spens Report, 1938). This was the great classical education that formed the minds of Milton and Shakespeare and would create some of Europe's most academically proficient individuals throughout the Renaissance and the Enlightenment.

Grammar schools found themselves in decline during the 19th century because their statutes, which meant they could only teach the trivium, made them increasingly irrelevant to a merchant class thriving on the dividends of the Industrial Revolution and seeking instruction in the sciences. The Endowed Schools Act (1869) restructured grammar schools, opened access to girls and created a committee that modernised the curriculum (Sutherland, 1990).

The 1944 Education Act allowed some grammar schools to operate with direct grants whereas others depended on LEAs. Despite some difference, what remained was a meritocratic approach: the schools were to offer a high standard to the brightest children in the UK over 14 years old. Although there were different categories of grammar school and some charged fees, the most iconic ones, such as Manchester Grammar School (founded in 1515), became synonymous with meritocratic, need-blind intellectual rigour. The school's famous headmaster from 1945 to 1962, Eric James, led the school with a strong belief in academic excellence that bore fruit with a high percentage of students gaining scholarships to Oxbridge every year. He argued that "intelligence mattered more than birth" (Briggs, 2001, p. 174) and defended the initial premise that the school should be free of charge.[1] James discussed his meritocratic elitist position in *Education and Leadership* (1951), which has been described as "the classical exposition of grammar school virtues" (McCullogh, 1989, p. 43).

There were well over 1,200 grammar schools in England and Wales in the mid-1960s, but by the mid-1980s this number had fallen to 160 in England (Richardson, 2016). The meritocratic elitism of grammar schools was not appreciated ideologically by the Labour government of the time, particularly Education Secretary Anthony Crosland who, in 1965, published the so-called Circular 10/65 that had LEAs in England and Wales convert all schools to comprehensives. One year later, the government refused to give any funding to non-comprehensive schools. The Circular stated the following:

> [C]onscious of the need to raise educational standards at all levels, and regretting that the realisation of this objective is impeded by the separation of children into different types of secondary schools, [the Circular] notes with approval the efforts of local authorities to reorganise secondary education on comprehensive lines.
>
> (Department of Education and Science, 1965)

Crosland, despite having benefited himself from a fee-paying independent education at Highgate, followed by Oxford, is reported to have said, "If it's the last thing I do, I'm going to destroy every fucking grammar school in England. And Wales and Northern Ireland" (1982, p. 148). The Labour government formally discontinued grammar schools in 1976.

Indeed, the meritocratic elitism of grammar schools, cherished by some as a chance for bright but poor children to have access to high standards, is a contentious issue that causes emotions to run high. Dickinson et al. (2014) point out that fairly rigorous studies show that despite good intentions, "grammar systems increase inequality, lowering earnings at the bottom as well as raising them at the top". Harris and Rose (2013) studied student attainment in Buckinghamshire and found that

> pupils in grammar schools have greater examination success but that this 'value-added' comes at a cost to those not in the schools. The low prevalence of FSM [Free School Meals—a measure of poorer students] eligible pupils in the grammar schools casts doubt on their ability to aid social mobility.
>
> (p. 151; see Bell, 2020)

Grammar schools today are not what they were in the 1950s. Perry and Morris point out that over 80% of previous grammar schools have become academies, which they describe as a mere "tick box exercise" (2016) in order to preserve their independence. Existing grammar schools often charge fees, as does Manchester Grammar School, meaning that the meritocratic dream of Eric James has been tainted somewhat. On the whole, Labour government favours the disbanding of grammar schools, whereas the Conservatives are in favour of preserving them. The Conservative Party's argument is that grammar schools represent academic high standards (while comprehensives do not), but the Labour Party's argument is that the idea of grammar schools allowing for social mobility is not a reality and that the schools do little more than reinforce class division.

This chapter will show how other countries with grammar and comprehensive systems do not necessarily find the dichotomy as difficult to sustain as the UK does, which begs the question of whether the debate on grammar schools is about education per se or more about class, something that has been seen as an obsession in British society and politics for many years (Young, 2012; Devine, 2020).

Plutocratic elitism: private schools, independent schools and public schools

While there are comprehensive schools, academies and grammar schools, some state funded, others funded by LEAs, still others by boards operating in partnership with government organs, and while these schools are either free or relatively inexpensive, the private sector, made up essentially of preparatory schools, independent schools and public schools, is much more expensive although not always academically selective. Therefore, these schools can be termed as plutocratically elitist, meaning that they are accessible to a minority of wealthy individuals. Many are both meritocratically and plutocratically elitist in their selective admissions policies.

An independent school is a non-state private school that is accredited by the National Association of Independent Schools and run by an independent board of governors, while a private school is a non-state school that is run by a board of governors but often is also run by a corporation. A public school is a subset of private secondary schools although, technically speaking, there is a purist and narrow definition for a public school (upon which I shall elaborate shortly) and a much broader informal one (essentially meaning any secondary private school).

Roughly 6% of children in the UK attend such schools and about 60% of children from families earning upwards of £300,000 per annum attend such schools, with the most expensive boarding schools such as Eton, Harrow and Winchester charging roughly £42,000 per annum in fees (Green & Kynaston, 2019, p. 2). According to a study carried out by the Organisation for Economic Co-operation and Development (OECD) in 2016, the UK "has one of the most socially stratified private school sectors in the [so-called] developed world" (OECD, 2012, p. 2).

Independent and private schools tend to get better results than state schools. The Independent Schools Council (2019) states that "more than 50% of independent schools' entries for A-level chemistry were awarded an A★ or A compared with less than 30% of state entries in the UK" (p. 4).

The Common Entrance examination

Running parallel to the 11-plus, designed for entrance to grammar schools, is the Common Entrance examination, instituted in 1904, designed for entrance to private schools. An academically rigorous, knowledge-centred evaluation, at the time of the writing of this book, the Common Entrance examination was due to be phased out in favour of assessments deemed to be more skills-based and contemporary in style (Horton, 2019).

Preparatory schools

Preparatory schools (known as Prep schools), which originated in the 1800s, are private primary schools (up till the age of 13) in the UK that essentially prepare children for the Common Entrance examination. Some preparatory schools also prepare children for the 11-plus to enter grammar schools. Some of the advantages of a preparatory school over a state primary school include small class sizes, more specialist teachers, strong provision for special needs and "high test scores [as children] will be virtually guaranteed to get a place in a good secondary school when they leave" (Knowles, 2017). Preparatory schools are foregrounded by pre-preparatory schools, which admit children at the age of three or four and prepare them for the preparatory school.

Public schools

The most famous private schools in the UK are known as public schools (although some use the term "public school" to denote, in a type of shorthand, any private school). In the Middle Ages, some of the earliest schools operated as charities for those professing the Christian faith who could not afford tuition. Winchester, Westminster and Eton College, for example, were all dedicated to offering an education explicitly for the poor (Green & Kynaston, 2019, pp. 65–66). Henry VI founded Eton College in 1440 to offer 70 poor boys an education that would make them eligible for King's College Cambridge (founded in 1441) (Serhan, 2019). These schools grew in reputation and status over time as did the intake of fee-paying students and, by the 19th century, they had become extremely wealthy institutions. The term "public", somewhat oxymoronically, meant that the schools were open to any member of the public who could afford the fees. By the mid-1800s, Eton College seemed to have fallen into a certain decadence and had become the brunt of complaints and accusations about unruly and violent behaviour among students and the misappropriation of endowments by the school's leadership (Shrosbee, 1988, p.3). A commission, led by Lord Clarendon, investigated Eton College's financial and student management along with eight other well-established schools (six boarding schools: Winchester, Westminster, Charterhouse, Harrow, Rugby and Shrewsbury; and two day schools: Merchant Taylors' and St Paul's).

In the years that followed, the Public Schools Act (1868) ensured that these schools were managed by independent boards that stipulated regulations over their financial management and the manner in which they handled bursaries (although this was only for the first seven of the original nine schools). These were, therefore, the original public schools.

Despite their charitable origins, public schools have become synonymous with extreme plutocratic elitism. Kynaston and Green in their anti-private school book *Engines of Privilege* (2019) go to considerable lengths to point out how opulently financed such schools are: in 2015, UK schools' net asset wealth was calculated as a figure per student, with state schools ranging from roughly £7,000 per student (in poorer areas) to £14,000 per student (in wealthier areas) alongside Rugby (roughly £140,000 per student) and Eton (roughly £280,000 per student) (p. 104). In other words, in 2015, the most wealthy public schools were 10–20 times richer than some of the poorer state schools. The teacher-to-student ratio in public schools is in the region of 1:8 (half that of the comprehensive school ratios).

The vast majority of Britain's 55 Prime Ministers were educated in the public school system, with 20 of them (almost half) attending Eton College. The list of alumni from public schools is impressive and includes politicians, artists, social activists and athletes. The ethos of public schools tends to be that of character, emblematised in the misquoted analogy that the Duke of Wellington once made between the victory at the Battle of Waterloo and the action on the playing fields of Eton ("the battle of Waterloo was won on the playing fields of Eton") (Oxford Academic, 2013)[2] and intellectual freedom (Westminster School speaks of an ethos of "loyal dissent").

Much has been written about the complex social codes that historically have characterised public schools: from distinctive uniforms such as the famous Etonian tailcoats and top hats, and "fagging" (now officially discontinued) through to tribalistic acts of debauchery, violence and sexual abuse that reached their zenith in the mid-1800s (Chandos, 1984, p. 7). Many of these practices, similar to initiation ceremonies and inner-circles at certain elitist universities, can be analysed sociologically as a way in which students form deep-seated bonds to set them apart from the lower class. As W.H. Auden said in the 1930s when discussing "the public school boy's attitude to the working-class … their lives and needs remain as remote to him as those of another species" (Green & Kynaston, 2019, p. 78). Some of the rituals at public schools such as the Wall Game at Eton (a type of rugby game) or the "pancake greaze" at Westminster School (where a pancake is thrown into a crowd of boys) are maintained to keep the schools steeped in their rich historical traditions, but one could argue that even these seemingly innocuous games carry a streak of in-grouping about them that can have the profound psychological effect of setting children apart from those outside the establishment. Public schools in the 21st century are not what they were in the Victorian age. They have made efforts to diversify and offer as many scholarships as possible, perhaps eager to escape their strong legacies of elitism that might be considered embarrassing from a contemporary cultural viewpoint.

Arguments against private schools

Arguments against private schools in general, particularly extremely expensive ones, is that they increase class division and wealth concentration, and create a system of unhealthy hothousing from the early years.

In 2015, UK government figures showed that private school graduates are five times more lightly to gain a place at Oxbridge than those from state schools (p. 12), while more granular information on Oxbridge college offers from 2017–2019 shows specific corollaries, mainly favouring graduates of private and public schools (Turner & Herrmann, 2020). This is not necessarily unfair but, given the cost associated with schooling in these sectors, can be considered an instance of wealth begetting wealth to the expense of poorer classes who cannot afford such fast-tracking or access to the "gilded path". It should be added that detractors of private schools are not convinced by their strong academic results seeing as they tend to be selective in the first place and might not be adding that much value. This has led to the proliferation of value-added testing in the UK to try and ascertain whether expensive schools really are worth the extra money.

There is also a bone of contention over the charitable status that so many private schools enjoy, which makes them eligible for tax breaks (something that will almost definitely be phased out in the future due to its widescale unpopularity). In 2019, the Labour Party suggested scrapping private schools altogether, or at least discontinuing their charitable status. Shadow Chancellor of the Exchequer John McDonnell declared that "private schools don't need to exist … and should not exist" (Serhan, 2019). It has been argued that the government should deploy such funds into the state sector to create a provision as robust as that in Nordic countries, allowing for universal access to quality education. A popular model is Finland, where the common belief is that there are no private schools (in fact there are over 80) and that education is free (in fact it is heavily subsidised, but not entirely free) (Watson, 2019).

Anti-private school viewpoints are mostly socialist and egalitarian in flavour.

Arguments for private schools

The arguments for private, independent and public schools are essentially conservative, sometimes elitist in flavour, but not always. First, there is the argument that academic standards and general learning conditions in state schools are not up to scratch (Nelson, 2007). Therefore, it is understandable that parents should wish to send their children to the higher quality private school sector where results are better (Henderson et al., 2019).

There is also the argument that private schools are not just about academic results but the whole educational experience, instilling in children growth mindsets and lifeworthy competences. In describing a preparatory school, an extract from the Good Schools Guide (2020) reads as follows:

> This is a school that offers boys with high academic potential a dazzling start in life. Most leave not only with great academic results, but excellent general knowledge, huge intellectual curiosity and an appreciation of all things cultural. Myths abound that these are boffins that are hothoused, but in fact we found they are boys with a great sense of fun and who are highly motivated, genuinely enjoying being stretched.

The Independent Schools Survey points out that many private schools are engaged in social impact projects with over 11,000 state schools. The study claims that in 2019 "beyond partnerships with state schools, between £10m and £15m was raised for charities at ISC schools this year and 901 ISC schools organise volunteering opportunities for their staff and/or pupils" (ISC, 2019, p. 4). The same study also points out that private schools are good for employment and the economy.

In response to the idea that private schools should be closed, the headmaster of Eton, Simon Henderson, said:

> I don't think that by abolishing some of the best schools in the world, by confiscating and redistributing their assets, that we are going to improve the life chances of young people who have been left behind by the education system.

He advocated, instead, increased partnership between private and state schools (Weale & Walker, 2019).

Therefore, the debate on whether education in the UK should be state-run (comprehensive) or independent is a debate about perceptions of resource distribution, the economic impact of the educational offering, access and quality. It is not only an archetypal debate that sustains itself throughout the chapters of this book, it is acutely developed in the UK for historical reasons. Class consciousness is so anchored in English society and class fragmentation is so nuanced that George Orwell famously described himself as being "born into what you might describe as the lower-upper-middle class" (1937, Ch. 8). The globalised economics of the 21st century have hollowed out the middle class to the extent that the class divide is even more stark, stuck between moderate to extreme poverty and extreme wealth, meaning that the debate is ever more heated.

The United States

Compared to the UK, the American system is far less complex and dichotomous. However, the impact of English colonialism on America has meant that traces of English-styled elitism are strongly embedded in the private school/state school divide.

Little has been documented on the educational practices of the hundreds of different Native American peoples that interacted across the continent before the arrival of the colonisers. It seems that education was holistic and conducted mainly in informal family units with specific skills taught to selected groups (Lomawaima, 2002, p. 425).

The first settler schools were Latin Schools, in the style of early English grammar schools. They suffered a similar fate in that while their initial premise was to open access to education to scholars irrespective of social standing, their reputation meant that over time they became extremely selective and, therefore, meritocratically elitist. The first, Boston Latin School (founded in 1635), to this day places Classics, including Latin and Greek, at the centre of its curriculum and admits roughly 20% of applicants (Encyclopaedia Britannica, 2020) and has long been associated with the so-called Boston Brahims, a group of upper-class families descended from the first New England settlers, known to congregate in exclusive clubs and to occupy elite positions in society (Greenwood & Greenwood, 2011).

Public schools and charter schools

State schools, called public schools (not to be confused with public schools in the UK), are tuition-free and are funded either by the state or by the federation. Structural elements such as class size and resources depend on the state in question and admission tends to be by residency. Some public schools are called charter schools, meaning that they "are tuition-free, and must still follow the established teaching standards in their state. However, these schools have a lot of freedom in how they reach those standards" (Educationdata, 2020). Estimates for 2020 state that in the United States, 56.5 million students attend school with 50.8 million at public schools where the teacher-to-student ratio national average is 16:1 (Educationdata, 2020). Public schools are well funded, to the tune of US $13,000 per student. This makes the United States the country that invests the most in public education.

Meritocratic elitism: magnet schools

In the early 20th century, the term "grammar school" in the United States was used to describe primary schools (known as elementary schools) and by the mid-20th century, the equivalent of British grammar schools in the United States (in other words, academically selective state schools) were so-called magnet schools. These are still in operation today and work on the premise that a high-quality educational experience should be given to children, irrespective of their financial means, who perform well on admissions criteria (usually the Independent School Entrance examination—a test roughly similar to the English Common Entrance examination also used for independent schools). There are many different types of magnet schools in terms of curriculum offer and organisational statutes. Essentially, they are academically selective and offer gifted education programmes or specialised education to students.

A strong feature of magnet schools' ethos is that they should not only be inclusive but ethnically diverse in student body. Some feel that magnet schools have been extremely successful in opening access to diverse ethnic groups and social integration (Hinds, 2017).

Not unlike grammar schools, despite the honourable intentions of magnet schools, their effect can be a concentration of one class, or even race, as is the case in the United States, over others. Orfield and Frankenberg (2013) have shown that when magnet schools do not offer free transportation to students, ethnic diversity is reduced to the point that roughly 12% of these schools become "one-race". This is because magnet schools tend to be situated in affluent neighbourhoods inhabited mainly by white people (due to the strong race-class matrix that is so prevalent in the United States) and in order to pull minority students to the school from less affluent areas, public transport must be provided (p. 118). Wang and Herman (2017) report "mixed results" in their thorough overview of the impact of magnet schools on learning and social integration (pp. 158–179).

Plutocratic elitism: private schools

There are over 34,000 private schools in the United States (roughly one-quarter of all schools in the country) (CAPE, 2020). Private schools are independent and many are denominational. In 2020, "the private elementary school average [annual fee was] $9,946 per year and the private high school average [annual fee was] $14,711 per year" (Private School Review, 2020).

The most expensive secondary private schools in the United States (the Berkshire School in Massachusetts, the Browning School, Collegiate School, Avenues New York and the Hotchkiss School, for example) charge in the region of US $50,000 per annum (Marchbank, 2020).

Parents are willing to pay these fees because of the schools' lavish infrastructure, peers' higher socio-economic status, small classes and character building through the historical ethos of each school and academics. This last point is contentious, however, since studies have not demonstrated any clear academic value added: a 2014 publication by Lubienski and Lubienski in which longitudinal studies and National Assessment of Educational Progress data were used and demographic variables were controlled, showed that public schools actually outperformed private schools in terms of academic value added. The provocative title of the book is *The Public School Advantage: Why Public Schools Outperform Private Schools*.

This begs the question of whether private school graduates have an advantage over public school graduates when it comes to university admissions, particularly to elite top-tier and Ivy League universities. In terms of pure academics and student profile, the answer is probably no, but in terms of resources allocated to preparation for college, the answer is more lengthy and nuanced:

> [C]ounselors in public high schools report spending only 22% of their time on college-related counseling while their private school counterparts spend a far healthier 55%. Moreover, three-quarters of private high schools employ a counselor who is solely dedicated to matters of college admissions, something very few public schools are able to offer. Private school students are also more likely to be completely surrounded by highly motivated, college-bound peers which research suggests raises expectations and performance. Roughly 95% of non-parochial private high school grads go on to four-year postsecondary institutions compared with 49% of public school grads. And it's also worth keeping in mind that only 10% of children in the U.S. attend private school, yet make up a disproportionately high percentage of accepted students at elite colleges.
>
> (Bergman, 2020)

Plutocratic elitism in the United States, not unlike the UK model, is based on a gilded path philosophy, where the social networking advantages of belonging to a select group as well as the extra scaffolding (not necessarily raw academics but university-track preparation scaffolding) set students apart from the public school population. Although voices in favour of plutocratic elitism will tend to be Republican and those against tend to be more Democrat-orientated, it is less clear cut and less polemical in the United States than it is in the UK, whereas viewpoints on colleges and universities are much more divided in the United States, as this book will show in Chapter 7.

Meritocratic elitism in the United States has had a less controversial experience than grammar schools in the UK and the effort of magnet schools to diversify student populations is generally appreciated even if it is not necessarily very effective. Interestingly, in both the plutocratic and the meritocratic systems at work in American education, there seems to be little palpable academic advantage to public (state) schools. This evokes another central question around elitism and education, which is whether parents choose selective pathways for their children for narrow educational quality or for broader social networking and image-related benefits.

Australia

The Indigenous peoples of Australia's education system, which was essentially destroyed by colonisation, does not appear to have been selective in any way.

Settler education started with the reading of religious texts to English convicts in the late 1700s. Following the arrival of fleets of new convicts, the need to set up schools arose and by 1814 there were 13 elementary schools funded or part-funded by the state (Education Encyclopaedia, 2020). A host of denominational grammar schools opened in the mid-1800s. In some states the schools were mainly Catholic, in others, they were chiefly Anglican. Schools, and in particular high schools, boomed after the discovery of gold in Victoria and New South Wales in the 1850s.

> Government schools account for 65.6 per cent of students in 2020. States and territories are the majority public funder of the government sector in line with their constitutional responsibility. The Australian Government is the minority public funder. Non-government schools account for 34.4 per cent of students in 2020. The Australian Government has historically been the majority public funder, reflecting its commitment to supporting parental choice and diversity in the schooling system. State and territory governments are the minority public funders.
>
> (Australian Government, 2020)

Although public schools are free, a "voluntary contribution" is expected of parents, which creates a complex situation. One report explains that in a public school in Australia,

> students whose parents had paid the voluntary contributions before the requested deadline received a packet of popcorn with their canteen lunch orders. Children whose parents had not yet paid got nothing. The scheme singled out the students whose parents hadn't paid their contributions and unsurprisingly left a few children in tears.
>
> (Shad, 2020)

So, in a sense, no school education is entirely free in Australia. Indigenous peoples receive a state education with specific endowments and "while there have been some encouraging improvements in the educational achievements of Aboriginal and Torres Strait Islander children and young people, such as improved levels of Year 12 attainment, the gap persists in other educational outcomes" (Government of Australia, 2020).

Meritocratic and plutocratic elitism: Catholic and independent schools

Private schools in Australia are mainly Catholic, grammar and independent. Reasons for attending these schools will vary from school to school but will invariably include specialised attention to learning, lavish infrastructure, religious values and general social distinction. Some of the most expensive schools in the country such as Sydney Church of England Grammar School, Cranbrook School, the Scots College and Geelong Grammar School charge in the region of A\$38,000 per annum (Allen, 2020). In general, the cheaper private schools will be mostly single-sex Catholic schools, whereas independent schools will be more expensive.

Schools tend to express the style and ethos of Victorian public and grammar schools: students wear uniforms and masters often wear gowns, and many schools are single-sex and include chapels. Social distinction clearly ranks as a major criterion for parents choosing these schools: one website boasts that "most of these schools were once home to the most successful and renowned leaders, professionals and talents across the world" (Allen, 2020).

There appears to be no positive correlation between price and academics, and the relationship might actually be inverse. Summarising the research findings of four rigorous studies carried out between the 1980s and 2005, Preston (2014) claims, surprisingly, that "graduates of lower-fee private schools (in Australia, Catholic schools) tend to do better than graduates of higher-fee private schools (in Australia, independent schools)".

South Africa

Traditional educational models in Xhosa, Zulu and other indigenous cultural practices in South Africa, transmitted through an oral tradition of learning, were based on respect for elders, ancestral wisdom, rites and laws, initiation and holistic agriculture and hunting. Notions of a common humanity ("Ubuntu"), based on reciprocity and community-based life were prominent and continue to feature as an important Africanist model for Southern Africa and beyond. Essentially, pre-colonial models of learning were inclusive.

Following successive waves of colonisation, it was under British colonists that schools were opened and to this day independent schools, as is the case in Australia and the United States, carry a strong colonial, British feel in their design and ethos. Apartheid education separated provision by race and ghettoised black populations with "Bantu education", an under-resourced system that reinforced apartheid iniquity. This has had damaging effects on the national education system in South Africa, which is one of the worst in the world today: an OECD 2015 league table ranked South Africa 75th out of 76 participating countries and reports have shown that over one-quarter of children cannot read after six years of schooling (*The Economist*, 2017). UNESCO statistics in 2018 placed the average teacher-to-student ratio at roughly 1: 33.6, but numbers are much higher in many rural schools (*Economic Times*, 2018).

Schools are divided into state and independent. The latter is made up of community schools, expensive private boarding schools and denominational schools. There are no clearly identified meritocratic elitist state structures in South African political or education systems (Tau, 2019), such as the original grammar schools in the UK or magnet schools in the United States, but some private schools award many bursaries to the brightest and poorest, a notable example being the Oprah Winfrey Leadership Academy for Girls.

Plutocratic elitism

The most expensive schools in South Africa were constructed under the British and are styled in the fashion of public schools. Similarly to Australia and the UK, cultural codes include uniforms, headmasters' gowns, houses and Latin mottos. The most expensive schools are Hilton and Michaelhouse, both of which charge over 300,000 rand per annum (around US $16,000). Other prestigious schools include St Andrew's College, Roedean and St John's College (*BusinessTech*, 2020). Again, as we have seen in other models, the most expensive schools are not necessarily those that yield the best academic results, although they do tend to feature among the highest scoring: the 2020 matriculation results showed Crawford (the seventh most expensive day school) to have achieved the best scores. The group of schools with the best results was a private company listed on the stock exchange, ADvTECH (Head, 2020).

In terms of social reform, while it is true that a growing group of black middle- and upper-class students are gaining access to the gilded path of expensive private schools, the majority remain undereducated in a poorly performing state system.

A school that is aiming to Africanise elitism is the African Leadership Academy, which is meritocratically elitist, screening applicants through a rigorous selection process and offering, where possible, financial support to learners based on criteria. However, the general fees are over US $30,000 per annum, making the academy even more expensive than the most expensive independent schools (ALA, 2020).

India

As Chapter 3 has shown, India's traditional education system is extremely rich both culturally and historically: the Gurukula model of schooling expressed an inclusive model. Formal schooling in a Western sense was imposed by the British under colonisation and Macaulay's education plan for the country, which educated selectively and not in the interest of providing a public good, but of exploitation. Nehru's independentist model involved a vision for universal access to education which he fought hard to implement, but the country has not managed this yet, despite education bills being passed and repeated efforts. For Sherman, the decentralisation of India has not helped:

> With scarce resources, Indian policy-makers faced the dilemma of whether to improve the existing system, which served a narrow, urban elite, or expand it to the entire population, as the Constitution promised they would … However, by relying on communities to use their own resources to build local schools, this DIY socialism entrenched existing inequalities.

(2018, p. 504)

Today, government education in India is complex and operates at the state level. Some government schools are run entirely by the state, others are partly financed by private entities. Children aged between six and 14 are entitled to a free education. Despite this, estimates show that about 32 million children in India are not in school (*India Today*, 2019). UNESCO statistics in 2018 placed the average teacher-to-student ratio at roughly 1:30–35, although for some states such as Bihar and Uttar Pradesh, it was more than 1:60 (*Economic Times*, 2018).

Meritocratic elitism

The Indian system, like many systems in the world, forks after middle school. Students take a secondary school leaving certificate at the end of Year 10 and, at that point, will either progress to a "polytechnic" or upper secondary education which, after a Year 12 certificate, will make them eligible for university (WENR, 2018).

Plutocratic elitism

The most expensive schools in India, not unlike schools in the United States, Australia and South Africa, are modelled on English public schools with extremely lavish facilities (Stonehill, for example, has a 34-acre campus). They tend to emphasise Victorian values such as sports and good manners. Well-known elitist institutions include Woodstock, the Ecole Mondiale World School and the Doon School, charging in the region of 10 to 15 lakh rupees per annum (approximately US $15,000).

India's 2009 Right to Education Act made it compulsory for private schools to offer a quarter of all admissions places to poor children, who are drawn from a lottery. This is certainly a strong step against any formal system of elitism but some critics feel it is a type of egalitarianism that is not fair on some members of the middle class who can miss out on the opportunity because they fall into the wrong income bracket (McInerny, 2013).

Switzerland

Switzerland is an example of a country with an extremely robust but selective national educational system that operates alongside some of the most expensive private schools in the world. The World Economic Forum has placed Switzerland in the top five countries in its Global Competitiveness Report over the last ten years, usually in first place (WEF, 2019).

School is compulsory until the age of 15 and in some cantons, such as Geneva, until the age of 18. State education is free with average class sizes of about 20 and excellent academic results. PISA, TIMMS and PIRRLS scores have consistently ranked Switzerland among the top European countries in maths and science even though reading scores put Switzerland below average (Leybold-Johnson, 2019). Education is decentralised with cantons presiding over general rules and regulations although there is a centralised, federal approach that is sometimes deployed across cantons.

Meritocratic elitism: the state pathway

Much like the German and French system, the Swiss school system consists of a general primary and middle school experience after which an entrance examination must be taken to continue to the highly academic secondary level, called the Gymnasium in German-speaking Switzerland. If students do not perform well in the test, they will go on to a vocational course or apprenticeship (some may choose to go straight into an apprenticeship, of course), at a Realschule, as they are called in the German-speaking cantons and also in Germany. There is also a third pathway for low-achieving students or students with special educational needs. Some cantons admit students to the corresponding secondary pathway depending on their grades rather than their scores on an entrance test.

This level of streaming means that it is difficult to pursue the academic route and the majority of students in Switzerland will follow the vocational pathway. For those who progress through secondary school with the academic qualification (the "maturité" as it is called in French-speaking cantons), much as it is in France, the first years of university are also typically difficult and most students drop out before reaching their bachelor degrees, meaning that there is a further layer of streaming at this level.

Unemployment, however, is low in Switzerland and vocational pathways are rigorous and highly regarded, often leading to employment in well-remunerated sectors of the economy. Approximately 95% of Swiss children attend state schools (Williams, 2019).

Plutocratic elitism

Switzerland is home to the most expensive boarding schools in the world, many of them offering an international curriculum rather than the Swiss pathway. The most expensive are the Institut auf dem Rosenberg, Collège Alpin Beau Soleil and Le Rosey, each charging in the region of 130,000–150,000 Swiss francs per annum. The country hosts a number of other international private boarding schools that cost anywhere between 80,000 and over 100,000 Swiss francs. For that amount of money, one can assume that parents are not looking for academic results alone but social networking and class preservation, although it should be said that the schools offer extremely rich sports and cultural programmes along with a strong character-building education.

One website detailing the costs of these schools explains it clearly: "the price range also creates its own inherent value – by sending your child to one of these boarding schools, chances are high they will make friends with members of royal families, future political figures or others with connections" (Williams, 2019). Not unlike the most expensive schools we have seen in other examples, these boarding schools carry with them many of the codes of the English public school: uniforms, an emphasis on manners, houses and a wide range of extra-curricular activities. It is important to note also that the medium of instruction of most of these schools is English.

Conclusion

This chapter has shown how different countries around the globe share similar superstructural approaches to education. On the one hand, there is the idea of state-run or -sponsored universal access to education with, in many cases, selective academic streams. Such models came into force in the mid-1800s in Western Europe, the United States and Australia, and in previously colonised countries such as India and South Africa after independence in the mid- to late 20th century.

Some of these schools, often funded by the state, are meritocratically elitist, meaning that they are academically selective. The English grammar school is an archetype for this model. Interestingly, a number of studies on educational achievement suggest that, once the demographics that are filtered by selective admissions have been controlled, these schools do not necessarily add as much academic value as one might imagine at face value: their grade averages are high but then again students are selected at entry. There are arguments for and against this type of establishment, particularly in the UK where discussion around grammar schools has been tense. Proponents of state selective systems argue that they allow for gifted and bright children to advance and retain quality. Egalitarian discourses will argue that such schools are divisive and therefore reinforce or even create social hierarchies.

On the other hand, there is the private sector that is not funded by the state and is, in most cases, economically selective. It is important to notice that not all private schools are extremely expensive: there is a considerable range. In order to demonstrate salient extremities of the spectrum, however, this chapter has focused on the most prestigious examples.

Most private schools, particularly the costly ones, set students apart from others socially. Some of these schools are academically selective, others are not. Many of them resonate with the symbols and codes of the archetypal public school model which, ironically, originates in the work of religious, charitable organisations of the Renaissance. These schools tend to obtain strong academic results, but like public selective schools, there are confounding variables that explain this: parents who are wealthy enough to send their children to such schools will invariably provide their children with a social educative background that puts them at an advantage right from the start, often meaning that they have been prepared for such schools certainly from primary school and even, in a sense, from birth, since they will have had access to elaborate linguistic codes and comfortable infrastructure all their lives long.

This is not to say that private schools are focused on wealth and class distinction cynically and purposefully as their driving force: most have mission statements that are about developing character. Nor is it to say that parents deliberately and consciously send their children to these plutocratically elitist schools to "get ahead" of the masses: many wish their children to benefit from small classes, extensive personalised care, high-quality infrastructure and school values, as would any parent given the means to do so.

The models investigated leave us with a dilemma that we will come back to again and again in this book: how can education preserve quality, open access and prevent class splintering?

Notes

1 For the prominent educational theorist Michael Young, who started his career as a strong socialist but ended as an academic conservative, Eric James' meritocratic worldview was an inspirational, normative vision necessary to ensure an ethical educational provision that would empower the lower class in the UK. However, in his dystopian work *The Rise of Meritocracy, 1870–2033*, Young warned of the danger of entrance tests becoming hegemonic and ultimately corrupt.
2 George Orwell (1941) wrote, in response, that "the opening battles of all subsequent wars have been lost there".

References

African Leadership Academy (ALA) (2020). *Fees and Financial Assistance*. www.africanleadershipacademy.org/apply/fees-financial-assistance/.

Allen, J. (2020). It is said that if you think education is expensive, then try ignorance! *Stay at Home Mum*. www.stayathomemum.com.au/my-kids/schooling/the-10-most-expensive-schools-to-attend-in-australia/.

Bergman, D. (2020). Is there a private school advantage in college admissions? *College Transitions*. www.collegetransitions.com/blog/private-vs-public-hs/.

Bell, T. (2020). Wage inequality is the price society pays for grammar schools. *The Guardian*. www.theguardian.com/commentisfree/2020/apr/26/wage-inequality-is-the-price-society-pays-for-grammar-schools-torsten-bell.

Bevan, G., & Wilson, D. (2013). Does "naming and shaming" work for schools and hospitals? Lessons from natural experiments following devolution in England and Wales. *Public Money & Management*, 33(4), 245–252. doi:doi:10.1080/09540962.2013.799801.

Briggs, A. (2001). *Michael Young: Social Entrepreneur*. London: Palgrave Macmillan.

Burgess, N. (2019). Ban school league tables: They're not just misleading, they're harmful. *The Guardian*. www.theguardian.com/commentisfree/2019/jan/26/school-league-tables-research-grammar.

BusinessTech (2020). 60 of the most expensive boarding and day schools in South Africa in 2020. *BusinessTech*. https://businesstech.co.za/news/lifestyle/365180/60-of-the-most-expensive-boarding-and-day-schools-in-south-africa-in-2020/amp/.

Chandos, J. (1984). *Boys Together: English Public Schools 1800–1864*. London: Hutchinson.

Council for American Private Education (CAPE) (2020). *Facts and Studies*. www.cap enet.org/facts.html.

Crosland, S. (1982). *Tony Crosland*. London: Jonathan Cape.

Department for Education (2019). *Schools, Pupils and their Characteristics: January 2019*. www. gov.uk/government/statistics/schools-pupils-and-their-characteristics-january-2019.

Department of Education and Science (1965). *Circular 10/65 (1965): The Organisation of Secondary Education*. www.educationengland.org.uk/documents/des/circular10-65.html.

Devine, F. (2020). *The British Obsession with Class* (lecture). Yorkshire Philosophical Society. www.ypsyork.org/events/the-british-obsession-with-class/.

Dickinson, M., MacMillan, L., & Burgess, S. (2014). Hard Evidence: Do grammar schools boost social mobility? *The Conversation*. https://theconversation.com/hard-e vidence-do-grammar-schools-boost-social-mobility-28121.

Durham University (2018). *Grammar Schools Are No Better Than Other State Schools, Shows New Research*. School of Education News Feed. www.dur.ac.uk/education/ news/?itemno=34151.

Economic Times (2018) India improves student-classroom, pupil–teacher ratios: Survey. *Economic Times*. https://economictimes.indiatimes.com/industry/services/education/ india-improves-student-classroom-pupil-teacher-ratios-survey/articleshow/62695301. cms?utm_source=contentofinterest&utm_medium=text&utm_campaign=cppst.

Education data (2020). *How Many Public Schools Are There in the U.S.?*https://educa tiondata.org/number-of-public-schools/.

Education Encyclopaedia (2020). *Australia: History and Background*. https://education.sta teuniversity.com/pages/75/Australia-HISTORY-BACKGROUND.html.

Encyclopaedia Britannica (2020). *Boston Latin School: American Secondary School*. www. britannica.com/topic/Boston-Latin-School.

Gorard, S. (2015). The uncertain future of comprehensive schooling in England. *European Educational Research Journal*, 14(3–4), 257–268. https://doi.org/10.1177/ 1474904115590214.

Gorard, S., & Siddiqui, N. (2018). Grammar schools in England: A new analysis of social segregation and academic outcomes. *British Journal of Sociology of Education*, 39 (7), 909–924. doi:doi:10.1080/01425692.2018.1443432.

Government of Australia (2020). *How Are Schools Funded in Australia?*www.education. gov.au/how-are-schools-funded-australia.

Green, F., & Kynaston, D. (2019). *Engines of Privilege: Britain's Private School Problem*. London: Bloomsbury.

Greenwood, A., & Greenwood, A. (2011). *An Introduction to the Unitarian and Universalist Traditions*. Cambridge and New York: Cambridge University Press. p. 60.

Harris, R., & Rose, S. (2013). Who benefits from grammar schools? A case study of Buckinghamshire, England. *Oxford Review of Education*, 39(2), 151–171. doi: doi:10.1080/03054985.2013.776955.

Hart, R.A., Moro M., and Roberts, J.E. (2012). Date of birth, family background, and the Eleven–Plus exam: Short- and long-term consequences of the 1944 secondary education reforms in England and Wales. Stirling Economics Discussion Paper, 2012-10, Stirling Management School. https://dspace.stir.ac.uk/handle/1893/6612#.X9Tnh9hKg2w.

Haydn, T. (2004) The strange death of the comprehensive school in England and Wales, 1965–2002, *Research Papers in Education*, 19(4), 415–432. doi:doi:10.1080/ 0267152042000295456.

Head, T. (2020). Matric results: This is the best-performing private school of 2019. *The South African*. https://www.thesouthafrican.com/lifestyle/matric-results-2019-best-performing-private-school/.

Henderson, M., Anders, J., Green F., & Henseke, G. (2019). Private schooling, subject choice, upper secondary attainment and progression to university. *Oxford Review of Education*. doi:doi:10.1080/03054985.2019.1669551.

Hinds, H. (2017). *Drawn to Success: How Do Integrated Magnet Schools Work?* http://rides.gse.harvard.edu/files/gse-rides/files/rides_-_drawn_to_success_how_do_integrated_magnet_schools_work.pdf.

Horton, H. (2019). Britain's oldest school exam to be scrapped amid diversity drive at private schools. *The Telegraph*. www.telegraph.co.uk/news/2019/09/29/britains-oldest-school-exam-scrapped-amid-diversity-drive-private/.

Independent Schools Council (ISC) (2019). *ISC Census and Annual Report*. www.isc.co.uk/media/5479/isc_census_2019_report.pdf.

India Today (2019). 32 million Indian children have never been to any school: How can we reform education for the underprivileged? *India Today*. www.indiatoday.in/education-today/featurephilia/story/32-million-indian-children-have-never-been-to-any-school-how-can-we-reform-education-for-the-underprivileged-1582293-2019-08-19.

James, E. (1951). *Education and Leadership*. London: Harrap.

Knowles, S. (2017). *What Is a Preparatory School?* Get the Right School. www.gettherightschool.co.uk/what-preparatory-school.html.

Kynaston, D. (2014). *Modernity Britain: A Shake of the Dice 1959–62*. London: Bloomsbury.

Leckie, D., & Goldstein, H. (2016). The evolution of school league tables in England 1992–2016: "Contextual value added", "expected progress" and "progress 8". Bristol Working Papers in Education #02/2016. Bristol: Graduate School of Education.

Levinson, D., Cookson, P.W., and Sadovnik, A.R. (2002). *Education and Sociology*. London: Taylor & Francis. pp. 215–218.

Leybold-Johnson, I. (2019). *PISA Study Finds Swiss Students "Still Behind" on Reading*. SWI. https://www.swissinfo.ch/eng/education_pisa-study-finds-swiss-students–still-behind–on-reading–/45406778.

Lomawaima, K.T. (2002). American Indian Education: By Indians Versus for Indians. In P. Deloria, & A. Salisbury, *Companion to American Indian History*. Malden, NJ: Blackwell.

Lubienski, C.A., & Lubienski, S.T. (2014). *The Public School Advantage: Why Public Schools Outperform Private Schools*. Chicago: University of Chicago Press.

McCullogh, G. (1989). Education for Leadership in the 1950s: The ideology of Eric James. *Journal of Educational Administration and History*, 21(1), 43–52. doi: doi:10.1080/0022062890210105.

McInerny, L. (2013). Selective schools may help poor, bright children; what about the rest? *The Guardian*. www.theguardian.com/education/2013/aug/19/selective-education-disadvantaged-pupils.

Marchbank, K. (2020). Most expensive private high schools in America. *Vocal Media*. https://vocal.media/education/most-expensive-private-high-schools-in-america.

Moumoula, I.A. (2006). Étude d'adaptation du questionnaire d'intérêts professionnels au contexte burkinabé. *L'Orientation scolaire et professionnelle*. doi:doi:10.4000/osp.2396.

Murray, J. (2012). Why I sent my child to a private school. *The Guardian*. www.theguardian.com/education/2012/jul/23/why-send-child-to-private-school.

Nelson, F. (2007). Look back in anger. *The Spectator*. www.spectator.co.uk/article/look-back-in-anger.

Northern, S. (2011). What became of the bog-standard comprehensive? *The Guardian.* www.theguardian.com/education/2011/feb/15/bog-standard-comprehensive-uniformit y-specialism-faith.

Orfield, G., & Frankenberg, E. (2013). *Educational Delusions?: Why Choice Can Deepen Inequality and How to Make Schools Fair.* Berkeley: University of California Press.

Organisation for Economic Co-operation and Development (OECD) (2012). *Public and Private Schools: How Management and Funding Relate to their Socio-economic Profile.* www. oecd-ilibrary.org/education/public-school-private-school_9789264175006-en m.

Orwell, G. (1937). *The Road to Wigan Pier.* London: Victor Gollancz Ltd.

Orwell, G. (1941). *The Lion and the Unicorn.* The Orwell Foundation. www.orwell foundation.com/the-orwell-foundation/orwell/essays-and-other-works/the-lion-and-the-unicorn-socialism-and-the-english-genius/.

Oxford Academic (2013). *Misquotation:"The battle of Waterloo was won on the playing fields of Eton".* https://oupacademic.tumblr.com/post/57740288322/misquotation-the-ba ttle-of-waterloo-was-won-on.

Perry, T., & Morris, R. (2016). Time for an honest debate about grammar schools. *The Conversation.* https://theconversation.com/time-for-an-honest-debate-about-gramma r-schools-62370.

Preston, B. (2014). State school kids do better at uni. *The Conversation.* https://the conversation.com/state-school-kids-do-better-at-uni-29155.

Private School Review (2020). *Average Private School Tuition Cost.* www.privateschoolre view.com/tuition-stats/private-school-cost-by-state.

Richardson, H. (2016). Grammar schools: What are they and why are they controversial? BBC News. www.bbc.com/news/education-34538222.

Royal Grammar School Worcester (RGSW) (2020). *History of Royal Grammar School Worcester.* www.rgsw.org.uk/worcester/history/.

Serhan, Y. (2019). Should Britain abolish private schools? *The Atlantic.* www.theatlantic. com/international/archive/2019/11/britain-labour-party-plans-abolish-private-schools/600412/.

Shad, S. (2020). A "free" public school education can cost $1,300 a year—and it's get-ting harder for parents to say no. ABC News. www.abc.net.au/news/2019-03-20/pa rents-pitch-in-for-the-high-cost-of-public-schooling/10917358.

Shrosbee, C. (1988). *Public schools and Private Education: The Clarendon Commission, 1861–64 and the Public Schools Act.* Manchester: Manchester University Press.

Sutherland, Gi (1990). Education. In F.M.L. Thompson, (ed.) *Social Agencies and Insti-tutions.* The Cambridge Social History of Britain 1750–1950. Vol. 3. Cambridge: Cambridge University Press. pp. 119–169.

Tau, R. (2019). Serious about taking South Africa forward? We need meritocracy. *Daily Maverick.* www.dailymaverick.co.za/opinionista/2019-03-18-serious-about-taking-south-africa-forward-we-need-meritocracy/.

The Economist (2017). South Africa has one of the world's worst education systems. *The Economist.* www.economist.com/middle-east-and-africa/2017/01/07/south-africa-has-one-of-the-worlds-worst-education-systems.

The Good Schools Guide (2020). *Prep and Pre-Prep Schools: What Do I Need to Know?*www. goodschoolsguide.co.uk/choosing-a-school/independent-schools/prep-and-pre-preps.

The Spens Report (1938). *Secondary Education with Special Reference to Grammar Schools and Technical High Schools.* London: HM Stationery Office. www.educationengland. org.uk/documents/spens/.

Turner, C., & Herrmann, J. (2020). Revealed: The schools which send the highest number of pupils to every Oxbridge college. *The Telegraph.* www.telegraph.co.uk/news/2020/01/12/revealed-schools-send-highest-number-pupils-every-oxbridge-college/.

Wang, J., & Herman, J. (2017). Magnet schools: History, description, and effects. In R. Fox & N. Buchanan (eds.) *Handbook of School Choice.* New York: John Wiley and Sons, pp. 158–179.

Watson, A. (2019). *12 "myths" about education in Finland debunked.* https://thecorner stoneforteachers.com/12-myths-about-education-in-finland-debunked/.

Weale, S., & Walker, P. (2019). Head of Eton hits back at Labour plans to abolish private schools. *The Guardian.* www.theguardian.com/education/2019/sep/23/head-of-eton-hits-back-at-labour-plans-to-abolish-private-schools.

Wiggins, A., & Tymms, Peter. (2002). Dysfunctional effects of league tables: A comparison between English and Scottish primary schools. *Public Money & Management*, 22, 43–48.

Williams, D. (2019). 6 top Swiss boarding schools where royalty and the super-rich send their children – and pay up to US$150,000-a-year in fees. *South China Morning Post.* www.scmp.com/magazines/style/luxury/article/3035693/6-top-swiss-boarding-schools-where-royalty-and-super-rich.

Wintour, D. (1995). Attack on 'incomprehensible' policy incenses Blunkett. *The Guardian.* www.theguardian.com/politics/1995/oct/05/education.education.

World Economic Forum (WEF) (2019). *The Global Competitiveness Report.* www3.weforum.org/docs/WEF_TheGlobalCompetitivenessReport2019.pdf.

World Education News & Reviews (WENR) (2018). https://wenr.wes.org/wp-content/uploads/2018/09/WENR-0618-Country-Profile-India.png.

Young, T. (2012). Why are we still obsessed with class? *The Spectator.* www.spectator.co.uk/article/why-are-we-still-obsessed-with-class-.

Chapter 5

Massification

Zach and Anthony

Zach rarely has enough space at his desk which he shares with four other students but for him it's enough; he only needs a small elbow's width of desk that he manages to carve out every day. They sit squeezed together, only just fitting on the bench, and the 80-odd students in the room mean that the noise is too disruptive for any real concentration. Mama Estelle has to shout over the din.

All the children in the village should be at school, and most do come, even if many stop coming after a while. There is never enough space to move around comfortably and there are so many students that the only real way learning can take place is through lectures that the teacher gives at the blackboard with the students copying everything down word for word or answering in unison. It is very rare for each individual student to be called upon to express an opinion and marked written work only comes back to the students once in a while. There are simply too many children for things to work otherwise.

Zach prefers to keep quiet in class. He does not bother to put his hand up when Mama Estelle asks a question, but this does not worry him. He listens carefully though and takes notes as best as he can.

Zach's father says that when he was at school there were fewer students and they were all able to participate in discussions with the teacher. Now that is no longer possible.

Anthony enjoys world-class conditions with small class sizes, an interactive mode of learning and excellent teachers. He knows this but he also knows that competition is stiff and across the globe there are many other students learning in excellent conditions like him. Worse still, children like Anthony who are being educated in similar schools will be competing for places at the same universities alongside children from South Korea, India and China.

Anthony's father tells how when he went to university, industries would offer jobs to students as soon as they graduated. Those days are over: not only do you have to get into an excellent university, you have to fight for a good job afterwards too. "The world is flat, my boy", his father tells him from time to time. "You are competing with a globalised workforce. Don't forget that!"

Anthony sometimes feels the pressure on him. It's like there's someone breathing down his neck, reminding him that there is little margin for error or for coming second best. But it's not deeply worrying.

A definition of massification

At the time of the first implementation of formal education, the global population numbered less than half a billion. Systems were designed for a fraction of that already small population. By the time education became standardised by the state and compulsory for all children, the global population had crept up to about one and a half billion.

When the dream of universal access to education was expressed in the 1948 Universal Declaration of Human Rights, the global population numbered roughly less than two and a half billion people. Today, that number has more than tripled and projections show that by the end of the 21st century the global population will be roughly 11 billion (UN, 2019).

Not only has the global population growth rate been high, the concept of access to education has been steadily widened to incorporate all young people. At the same time, access to standards of middle-class wealth and many of the social expectations that come with it, primarily involving education, have become increasingly widespread throughout the world. For example, "in France, whereas just under a quarter of each generation reached Baccalaureate level as at the start of the 1980s, nearly two-thirds did by the end of the 1990s" (Coulangeon, 2008, p. 281).

The idea of graduating from school and attending university is now a globalised, widespread expectation. United Nations (UN) and UNESCO initiatives such as Education for All (2015) and Sustainable Development Goal 4 (2018) have put pressure on systems to accommodate a mass of students that the initial infrastructure and purpose of education had not been designed to incorporate.

The pressure on capacity is particularly acute in universities, especially since they now admit senior students, part-time students and offer degrees of specialisation that require expensive and multifaceted resources, both human and material. Furthermore, many national education schemes, such as those in Switzerland and France, make universities accessible to any student who passes secondary school certification, meaning that numbers in undergraduate classes tend to be very large. Projections suggest that this sector in particular will become more and more cramped over time. A study in 2015 predicted that "Global post-secondary enrolments [are] projected to increase from 214.1 million in 2015 to 594.1 million in 2040" (Calderon, 2018). In other words, the number of university places will have to double in the next 20 years.

In theory, countries should be able to cope with the notion of educating all young people with a free, high-quality education. Most countries spend in the region of 2%–6% of tax revenue on education: the Centre on Budget and

Policy Priorities estimates that in the fiscal year 2019 the US government spent only 2% of its budget on education (CBPP, 2020) and India roughly 4.6% (*Business Today*, 2020), whereas in the UK spending over the past 40 years has hovered between 4% and 6% (Bolton, 2019). At face value, leveraging more funding for education in order to expand facilities, and increase teacher training and teaching conditions should be quite easy.

However, the situation is far more complex for four fundamental reasons:

1   Tax revenues need to be spread across multiple sectors such as health care, infrastructure, armed services and social security.
2   It is not because a country spends more on education that quality or access will necessarily improve. Organisation for Economic Co-operation and Development (OECD) statistics show that countries that invest comparatively more in education do not necessarily yield the best PISA, PIRRLS or TIMMS results. For example, 2015–2016 data showed that Costa Rica and Brazil spend almost twice as much as Japan and Germany (OECD, 2016). Increasingly, analysis carried out by McKinsey and the OECD suggest that it is the approach that makes an impact rather than the size of investment.
3   Taxation systems are broken in many so-called developing countries, meaning that there is not enough capital to invest in education purposefully.
4   Multiple recessions such as the 2008 global financial crisis and the aftermath of the COVID-19 pandemic have made it increasingly difficult for governments to invest more in education.

At the centre of this dilemma is a burning question about education and elitism. On the one hand, following classical elite theory in the vein of Pareto, the whole purpose and assessment structure of education are elitist processes whereby fewer and fewer learners pass certification as different strata become necessarily more difficult. After all, what would be the value of a doctorate if everybody had one? How would it be possible to talk about an excellent education if that precise experience did not rise above others, making it unique and, therefore, valuable? Therefore, the pro-elitist position (be that meritocratic or plutocratic elitism) is that universal access to education does not imply universal certification and that it is an illusion to try and design structures that would allow maximum access. This would apply in systems where there are minimal entry requirements for admission to national universities, such as being required to achieve a particular high school score. If this were the case, standards would be mediocre and even meaningless. It is acceptable and perhaps even desirable, in this worldview, to select access.

The classical model of education tends to be a hierarchy of access, starting with inclusive state institutions consolidating the basics of numeracy and literacy for the early years—therefore compulsory primary education—following degrees of selectivity as students progress to secondary and then tertiary learning. The advantage of this model is that it allows resources to be concentrated in such a way that high levels of quality are attained: schooling is massified and can be accommodated at the base level, but as students progress fewer continue and therefore resources can be shared out among the places available at higher rungs of the educational ladder. The disadvantage of this pyramidal model is that it depends on an attrition rate that excludes many.

On the other hand, diametrically opposed to this view is the universalist, social democratic view that not only is education a right, but that it is a social responsibility. The more people the state educates, the higher literacy levels rise, and the more widespread that levels of critical independent thinking become, the healthier society will be. Schools and universities should not only be free, they should be considered a human right. Rather than viewing the situation as a zero-sum game with winners and losers, applying classical economic theory of the scarcity principle to a resource that is not a physical construct but one that can be shared and duplicated quite easily, it is healthier to view education as entirely inclusive and communal. This view has been supported rhetorically by post-Enlightenment policy writers and structurally by Marxist and socialist countries. The advantage of the position is that it allows a groundswell of people to experience education and, potentially, to live better lives because of it. The disadvantage is that by opening up access and encouraging maximum certification it becomes difficult to retain quality and the comparative value of education and certification is lessened because everyone is certified and no one stands out.

The post-Second World War approach to education, at least in primary and the majority of secondary schooling, has been geared towards an anti-elitist approach, emphasising access. What this has meant is that a service that historically was reserved for the few has been opened to the masses. What are the implications of this widening of access?

Massification

The term "massification" stems first and foremost from the business sector and refers, historically, to expansion strategies employed by luxury goods companies to increase the diffusion and consumption of their products. Typically, products will be massified by so-called diffusion lines (which are subsidiary, cheaper sub-brands) and can be done by extending a product or brand's repertoire so as to make elements of it accessible to the masses (Albrecht, et al., 2013).

The idea behind massification is that the quality or prestige of a luxury brand should be maintained while more people should be able to afford it. As this is not entirely possible (since luxury goods are, by definition, expensive and therefore exclusive), new affiliations, sub-brands and extensions are established.

To extend this narrow definition of massification to education, the idea is that the hitherto selective process of education, with its historically elitist agenda, is democratised and designed for many while remaining rigorous and of high quality.

The term is used in education primarily with reference to tertiary education, essentially because it has been difficult for the tertiary education sector to keep up with demand. One of the consequences of the democratisation of primary and secondary education has been a greater mass of school leavers seeking university places.

The historical periods of the massification of tertiary education, mainly due to political changes, have been as follows: Russia during the early period of the 20th century; the United Kingdom and the United States shortly after the Second World War; and the rest of the world mainly after the 1990s (although there are, of course, a number of exceptions).

Trow (2007) has grouped the massification of higher education into three different historical phases: first there is an elite phase, when universities are inaccessible to most high school leavers and represent a scarce resource (essentially from the origin of universities to the Second World War, with national enrolment ratios of up to 15%), then there is a mass phase, meaning that after the Second World War, following a surge in wealth and middle-class populations, particularly in the United States, it becomes a middle-class expectation to attend university and, therefore, demand increases (by up to 50%), and finally there is a universal phase, meaning that national enrolments are in excess of 50% as most high school leavers choose to study at university. Furthermore, the universal phase expands this worldview beyond the United States and Europe to all parts of the world.

This increased demand on universities is projected to increase steeply in the next 20 years. According to Calderon (2018), by 2040, global tertiary education enrolments will be in the region of 595 million with the following enrolment figures by region:

East Asia and the Pacific: 257.6 million;
South and West Asia: 160.4 million;
Latin America and the Caribbean: 65.6 million;
The Arab states: 22.3 million;
Sub-Saharan Africa: 21.7 million;
The United States and Western Europe: 43.7 million.

These figures suggest that demand will double (and even triple in sub-Saharan Africa) in all regions but Europe and the United States where population size will grow more slowly than in other regions.

Schools

Although the term "massification" is very rarely used to describe schools, clearly the same phenomenon is at work and has developed through history in phases much like the ones Trow (2007) delineates for universities: over time it has become a universal expectation not only for the majority of young people to attend school but for every young person to be schooled as a fundamental right, therefore taking school as a social construct through phases of elitism, massification and universalism.

Worldwide, primary school enrolment has increased from less than 20% in the early 1800s to close to 100% in the post-Second World War period, while the average amount of time in school has lengthened from less than three years before the end of the 19th century to closer to ten years by 2010 (Roser & Ortiz-Ospina, 2020). Government expenditure on education has increased but not commensurately. Only a few countries, such as Norway, invest more than 6% of gross domestic product in schooling and there are still about 258 million children out of school, of which "59 million children [are] of primary school age, 62 million of lower secondary school age and 138 million of upper secondary age", mainly in Sub-Saharan Africa (UNESCO, 2020).

The United Kingdom

The issue in the UK is not so much one of school massification outweighing the number of available places, but more the inability of the system to meet parents' choice of school satisfactorily. In 2018, "about 20% of families in England failed to gain a place at their first preference school, with … one in eight families in London failing to gain a place at any of their choices" (Adams, 2019).

In 2019, Department for Education data showed that the number of pupils in state-funded schools had risen for five consecutive years (p. 1), that "15.4% of pupils were eligible for and claiming free school meals … the highest proportion since 2014" (p. 6), and that the average secondary class size has been increasing since 2015 (although it only hovered at above 20 students in a class) (p. 10). Furthermore, in 2019, only 85% of the so-called teacher supply model was reached with not enough teachers in mathematics and some of the sciences (Department for Education, 2019b, p. 1).

This suggests that teacher conditions are not attractive enough to meet the demands of an increasingly massified demand.

The United States

With a little under 51 million children in public schools and just under six million in private schools (National Center for Education Statistics, 2019), the United States has a well-resourced educational response to the massification of demand and has been able to accommodate the numbers of students adequately.

However, budget cuts have led to increased class sizes and increasingly difficult learning conditions in many schools across the country: reports of large classes (up to 40 students) in Philadelphia, Arizona and Ohio, for instance, suggest that some parts of the country struggle with the numbers (Jerkins,

2015). A 2015 study by the National Center for Education Statistics reported that 14% of schools in the United States exceeded capacity (Lynch, 2015).

There is also a shortage of teachers, particularly in schools in poorer neighbourhoods, a problem that has become more and more emphatic over time. Sutcher, Darling-Hammond and Carver-Thomas (2016) predict that by 2025 the number of actual supply teachers available in the United States will be just over 100,000 but that demand will exceed 300,000. Reasons for a shortage of teachers range from low pay (the pay gap between teachers in public education and professionals in other sectors of the economy having a similar standard of qualification has been widened over the past few decades, see Garcia & Weiss, 2019) and the nature of the work (often demoralising in poorer areas).

Private schools in the United States have been witnessing declining enrolment numbers since the 1970s. At the same time, admission fees have skyrocketed: " the average tuition at Catholic elementary schools in 2010, the most recent year for which comparable data are available, was close to $6,000 in 2015 dollars, six times more than what it was in 1970 ($873 in 2015 dollars)" (Wong, 2018). The initial effects of the massification of education spilled into the private sector with the post-Second World War surge of the middle class, but as a result of the steady erosion of that sector, the situation has become more extreme and, arguably, private schools have become much more elite.

Australia

Australia's population growth, despite slowing down somewhat in the 1990s, increased by 25% between 2001 and 2016 with over half of that population increase being immigrants (Australian Bureau of Statistics, 2019). As globalised immigration continues, the population booms and forecasts in 2016 led to predictions that by 2026 a 17% increase in students would need to be accommodated by school growth (Goss, 2016). Statistics are higher in the major cities, suggesting a steeper increase.

Some states in Australia have struggled to meet the needs of a massified, globalised increase in demand. In 2018, in New South Wales, temporary schools had to be built as there were not enough classrooms (*Sydney Morning Herald*, 2018).

While the government has projected adequate investment, building projects and planning to ensure that demand is met, private schools have experienced a softening of enrolment (Mogato, 2019).

India

The massification of schooling in India has put tremendous pressure on an infrastructure that was underdeveloped under British colonialism and, since 1947, it has been the subject of much renewed government policy to cater sufficiently for the country's huge population.

Gains have been considerable with an increasing number of students completing education to a high level, progressing to PhD level (one in ten doctoral graduates in G20 countries were Indian in 2017). However, "71% of adults do not have upper secondary education. Even among younger adults, 70% of women have not attained upper secondary education, compared to 58% of men" (OECD, 2019).

Class sizes are in the global norm established by UNESCO: the average class size in India reached 32 students per class for primary schools in 2017 (Jagan-mohan, 2019). Some schools, however, push well beyond that: City Montessori school in Lucknow admits over 50,000 students to its 20 campuses and has classes of 45 students (Overdorf, 2015).

Estimates show that there are more than 600 million people under the age of 25 in India, and the country's population is rapidly becoming the largest in the world (it is predicted that the Indian population will number 1.5 billion people by 2030) (Trines, 2018). Therefore, the educational infrastructure will have to develop accordingly.

As pressure on places increases and India's economy becomes more and more dominant, the private school industry is growing with a surge in particularly expensive private schools, thus exacerbating the wealth gap (Singh & Sharma, 2019).

The African context

The broader African context sees large numbers of students leaving school before graduation: for example, reports in 2012 indicated that only 50% of children in Ghana completed grade 5 (Epstein & Yuthas, 2012). Similar statistics can be found for many other countries in Africa. This is largely due to the poor quality of education received, unwieldy class sizes, lack of availability of sufficient resources and a questioning by students of the relevant value and opportunity cost of an education—in other words, whether it is worth the investment of time given that opportunities directly correlated with secondary school graduation are not always palpable:

> Too few graduates gain the skills they need to find work. Nowhere is this quality challenge more evident than in the transition to the labour market. Graduate unemployment rates are high in many countries and employers across the region complain of a lack of basic, technical and transferable skills.
>
> (British Council, 2014a, p. 3)

Indeed, the fact that high-skilled jobs are often concentrated in the hands of a few with little real access to social ascension and the brain drain phenomenon whereby talented Africans decide to complete their studies overseas do not help this situation.

The critical problem of class size, with an average well over 30 and many instances on the African continent running well over 40 students per class, suggests that the entire educational infrastructure is underfunded and cannot cope with the massification of schooling. A 2016 study by UNESCO showed that average class sizes exceeded 70 students per class in Malawi, the Central African Republic and Tanzania with more than 80 students per class in the first three years of primary schooling in the Central African Republic (UNESCO, 2016). This is a problem that will become increasingly acute as Africa's population grows quickly and some analysts have forecast that one in four people will be African by 2050 (Ferris, 2015).

Educational resources are often not available to cope with the demands of massification. In 2016, in Cameroonian schools, mathematics textbooks were shared by 14 students on average. Physical resources are often not sufficiently available either (one in three primary schools did not have toilets in 2016 and the vast majority of schools were without access to electricity, UNESCO, 2016).

South Africa

South Africa is a unique case because of its history of apartheid, but it still manifests some of the more typical problems relating to the massification of education that can be found on the continent. The state runs over 23,000 schools providing education for over 12 million students (Ryan, 2019). Nationwide student surveys in 2018 put large class sizes and an insufficient number of books as the two most significant issues disturbing the quality of learning (South African Market Insights, 2020).

Worryingly, 2018 statistics showed a lower percentage of students of black ethnicity progressing to a bachelors' level degree after matriculating from school than was the case in 1975, which was during the dysfunctional system of Bantu education under apartheid. This suggests that as primary and secondary education becomes increasingly massified, more investment must be made in the sector to enable more successful pathways.

As the state system struggles to meet massification in South Africa, the private education market has expanded in recent decades (Ryan, 2019). However, the cost of a private education is becoming increasingly heavy for parents to bear and there are reports of decreases in enrolment numbers (*BusinessTech*, 2018), a trend that can be expected to increase in the financial wake of the COVID-19 pandemic. Indeed, periods of economic recession halt the overall proclivity of access to elite circles.

Analysis of the massification of schooling

These case studies show that the situation is by no means the same across the globe: there is a dearth of baseline infrastructural support for learners in many African countries with a dramatic spike in demographics on the horizon. South Africa faces the challenge, as do so many African countries, of ensuring that state education keeps up with the needs of a massified demand.

Both the UK and the United States, neither of which has a population that is growing as rapidly as it is in sub-Saharan Africa, offer strong educational models to their students but they still struggle to give parents the choice they would like and there is a dearth of teachers and supply teachers, and this is likely to become more and not less of a problem in time. Teachers' salaries and working conditions are not attractive enough to create the pipeline that is needed to cater for demand.

Australia, like South Africa, has seen a spike in private schools as parents look for better conditions for their children, but recent periods of economic recession have softened enrolment in that sector and are forcing school fees down. India, on the other hand, has witnessed increasing demand from the private sector, thereby allowing some schools to push fees up even more.

If there is a pattern in these stories, it is that the appetite for an elite education is strong, even if pockets are not always deep enough to foot the bill: the public sector in these countries, like most in the world, struggles greatly to accommodate the needs and aspirations of a massified demand for education. It is only in extremely wealthy countries with small and/or declining populations, a tradition of heavy investment in education (Norway, Switzerland, Finland) or wealthy countries with a long tradition of developed formal education (Canada, the United States, the UK) that the quality of education that Sustainable Development Goal 4 preaches can be met across the board and for free.

Universities

If schools are struggling to keep up with massification, this is even more the case for universities. This is essentially because demand for university places is increasing while they are extremely expensive educational units to run and many receive relatively little government funding. Global enrolment has increased dramatically and doubled from about 100 million in 2010 to twice that in 2014 (British Council, 2014a). At the same time, the status of postgraduate degrees and the globalised normalisation of university as an expected post-secondary school outcome have increased demand for places.

The COVID-19 pandemic has placed a supplementary weight on the shoulders of universities, as Chapter 8 in this volume discusses in detail. Further disruptions to society, such as environmental or health crises, will no doubt hit the university sector hard, possibly reversing the trend of massification as the means to support large populations of tertiary learners are diminished.

The United Kingdom

UK universities are commonly seen as having undergone massification from the 1970s to the present day (Bronwen Night, 2017). Post-Second World War expansion in the fields of science and medicine in the context of general economic prosperity led to more and more people seeking tertiary degrees, essentially in order to access employment in these booming sectors. The Robbins Report of 1963 stated that undergraduate university places "should be available to all who [are] qualified for them by ability and attainment" (Burnett, 2018). Mayhew, Deer and Dua (2004) argue that the public funding necessary to meet the philosophical ambitions of this expansion has not been sufficient.

One analysis is that the increase in demand was catered for by polytechnics (institutions offering vocational degrees): "Polytechnics, and later post-1992 universities, did the heavy lifting in the massification of UK higher education. They took more students and taught them for less money than their pre-1992 counterparts" (*University Business*, 2020). There is some debate about the quality of polytechnics and where they sit in the stratified UK system of educational institutions.

University education has been further massified by an important influx of international students, especially from India and China, with more than 400,000 every year and a hike of approximately 5% per annum in recent years (Kennedy, 2020).

Giannakis and Bullivant (2016) argue that the overall quality of service in tertiary education in the UK has deteriorated, mainly due to an increase in student numbers (p. 630). Marketing strategies are more and more explicitly focussed on international students, who, by paying extra fees, help the industry to thrive.

The United States

Massification in the tertiary education sector in the United States accelerated after the Second World War. Prior to this, a small, essentially white and male population attended university but after the war, the Servicemen's Readjustment Act of 1944, also known as the G.I. Bill of Rights, offered financial assistance to war veterans wishing to pursue university studies. This, coupled with economic growth between the 1950s and the 1970s, led to a spike in demand for university places. The Civil Rights movement opened access yet further to women and students of colour. Part-time and senior student enrolment increased over time. An increase in funding from the federal government in research, particularly in the sciences (directly linked to the Cold War space race competition that had arisen between the United States and the Soviet Union) led to an increase in the economic activity of universities, their staffing and the general social value of university qualifications. University-level certification became a massified middle-class expectation.

The prestige of top-tier and Ivy League universities with their lavish facilities and research laboratories has attracted many international students, especially to postgraduate degree programmes and, therefore, the massification of many American universities has been become as globalised as it has in the UK. There are approximately 20 million students in American universities with roughly three-quarters in state universities and one-quarter in private colleges (Duffin, 2020).

Although the percentage of international students in American universities rose from 1% in the 1950s to 5% in the early 21st century, recently enrolment has softened, possibly as a result of the

> rising cost of U.S. higher education, student visa delays and denials, and an environment increasingly marked by rhetoric and policies that make life more difficult for immigrants, as well as changing conditions and opportunities in home countries and increasing competition from other countries for students.
>
> (Zong & Batalova, 2018)

The COVID-19 pandemic hit US universities hard, reducing enrolment of international students for the 2020–2021 period (Hartocollis & Levin, 2020). Furthermore, the Trump Administration expressed its intention to discontinue or refuse to grant international student visas if courses were offered online (*Al Jazeera*, 2020), which could have an adverse effect on international student numbers since the prospect of an online course is not necessarily the same as a face-to-face one, for which international students are prepared to invest in significantly. Although this decision was later revised and rescinded, it acted as a strong deterrent to international students.

The university industry remains extremely competitive in the United States and represents a major source of economic activity. The massification of demand, in particular from international students, has made entry requirements more rigorous, especially for the so-called top-tier and Ivy League colleges. The response to massification has essentially been successful but is based on a meritocratically and plutocratically elitist enrolment philosophy: from the 1990s, state universities started to shift the costs of enrolment from the state to students (Lewin, 2011), while selective private colleges demanded higher scores on admissions tests.

Australia

Australian universities became massified after 1980s legislation made tertiary education free and, in 1989, increased funding (Dobson, 2001, p. 395). From the late 1980s full fee-paying international students increased in number to the point that tertiary education became Australia's third-largest export industry (Bradley et al., 2008, p. 4). Between 1989 and 2007, the university student population increased tenfold (up from 21,000 to 250,000). This trend has fluctuated since then depending on the government in power and type of visa restrictions that are in place.

The result has been a dramatic increase in enrolment (for example, from 2005 to 2014, the number of university students rose from 957,000 to 1.3 million (Engel & Halvorson, 2016, p. 548). Engel and Halvorson argue that the management of Australian universities, which is heavily focused on rankings and prestige, means that not enough attention is paid to teaching: "by international comparisons, Australian academics have a low reported preference for teaching, which is not surprising given prevailing incentive structures" (p. 552).

As strong immigration into Australia continues, immigration laws curtail or exacerbate international student numbers as it is these that create the narrative around massification in Australian universities. The Australian Population Research Institute forecasts a decline in international student enrolment for 2021 by up to a staggering 50% (Maslen, 2020).

The African context and South Africa

Despite the existence of a number of ancient universities in Africa (Al-Qarawiyyin in Morocco, Al-Azhar in Egypt and Timbuktu in Mali), most have been modelled on a European system imposed during the colonial period. Like colonial schools, universities were concentrated in urban areas, offering an education to a minority. At no point were they designed for massification. Reputed universities in the early postcolonial period (1960s) such as Ibadan (Nigeria), Makerere (Uganda) and Cheikh Anta Diop (Senegal) were not able to survive the general decline that most African universities fell into during the 1970s, 1980s and 1990s due to low operational budgets, cost-cutting by the World Bank and dictatorial governments that caused many academics to leave and standards to drop. A number of universities closed after independence (Makere was closed by the Ugandan President Museveni for example).

Mohamedbhai (2014) claims that "most public higher education institutions in Africa, in response to historical conditions, have enrolled students in excess of their capacity, resulting in massification and negative consequences on educational quality" (p. 59).

South Africa has a tradition of well-reputed universities, the most famous being the University of Cape Town, the University of the Witwatersrand, Stellenbosch, Rhodes University and the University of Pretoria. After apartheid, a groundswell of demand has put pressure on systems but, according to Jansen, "massification did not really happen. Where it did, it was restricted to a small number of historically white institutions capable of expanding their market share" (2017, p. 292). Instead, Jansen has argued that mergers of universities and technical colleges have attempted, with mixed success, to cater for rising student numbers and associated costs. Much frustration persists in South Africa over the question of tertiary education as the Rhodes Must Fall movement showed, when large numbers of students protested against high fees and an elitist, even neo-colonial ethos in most traditionally white universities.

According to Tutu (2020), one of the pressures on South African universities comes from junior graduates who return to complete postgraduate studies because there are not enough jobs on the market. In the wake of the COVID-19 recession, "a spike in postgraduate applications can be anticipated but the majority of these applications will not be from students who genuinely want to pursue postgraduate studies, but those who seek refuge on campuses because they cannot find jobs".

Jansen's thesis is that the massification of tertiary education in South Africa is not just a question of academics but of a welfare system:

> The continuity of welfare provision from school to university is now being strengthened along the education pipeline as poor students move through the system in large numbers with the expectation that their basic material needs will be satisfied during the transition from one level of education to the next.
>
> (2017, p. 175)

Therefore, South African universities are faced with a problem concerning massification that goes beyond academics into the very tissue of societal well-being. Future years of a globalised market, successive disruptions and other challenges to South Africa's economy will make it even more difficult for systems to cope with the massification of demand, expectation and need.

India

Varghese describes the massification of higher education in post-independent India in three successive stages: (1) high growth and limited access (1950–1970); (2) declining growth in enrolment (1970–1990); and (3) revival and massive expansion after 1990 (2015, p. 3). He attributes the most recent growth spate as essentially being driven by the privatisation of higher educational institutions (p. 8).

Massification in the tertiary education sector in India has increased at a significant magnitude: enrolment has increased fourfold since 2001 at a rate of roughly one million students per annum over the past five years (p. 33). This trend is set to continue as the population grows and more and more graduates look to register for undergraduate programmes.

India has approximately "993 Universities, 39931 Colleges and 10725 Stand Alone Institutions [with] 385 universities privately run" (AISHE, 2019, p. 1). "India had 37.4 million students enrolled in higher education in 2018–19. Gross Enrolment Ratio in higher education reached 26.3 per cent in 2018–19" (IBEF, 2020).

To give some comparison with other BRICS countries (an informal grouping of five major emerging national economies—Brazil, Russia, India, China and South Africa):

> India's higher education system, meanwhile, does not have the capacity to achieve enrollment ratios anywhere close to those of other middle-income economies. The country's tertiary gross enrollment rate is growing fast, but remains more than 20 percentage points below that of China or Brazil,

despite the creation of large numbers of higher education institutions (HEIs) in recent years.

(Trines, 2018)

A large number of Indian students leave the country to study abroad. The Indian student abroad community is the second largest globally after China. The number of Indian nationals studying abroad has risen from "134,880 students in 2004 to 278,383 in 2017" (UNESCO, 2020).

However, the return on investment is sporadic. As is the case in South Africa, a number of students will leave universities qualified but unable to enter the job market: in 2017 it was estimated that 60% of engineering graduates remained unemployed (Gohain, 2018).

Analysis of the massification of universities

These case studies have shown one essential pattern: that the concept of a university education went from something that was relatively rarefied, and therefore elitist, to a much more democratised universal expectation after the Second World War. This pattern has increased demand and put pressure on systems to accommodate increased enrolment, be it locally or through the influx of international students.

The response to this pressure, however, has varied in each country. In the UK, it led to the expansion of polytechnics in the 1990s. In the United States, it has meant shifting enrolment costs from the state to students. Meanwhile, in Australia (and also in the UK and the United States), the international student market has allowed universities to expand, thereby both catering for massification and creating it. In South Africa and India, the major challenge has been to provide rapidly growing local populations with a quality educational experience that allows them access to the workplace.

From the perspective of elitism, the massification of universities has intensified the concept of scarcity since the increase in pressure on admissions has meant that selective institutions have become statistically less accessible. For example, Harvard accepted more than 7% of applicants in 2012 but less than 5% for the 2022 intake (Franklin & Zwickel, 2018). It is likely that the situation will only become worse as more and more students with the financial means to do so apply to the same institutions globally, while local institutions struggle to accommodate demand. The COVID-19 pandemic and other societal or environmental phenomena in the future that cause recessions could dampen this trend, however.

From massification to privatisation

For both schools and universities across the globe, pressure on state systems as a result of massification has meant that education has been outsourced to the private sector. For example, "the majority of Indian students in tertiary education are enrolled in private institutions, where the ratio of students to teachers is much lower than in public institutions" (OECD, 2019), whereas "in Brazil, more than three quarters of the enrolment is now in private institutions" (British Council, 2015).

Of course, this is not necessarily the case in all countries but even those with strong national systems such as Finland, Norway, Denmark and Switzerland still have a plethora of private schools and universities open that, from the perspective of parents and students, offer either a better or a more specialised service than the national sector:

> The paradigm shift away from centralised and primarily state-facilitated forms of higher education, and towards a consumer market model is not merely the result of pressures exerted on the state by demographic growth, and an expanding participation rate. In several countries this shift gains traction from growing emphasis on the private value of education.
>
> (British Council, 2015)

It can be pointed out that numerous national systems in countries such as the United States and the UK, by shifting university costs to students, have commercialised education to the effect that it is not entirely dissimilar to private education:

> In the UK, for example, fees capped at £9000 have been introduced, enabled by the provision of universal government-backed loans, to be repaid only after the graduate has reached a salary threshold. Students are increasingly framed as 'consumers', exercising their choice within a market of possible course 'products'.
>
> (British Council, 2015)

However, state system learning environments are often negatively affected by large classes and insufficient teacher supply. This problem is likely to increase over time as the global population grows and finances are strained by economic recessions such as the 2008 financial crash and the fallout of the COVID-19 pandemic, weakening many national systems and causing parents and students to flock to the private sector for better infrastructures.

At the same time, private education costs and enrolments will no doubt continue to be affected by macro-economic fluctuations, meaning that fewer people will be able to afford expensive private pathways, forcing them to stay in national systems. Chapter 6 looks into the fast-growing phenomenon of cheap international schools offering an alternative to the state system that is within reach of lower-middle-class incomes. However, this system too can quickly become massified and therefore saturated.

A number of English public schools such as Westminster, Dulwich, Wellington and Harrow have set up campuses in China, thereby massifying their brand and extending their prestigious ethos to an external market. This allows upper-middle-class parents who cannot afford to send their children to prestigious international boarding schools to have their children educated locally but with the promise of English exclusivity.

Another way in which one can view the commercialisation of education as a response to massification is in the international student market drive, which has taken over so many universities, particularly in the UK where many universities have come to depend on Chinese and Indian students. Since international students pay higher fees, they are highly desirable. Aggressive marketing campaigns targeting international students can be viewed cynically:

> Tony Blair's Prime Minister's Initiative for International Education (PMI) encouraged them to regard the recruitment of international students as a commercial venture. The reduction of international students to government-endorsed targets has meant that they are treated as a commodity, not as young people making the most important decision of their life. Rather than being guided towards the best educational experience, they are harassed and cajoled by agents and recruitment teams into universities desperate to meet targets – all watched by admiring media and government agencies, excited that education is now one of the UK's largest exports.
>
> (*University Business*, 2020)

From the analytical perspective of elitism and education, the commercial angle that many institutions have taken and the flourishing of private schools has created a global augmentation of both meritocratic and plutocratic elitism. The underlying premise is the differentiation between state and private, the latter clearly perceived as more exclusive and of higher quality than the former.

Remote learning

One way of coping with the massification of education has been online learning. Some American universities started offering their courses online through Massively Open Online Courses (MOOCs) in 2008. The experiment started at the University of Manitoba and quickly sparked interest from other establishments: Stanford followed in 2011, then Harvard and MIT and today many universities offer at least part of their curriculum online (MAUT, 2020). India has become the second largest market for e-learning after the United States. "The sector is expected to reach US$ 1.96 billion by 2021 with around 9.5 million users" (IBEF, 2020).

"Evidence points to rising numbers of learners signing up for 'wholly online learning' as an indication that there is a real demand for such courses" (Patru & Balaji, 2016, p. 24), and there is a strong argument to be made for MOOCs opening access to higher education in such a way that it democratises it completely and removes the elitist barrier that has kept it out of reach to so many for hundreds of years:

> MOOCs are considered a tremendous opportunity to provide groups of people, particularly those who cannot afford a formal education and are disadvantaged, with access to HE. As courses are offered free of charge to people all over the world, thus giving them the opportunity to decide for themselves what, where and when to study, MOOCs may be regarded as contributing to the democratisation of HE, not only locally or regionally but globally as well.
>
> (Patru & Balaji, 2016, p. 24)

Bennet and Kent's detailed 2017 study of MOOCS points out that drop-off rates are high and many MOOC initiatives were not able to sustain themselves for any significant period. Nevertheless, in the wake of the nationwide lockdowns and imperative for social distancing as a result of COVID-19 it is likely that MOOCs will become even more important in the future than they have in the past, by being open to anyone with a broadband connection and democratising access to education.

Indeed, MOOCs partly deconstruct the discourse around plutocratic elitism and education although there is a material divide between those who have the means to access MOOCs and those who do not. The digital divide between learners, exacerbated and made so palpable during school closures related to COVID-19, is likely to endure as learning is digitised and available to those with the devices and broadband connections needed to enjoy such a service, primarily in Europe, East Asia and North America (Hughes, 2020b). Furthermore, some studies have shown than those who register for MOOCs are not necessarily from disadvantaged backgrounds:

> [A] team from the University of Pennsylvania, led by Gayle Christensen, found that the majority of the people enrolled in thirty-two of the courses offered through Penn's Coursera platform were young, already well educated, from developed countries, and, for the most part, employed … And most of the students weren't taking classes in order to gain an essential education that they wouldn't receive otherwise; predominantly, they said they had enrolled to satisfy curiosity or advance in a current job—both of which are worthy pursuits, to be sure, but they are not the main needs that MOOCs were created to meet.
>
> (Konnikova, 2014)

Virtual schools

Virtual schools started to open in Australia, the United States and the UK in the 1990s, first to offer schooling in areas that were sparsely populated and in which travel to the nearest school was difficult. Learning takes place synchronously or asynchronously through virtual learning environments. Although more research has been done at adult rather than school level, the challenges are similar:

The challenges associated with virtual schooling include the conclusion that the only students typically successful in online learning environments are those who have independent orientations towards learning, highly motivated by intrinsic sources, and have strong time management, literacy, and technology skills.

(Barbour & Reeves, 2009, p. 402)

Some research suggests that online learning is more effective in a number of domains, leading to better information retention (Gutierrez, 2016; Chernev, 2019).

In general, the advantages of online learning reduce elitist barriers: it tends to be less expensive; opens access to students with physical disabilities; and washes out some of the social differences between students that are more apparent in face-to-face environments. However, there are clear disadvantages that come with the removal of a physical leaning environment and problems of access to broadband connection affect students just as they do adults (Kumar, 2019).

The COVID-19 crisis meant that most of the schools around the world had to convert to virtual schooling despite different levels of preparedness. Estimates show that 1.2 billion children were learning outside of the classroom from early 2020 onwards. The so-called digital divide exacerbated gaps in learning for those in underdeveloped environments and those studying in technologically prepared schools (UNCTAD, 2020).

At the same time, the massification of online learning has accelerated like never before, changing the dynamics and morphology of schooling for the foreseeable future.

BYJU'S, a Bangalore-based educational technology and online tutoring firm founded in 2011 … is now the world's most highly valued edtech company. Since announcing free live classes on its Think and Learn app, BYJU'S has seen a 200% increase in the number of new students [whereas] Tencent classroom … has been used extensively since mid-February after the Chinese government instructed a quarter of a billion full-time students to resume their studies through online platforms. This resulted in the largest "online movement" in the history of education with approximately 730,000, or 81% of K-12 students, attending classes via the Tencent K-12 Online School in Wuhan.

(Li & Lalani, 2020)

Virtual schooling will no doubt become more of a norm than an exception in the future, making it more of a challenge for highly elitist institutions to operate as they have in the past since virtual schooling is less expensive than physically present learning and the value added of infrastructure and resources is no longer apparent.

The COVID-19 pandemic caused some elitist educational institutions to open their doors to a virtual audience, thereby massifying their hitherto exclusive offer. For example, Eton College created EtonX, an online platform that the school claimed would prevail in "widening access to the most effective educational methods and resources" (Eton, 2020).

Private and state cooperation

One way of catering for the increased massification of demand in education is to combine public and private forces, allowing for greater capacity absorption and diversification.

Fennell (2014) has argued for the efficacy of public-private partnerships (PPPs) in India and Pakistan with specific emphasis on the positive effects this has brought about for gender equality while Patrinos, Barrera-Osorio and Gàqueta's comprehensive 2009 study across different countries point out the essential advantages of such partnerships for the public good (competition in the market; flexible contracts; open bidding processes; sharing of risk) (p. 4). However, they also point out some of the dangers of PPPs such as "loss of government control" and, importantly for this study:

> Increasing the educational choices available to students and their families may increase socioeconomic segregation if better prepared students end up self-selecting into high-quality schools, thus further improving their outcomes ... PPPs will lead to poorer students being left behind in the deteriorating public schools that lose the support of more educated parents.
>
> (Patrinos et al., 2009, p. 4)

However, they argue that the evidence, based on OECD and World Bank studies, is that PPPs generally have a positive impact (p. 5), quoting success stories in Tanzania, Senegal, Colombia, Venezuela and Bangladesh (p. 6).

Conclusion

The massification of education, both in the realm of schools and universities, has changed the morphology of the educational experience for millions of learners across the globe in the space of 70 years. Just 100 years ago, only the few were formally educated, but after the ending of the Second World War, an intense augmentation in demand has put enormous pressure on educational infrastructures and continues to do so, leading to large class sizes, teacher shortages and the flocking of parents to the private sector.

At the centre of the massification of education is the perception of the quality of state education that, according to Katz, has been irrevocably damaged: "the value of the welfare state as a normative concept ... has effectively been destroyed. The image of welfare has been shifted from its positive connotations in supporting the common good to a negative association with the undeserving poor" (2001, p. 237). This oversimplification has not only led to a haemorrhaging of state systems but to new models that blend funding from the government with the private sector:

> A growing number of formal and informal public-private relationships have been formed, linking public and private efforts in education … education has become much more than before a 'public matter' but also a space for exercising social and corporate responsibility.
>
> (Acedo et al., 2012, p. 9)

It can be argued that this blended model of private and state cooperation could lead to a greater degree of accountability: "when communities can hold teachers, administrators and government officials accountable through formal institutional mechanisms, community members become more interested in school improvement – more willing to commit their own resources to the task" (Narayan, 2002, p. 231). Indeed, it may be that the future of quality of education depends on such synergies.

One of the ways in which this pressure cooker has been opened has been through the valve of online learning, a way of learning that was massively augmented during the 2020 COVID-19 pandemic. There is a strong likelihood that online learning will continue to expand in the future.

References

Acedo, C., Popa, S., & Adams, D. (2012). *Quality and Qualities: Tensions in Education Reforms*. Rotterdam: Brill.

Adams, R. (2019). England school places shortage "made worse by academies". *The Guardian*. www.theguardian.com/education/2019/aug/26/england-school-places-shortage-made-worse-by-academies.

Albrecht, C.M., Backhaus, C., Gurzki, H., & Woisetschläger, D.M. (2013). Drivers of Brand Extension Success: What Really Matters For Luxury Brands. *Psychology & Marketing*, 30(8): 647–659.

Al Jazeera (2020). US now says new foreign students can't enter if courses online. *Al Jazeera*. www.aljazeera.com/news/2020/07/ice-announces-rules-blocking-international-students-200724191429978.html.

All India Survey on Higher Education (AISHE) (2019). *All India Survey on Higher Education, 2018–2019*. New Delhi: Government of India, Ministry of Human Resource Development, Department of Higher Education. http://aishe.nic.in/aishe/viewDocument.action?documentId=262.

Australian Bureau of Statistics (2019). *Historical Population*. www.abs.gov.au/AUSSTATS/abs@.nsf/mf/3105.0.65.001.

Barbour, M.K., & Reeves, T.C. (2009). The reality of virtual schools: A review of the literature. *Computers & Education*, 52(2), 402–416. https://doi.org/10.1016/j.compedu.2008.09.009.

Bennet, R., & Kent, M. (eds.) (2017). *Massive Open Online Courses and Higher Education. What Went Right? What Went Wrong? And Where to Next?* Oxford: Routledge.

Bolton, P. (2019). Education spending in the UK. House of Commons Library. https://commonslibrary.parliament.uk/research-briefings/sn01078/.

Bradley, D., Noonan, P., Nugent, H., & Scales, B. (2008). *Review of Australian higher Education: Final Report.* Canberra: Department of Education, Employment and Workplace Relations.

British Council (2014a). *Can Higher Education Solve Africa's Job Crisis? Understanding Graduate Employability in Sub-Saharan Africa.* www.britishcouncil.org/sites/default/files/graduate_employability_in_ssa_final-web.pdf.

British Council (2014b). *Massification of Higher Education in Large Academic Systems.* www.britishcouncil.org/sites/default/files/massification_seminar_in_delhi_-_a_summary_report.pdf.

British Council (2015). *Managing Large Systems: A Comparative Analysis: Challenges and Opportunities for Large Higher Education Systems.* www.britishcouncil.org/sites/default/files/3.6_managing-large-systems.pdf.

Bronwen Night, E. (2017). *The Impact of Massification of the Higher Education Sector on the Idea of a Degree in the UK.* Unpublished doctoral thesis, Monash University. https://bridges.monash.edu/articles/The_Impact_of_Massification_of_the_Higher_Education_Sector_on_the_Idea_of_a_Degree_in_the_UK/5732178/1.

Burnett, K. (2018). UK universities face a crisis of over-ambitious expansion. *Financial Times.* www.ft.com/content/6f0d7502-90f5-11e8-9609-3d3b945e78cf.

BusinessTech (2018). South African Private Schools See Major Drop-Outs Due to Rising Costs: Report. *BusinessTech.* https://businesstech.co.za/news/finance/239759/south-african-private-schools-see-major-drop-outs-due-to-rising-costs-report/.

Business Today (2020). Union budget 2020: How much will modi govt spend on education? *Business Today.* www.businesstoday.in/union-budget-2020/news/budget-2020-how-much-will-modi-govt-spend-on-education/story/395077.html.

Calderon, A. (2018). *Massification of Higher Education Revisited.* Melbourne: RMIT University. www.academia.edu/36975860/Massification_of_higher_education_revisited.

Centre on Budget and Policy Priorities (CBPP) (2020). *Policy Basics: Where Do Our Federal Tax Dollars Go?* www.cbpp.org/research/federal-budget/policy-basics-where-do-our-federal-tax-dollars-go.

Chernev, B. (2019). 21 Astonishing E-Learning Statistics For 2020. *Techjury.* https://techjury.net/stats-about/elearning/#gref.

Coulangeon, P. (2008). The cultural disillusionment of school massification in France from 1981 to 2003. *Journal of Cultural Economy,* 1(3), 281–304. doi:doi:10.1080/17530350802477002.

Department for Education (2019a). *Schools, Pupils and Their Characteristics: January.* https://assets.publishing.service.gov.uk/government/uploads/system/uploads/attachment_data/file/812539/Schools_Pupils_and_their_Characteristics_2019_Main_Text.pdf.

Department for Education (2019b). *Initial Teacher Training (ITT) Census for 2019 to 2020, England.* https://assets.publishing.service.gov.uk/government/uploads/system/uploads/attachment_data/file/848851/ITT_Census_201920_Main_Text_final.pdf.

Dobson, I.R. (2001). How has massification changed the shape of Australian universities? *Tertiary Education and Management,* 7, 295–310. https://doi.org/10.1023/A:1012789128839.

Duffin, E. (2020). College enrollment in public and private institutions in the U.S. 1965–2029. *Statista*. www.statista.com/statistics/183995/us-college-enrollment-and-projections-in-p ublic-and-private-institutions/.

Engel, S., & Halvorson, D. (2016). Neoliberalism, massification and teaching transformative politics and international relations. *Australian Journal of Political Science*, 51(3), 546–554.

Epstein, M.J., & Yuthas, K. (2012). Scaling effective education for the poor in developing countries: A report from the field. *Journal of Public Policy & Marketing*, 31(1), 102–114. doi:doi:10.1509/jppm.11.066.

Eton College (2020). *Eton X*. https://etonx.com/.

Fennell, S. (2014). Public-private partnerships in education and the pursuit of gender equality: A view from South Asia. *International Development Policy*. http://journals.op enedition.org/poldev/1798.

Ferris, R. (2015). World population: Quarter of Earth will be African in 2050. *CNBC*. www. cnbc.com/2015/07/30/world-population-quarter-of-earth-will-be-african-in-2050.html.

Franklin, D.R., & Zwickel, S.W. (2018). Record-low 4.59 percent of applicants accepted to Harvard class of 2022. *Harvard Crimson*. www.thecrimson.com/article/ 2018/3/29/harvard-regular-admissions-2022/.

Garcia, E., & Weiss, E. (2019). The teacher shortage is real, large and growing, and worse than we thought. *Economic Policy Institute*. www.epi.org/publication/the-teacher-shorta ge-is-real-large-and-growing-and-worse-than-we-thought-the-first-report-in-the-perfe ct-storm-in-the-teacher-labor-market-series/.

Giannakis, M., & Bullivant, N. (2016). The massification of higher education in the UK: Aspects of service quality. *Journal of Further and Higher Education*, 40(5), 630–648. doi:doi:10.1080/0309877X.2014.1000280.

Gohain, M. (2018). 60% of engineering graduates unemployed. *Times of India*. http://timeso findia.indiatimes.com/articleshow/57698133.cms?utm_source=contentofinterest&utm_m edium=text&utm_campaign=cppst.

Goss, P. (2016). Should you worry about a school's shortage? It really depends on where you live. *The Conversation*. https://theconversation.com/should-you-worry-a bout-a-schools-shortage-it-really-depends-on-where-you-live-53296.

Gutierrez, K. (2016). Facts and stats that reveal the power of eLearning [Infographic]. *SHIFT*. www.shiftelearning.com/blog/bid/301248/15-facts-and-stats-that-reveal-the-p ower-of-elearning.

Hartocollis, A., & Levin, D. (2020). As students put off college, anxious universities tap wait lists. *New York Times*. www.nytimes.com/2020/05/01/us/coronavirus-college-enrollm ent.html.

Hughes, C. (2020b). Some implications of COVID-19 for remote learning and the future of schooling. *UNESCO International Bureau of Education*. https://unesdoc. unesco.org/ark:/48223/pf0000373229.

India Brand Equity Foundation (IBEF) (2020). *Education and Training Sector in India*. www.ibef.org/industry/education-sector-india.aspx.

Jaganmohan, M. (2019). Pupil-teacher ratio in India by school type 2013–2017. *Statista*. www.statista.com/statistics/603889/pupil-teacher-ratio-in-india-by-school-type/.

Jansen, J. (2003). *The State of Higher Education in South Africa: From Massification to Mergers*. In J. Daniel, A. Habib, & R. Southall (eds.) *State of the Nation: 2003–2004*. Cape Town: HSRC Press.

Jansen, J. (2017). *As by Fire: The End of the South African University*. Cape Town: Tafelberg.

Jerkins, M. (2015). Too many kids. *The Atlantic*. www.theatlantic.com/education/archive/2015/07/too-many-kids/397451/.

Katz, M. (2001). *The Price of Citizenship: Redefining the American Welfare State*. New York: Holt.

Kennedy, K. (2020). UK: growth in int'l student numbers, jump in new enrolments from India. *The Pie News*. https://thepienews.com/news/uk-hesa-data-shows-another-year-of-growth-in-international-student-numbers/.

Konnikova, M. (2014). Why MOOCs are failing the people they are meant to help. *New Yorker*. www.newyorker.com/science/maria-konnikova/moocs-failure-solutions.

Kumar, D. (2019). *Pros and Cons of Online Education*. Raleigh: North Carolina State University. www.ies.ncsu.edu/resources/white-papers/pros-and-cons-of-online-education/.

Lewin, T. (2011). Public universities relying more on tuition than state money. *New York Times*. www.nytimes.com/2011/01/24/education/24tuition.html.

Li, C., & Lalani, F. (2020). The COVID-19 pandemic has changed education forever. This is how. World Economic Forum. www.weforum.org/agenda/2020/04/coronavirus-education-global-covid19-online-digital-learning.

Lynch. E. (2015). 10 Reasons the U.S. education system is failing. *Education Week*. https://blogs.edweek.org/edweek/education_futures/2015/08/10_reasons_the_us_education_system_is_failing.html.

McGill Association of University Teachers (MAUT)2020. *A Brief History of MOOCs*. www.mcgill.ca/maut/current-issues/moocs/history.

Maslen, G. (2020). 50% drop in foreign student enrolment by 2021 predicted. *University World News*. www.universityworldnews.com/post.php?story=20200601150411139.

Mayhew, K., Deer, C., & Dua, M. (2004). The move to mass higher education in the UK: Many questions and some answers. *Oxford Review of Education*, 30(1), 65–82. www.jstor.org/stable/4127152.

Mogato, A. (2019). Are schools keeping up with booming enrolments? *The Educator*. www.theeducatoronline.com/k12/news/are-schools-keeping-up-with-booming-enrolments/266827.

Mohamedbhai, G. (2014). Massification in higher education institutions in Africa: Causes, consequences and responses. *International Journal of African Higher Education*, 1(1). https://doi.org/10.6017/ijahe.v1i1.5644.

Narayan, D. (2002). *Empowerment and Poverty Reduction: A Sourcebook*. Washington, DC: World Bank.

National Center for Education Statistics (2019). *The Condition of Education*. https://nces.ed.gov/programs/coe/indicator_cgc.asp.

Organisation for Economic Co-operation and Development (OECD) (2016). *Public Spending on Education*. https://data.oecd.org/eduresource/public-spending-on-education.htm.

Organisation for Economic Co-operation and Development (OECD) (2019). *Education at a Glance 2019: OECD Indicators*. Paris: OECD Publishing. https://doi.org/10.1787/f8d7880d-en.

Overdorf, J. (2015). 52,000 students and 1,050 classrooms: Inside the world's largest school. *The Guardian*. www.theguardian.com/teacher-network/2015/dec/16/52000-students-and-1050-classrooms-inside-the-worlds-largest-school.

Patrinos, H.A., Barrera-Osorio, F., & Gàqueta, J. (2009). *The Role of Public-Private Part-nerships in Education*. Washington, DC: World Bank.

Patru, M., & Balaji, V. (2016). *Making Sense of MOOCs: A Guide for Policy-Makers in Developing Countries*. Paris: UNESCO.

Roser, M., & Ortiz-Ospina, E. (2020). Global education. *Our World in Data*. https://ourworldindata.org/global-education.

Ryan, C. (2019). Private schools are thriving in SA. *The Citizen*. https://citizen.co.za/business/2167297/private-schools-are-thriving-in-sa/.

Singh, N., & Sharma, K. (2019). India's elite schools are good enough for the rich and famous, but our colleges aren't. *The Print*. https://theprint.in/features/indias-elite-schools-are-good-enough-for-the-rich-and-famous-but-our-colleges-arent/177439/.

South African Market Insights (2020). *South Africa's Education Statistics*. www.southafricanmi.com/education-statistics.html.

Sutcher, L., Darling-Hammond, L., & Carver-Thomas, D. (2016). *A Coming Crisis in Teaching? Teacher Supply, Demand, and Shortages in the U.S. Learning Policy Institute*. Palo Alto, CA: Learning Policy Institute. https://learningpolicyinstitute.org/product/coming-crisis-teaching.

Sydney Morning Herald (2018). School overcrowding must be addressed sooner rather than later. *Sydney Morning Herald*. www.smh.com.au/national/nsw/school-overcrowding-must-be-addressed-sooner-rather-than-later-20180208-p4yzqe.html.

Trines, S. (2018). Education in India. *WENR*. https://wenr.wes.org/2018/09/education-in-india.

Trow, M. (2007). Reflections on the Transition from Elite to Mass to Universal Access: Forms and Phases of Higher Education in Modern Societies since WWII. *International Handbook of Higher Education*. Dordrecht: Springer, pp. 243–280.

Tutu, O. (2020). SA universities should brace for "massification of higher education" as first-time graduates battle to find jobs. *City Press*. https://city-press.news24.com/Voices/sa-universities-should-brace-for-massification-of-higher-education-as-first-time-graduates-battle-to-find-jobs-20200424.

University Business (2020). The post-1992 universities: Overseas, overstretched? *University Business*. https://universitybusiness.co.uk/Article/post-1992-universities-overseas-overstretched/.

United Nations (2019) *Growing at a slower pace, world population is expected to reach 9.7 billion in 2050 and could peak at nearly 11 billion around 2100*. Department of Economic and Social Affairs. www.un.org/development/desa/en/news/population/world-population-prospects-2019.html.

United Nations Conference on Trade and Development (UNCTAD) (2020). *Coronavirus Reveals Need to Bridge the Digital Divide*. https://unctad.org/en/pages/newsdetails.aspx?OriginalVersionID=2322.

United Nations Educational, Scientific and Cultural Organization (UNESCO) (2016). *School Resources and Learning Environment in Africa*. http://uis.unesco.org/sites/default/files/school-resources-and-learning-environment-in-africa-2016-en/school-resources-and-learning-environment-in-africa-2016-en.pdf.

United Nations Educational, Scientific and Cultural Organization (UNESCO) (2020). *Out of School Children and Youth*. http://uis.unesco.org/en/topic/out-school-children-and-youth.

United Nations Educational, Scientific and Cultural Organization (UNESCO) (2020b). *UNESCO Institute for Statistics*. http://data.uis.unesco.org/Index.aspx.

Varghese, N.V. (2015). *Challenges of Massification of Higher Education in India*. Centre for Policy Research in Higher Education. www.niepa.ac.in/download/Publications/CPRHE/March_2016/CPRHE_Research%20_%20Paper-1.pdf.

Wong, A. (2018). Private schools are becoming more elite. *The Atlantic*. www.theatlantic.com/education/archive/2018/07/why-private-schools-are-becoming-more-elite/566144/.

Zong, J., & Batalova, J. (2018). *International Students in the United States*. Migration Policy Institute. www.migrationpolicy.org/article/international-students-united-states.

Part II

Today's global context

Chapter 6

International schools, global citizenship and elitism

Zach and Anthony

Zach has never travelled outside Burkina Faso. His siblings and mother have been to neighbouring countries like Mali and Niger but no one in his family has been outside of Africa. Nor has Zach seen the sea. It is one of his projects, to get down to Côte d'Ivoire to see the coast one day, maybe after he has finished school.

Zach feels proud to be from Burkina Faso. In his classroom, there is a poster of his country's flag, flanked by two white horses. At the foot of the image are the words *Unité, Progrès, Justice*. It is difficult for Zach to envision what life outside Burkina Faso might be like but he imagines skyscrapers, lavish cars, vistas and glamorous images he has glimpsed occasionally on other people's iPhones.

On another wall in the classroom there is a map of the world. It is weather-beaten and tired but children still gather around it often, pointing at different countries, speaking their names out loud, testing each other on capitals. Zach's favourite country on the map is Brazil. When he looks at it he thinks of his favourite football player Neymar and the great Brazilian footballers that his father used to talk about with so much passion: Ronaldinho, Ronaldo, Kaka.

For Zach, travel is a far-flung dream that hardly ever enters his imaginary orbit. The major towns of Burkina Faso and its capital seem far enough away for him to look at them with some awe and bewilderment, let alone the prospect of travelling to another continent.

In class, students have discussed other parts of the world and what is happening in them. Zach has been told that the COVID-19 pandemic started in China, that it is dangerous to be a black person in America and that the recent terrorist attacks in Ouagadougou were carried out by extremists in Mali. He can sense that the world is connected and that while he might not be able to travel to see the world, the world travels to see him, even if it does so indirectly.

For Anthony, on the other hand, travel is second nature. Anthony has been to four continents and travels internationally every winter and some summers.

His father is constantly travelling although more recently, with the onset of the COVID-19 pandemic, he has been working from home.

Anthony's favourite country is Australia. He has been twice and loved surfing in Torquay, south of Melbourne. He also has fond memories of Hawaii as it was one of those trips that took place so long ago that it remains in his memory in a faded, nostalgic manner that is pleasing to recall.

Although Anthony holds a Russian passport, he doesn't really feel Russian: he considers himself more as a citizen of the world. Most of his classmates are the same—they are "global citizens". Anthony knows that whatever industry he chooses to enter in the future, it will involve working with people from all over the world and that it is therefore in his interests to speak more than one language and to know how to communicate with others well.

In his school, the headmaster talks about collaboration and soft skills a lot, explaining that these will be necessary for the future and that the students are lucky to be learning them from a young age. Anthony understands that soft skills are things like knowing how to listen to other people, how to negotiate and leadership qualities.

There are over 60 nationalities in Anthony's school and at the entrance there is a large screen that often plays a promotional film. It says, "At our school, we learn to be global citizens".

Introduction to the scope of the chapter

This chapter investigates the question of education and elitism from the angle of international education. The international schools industry is expanding and, in many contexts, it is competing with national systems. Although international schools were originally designed to offer an education to the children of mobile expatriate communities, during the 21st century there has been an increase in the number of international schools operating at the national level as an alternative to local schooling systems and they are experiencing enrolment from local students. Why is this the case and what are the implications for any discussion about elitism?

By investigating the different types of international school in operation and the extent to which they either mitigate or augment elitism, I will analyse the construct of global citizenship and its potential implications for the individual and for society. Indeed, just as there are different interpretations of the term global citizenship (critical, radical or neoliberal, for example), so there are different imperatives at work in international schools, often coexisting somewhat incongruously (an egalitarian function rhetorically but an elitist function administratively).

The chapter discusses how the design of international education can augment elitism but, at the same time, has the potential to offer greater access to high-quality education for students, thereby addressing Sustainable Development Goal 4 (SDG 4). Examples are given of state/international partnerships that are widening access and are worth investigating as possible models for future reforms in education.

The origins of international schools

In 1924, in the aftermath of the First World War, a group of educators versed in the constructivist pedagogic theories of Montessori, Dewey and Froebel and functionaries working for international not-for-profit organisations such the League of Nations and the International Labour Office came together to found the League School, later named the International School of Geneva. This was the world's first international school.

From the outset the vision of the school was to educate children of different nationalities with a view to creating a more peaceful world through principles of open-mindedness and cooperation. At the same time, the school's administrative function was to provide schooling for employees of the international organisations affiliated with the newly founded League of Nations.

During the 1920s, other international schools were opened in Yokahama, Japan, and New York, USA. More international schools opened across the globe over the next few decades.

In the late 1960s, the International Baccalaureate (IB) diploma programme was developed as the school leaving certificate that would give children, mostly those studying in international schools, access to universities around the world. The tenets of the IB were, very much like the foundations of the International School of Geneva, focused on accessing a better world through education: students were to engage in community service and to study a variety of subjects so as to broaden their perspectives. At the same time, the IB had a pragmatic function, which was to provide students who were not in their homeland with an educational experience that was different to the local system. This allowed, for example, British and American children to be schooled in English and to encounter a curriculum that was not too far removed from what they might have experienced in the United Kingdom or the United States and to do so in a system that would be recognised by British and American universities.

Early international schools and the International Baccalaureate Organization started as small experiments with relatively little funding behind them. At one point, the organisation's financial situation was so difficult that the head of the organisation, Gerard Renaud, mortgaged his own house in order to pay the staff their wages.

Today, the international schools market is vast, global and growing: there are over 11,000 international schools in the world (ISC Research, 2020) and the IB is offered in over 5,000 schools across the globe (International Baccalaureate Organization, 2020). Although the first international schools were explicitly designed to cater for expatriate populations, out of the 5.6 million students experiencing an international school experience, "the vast majority of enrolments (approximately 80%) are now children of local families attending an international school in their native country" (ISC Research, 2020).

Not only are international schools prominent on the landscape of education, they are becoming more widespread. A 2018 Global Report from ISC

Research counted "a compound annual growth rate of nearly 6% over the last five years ... with Dubai leading the way (followed at some distance by Shanghai, Abu Dhabi, and Beijing") (ICEF, 2018).

A 2017 report on educational trends in India showed that

> The number of students being taught at English-medium K–12 international schools now totals 268,600 – up from 151,900 five years ago, according to ISC Research's latest market report for India. Meanwhile, the number of schools has also significantly increased over the same time period, from 313 in 2012, to 469 [in 2017].
>
> (Marsh, 2017)

Why exactly international schools are growing so fast and what, therefore, the relationship is between international schooling and elitism is something that will be developed throughout this chapter.

Defining international schools

Trying to define international schools is not as simple as one might think and the difficulty in finding a coherent definition is at the core of the debate around elitism and international schools. First, there is no single binding definition of an international school and the title "international school" is not protected in any way. In fact, any school can call itself an international school if it wishes to. Second, there are different types of international school, some are simply called "the International School of (whatever the city is), others "the American International School" or "the British International School". Third, different international schools emphasise different areas of their operational impact. Nonetheless, it is possible to define, broadly speaking, certain ideas and trends in international schools.

As far back as the 1960s, when international schools were relatively scarce compared to today, Knight and Leach (1964) argued that there were seven different types of international school, whereas more recent researchers in international education such as Hayden and Thompson (2013) argue that there are at least three types of international school.

Walker suggests that while there are several different formats and structures, there is a recognisable international curriculum which runs through all of them and constitutes the main definition of an international school:

> An international school is an organization that offers its students an international education through the medium of its curriculum, its planned learning. An international curriculum is the thread that connects different types of international schools be they formally associated with the United Nations; be they state or privately funded, profit or not-for-profit; be they multicultural in terms of staff and students; be

they located in the northern or southern hemisphere, housed in a medieval castle or on a concrete and plate-glass campus.

(2015, p. 79)

The quotation is interesting for what it says by dint of imagery: the typology of schools mentioned is revealing: on the one hand, we could group "northern hemisphere", "medieval castle" (no doubt a reference to the world's first United World College, Atlantic College in Wales), "privately funded" and "profit" as suggesting expensive, possibly elitist institutions and, on the other we might group "southern hemisphere", "not-for-profit", "state" and "concrete and plate-glass" as referring to less well-resourced schools representing greater socioeconomic access. In other words, international education appears to span both elitist and non-elitist institutions.

Needless to say, this dichotomy is an over-simplification: some for-profit schools offer greater access to socioeconomically deprived learners and some not-for-profit schools are selective and/or expensive. However, the tension between the purpose and practical outcome of international schools is apparent and this is precisely why it is so difficult to define international schools with a single coherent description.

From internationalism to globalisation and implications for elitism

The fall of the Berlin Wall in 1989 and the acceleration of modern capitalism throughout the 1990s, as well as seminal dates upon which the world essentially became "flatter", to use Thomas Friedman's phrase, changed the face of world politics. The European Union was created in 1993 and by 2002 a common European currency was minted. In 1998, George Soros described a situation that is still very much de rigueur today:

We live in a global economy that is characterised not only by free trade in goods and services but even more by the free movement of capital. Interest rates, exchange rates, and stock [markets] in various countries are intimately interrelated and global financial markets exert tremendous influence on economic conditions.

(1998, p. 101)

One could contrast this market-driven globalised economy, or "globalisation" to put it in brief, with internationalism, a term that denotes less a system of boundless free market capitalism and more a system of international law between nation states built on principles of sovereignty, diplomacy and intergovernmental agreements.

Of course, 21st-century globalisation has been augmented and accelerated by technology and we are entering a phase of biocognitive capitalism where data control by all-powerful technological companies can be considered a new mode of production to be manipulated and exploited (Zuboff, 2019), whereas trading is increasingly done by algorithms, leading to an unprecedented level of deregulation and also a disconnect between the behaviour of the stock market and the real economy on the ground where salaries are earned and jobs lost. These developments go hand in hand with the increased power of monopolies like the GAFA and FAANG groups which have intensified wealth in the hands of a few to the point where the global wealth gap has never been greater: a 2017 study by Oxfam showed that "eight men own the same wealth as the 3.6 billion people who make up the poorest half of humanity". Globalisation in 2020 means something very different to what it did in the early 1980s.

Today, the concept of globalisation is a slippery signifier with a number of different readings attached to it. On the one hand, it represents the free market economy, a concentration of power and neoliberal interconnectedness. However, it also represents new affiliations and partnerships between marginalised political groups through global networks, a knowledge economy in which there is greater transparency and access to knowledge than ever before and a certain "calling out" of abuses of power that will be criticised and sometimes even brought to an international tribunal by international groups such as Human Rights Watch or Amnesty International. For example, one could argue that the Black Lives Matter protest marches that took place across the globe in the wake of the killing of George Floyd in Minneapolis, USA, is an example of globalisation.

Just as there is some ambivalence in defining the exact purpose of international schools, since they can span exclusive, selective, well-resourced and elitist institutions to open, accessible and often under-resourced institutions; so too is there some ambivalence and difficulty in giving a cohesive and satisfactory definition of globalisation and, by extension, the concept of the global citizen.

Essentially, international schools and global citizenship represent the same construct that can be interpreted in two conversely different ways: elitist cosmopolitanism or egalitarianist social activism.

It is worthwhile examining the concept of global citizenship to make clear the polyvalence in question and how it relates to internationalism, international schools and education in general.

Global citizenship

Akkari and Maleq (2019) point out that there are three types of global citizenship, outlined briefly below.

The first is a critical approach, focused on the individual as a critical thinker with agency who is able to choose responsible and active citizenship through rational and constructive processes. Indeed, the amount of information that circulates in a modern globalised knowledge economy requires precise thinking and the ability to sift through claims in the search for accuracy and possibly truth. The COVID-19 pandemic, for example, has presented the public with dozens of different health approaches and studies. The only way to navigate such an "infodemic" would be through critical thinking, and therefore this is a vital skill for a global citizen. In the critical model, there is an emphasis on action or social transformation that should come out of this critical stance (Boni & Calabuig, 2015; Torres, 2009). This approach is in line with Torres's (2009) work that advocates for critical social and political perspectives in citizenship.

To take the critical stance a step further, a so-called radical approach to global citizenship is articulated by Andreotti (2006). This second category of global citizenship is essentially a position of anti-neoliberalism whereby awareness is raised about the plight of disenfranchised and marginalised groups and social participative action is stressed. Within this approach, "the role of the global citizen is to challenge the hegemony of economic globalization and build solidarity across marginalized groups to fight oppression rather than focusing on building economic relationships across the globe" (Akkari & Maleq, 2019). This type of global citizenship can be seen in movements of solidarity with the plight of oppressed groups in different parts of the world. It follows some of the fault lines of critical pedagogy (Paolo Freire in particular) and carries overtones of Marxism in its worldview. Contemporary proponents of this position include the social activists Naomi Klein and Angela Davis.

Many definitions of global citizenship make a point of underlining the question of social justice. For example, Reysen and Katzarska-Miller (2013) describe global citizenship as "promoting social justice and sustainability, and a sense of responsibility to act" (p. 858), Oxfam (2006) states that a global citizen should be "outraged by social injustice", and UNESCO (2018) describes global citizenship education as something that builds "inclusive and secure societies". Therefore, we could argue that a normative philosophy of global citizenship leans in the direction of human rights and social justice, whether it be critical or more radical.

The third category of global citizenship, which detaches itself markedly from the critical and radical schools, is that of neoliberal global citizenship, delineated by Aktas et al. (2017) and Rizvi (2007). This approach, more empirical and pragmatic than normative, is centred on the development of global competences "that would enable students to become internationally mobile and readily employable in a variety of cultural and national contexts" (Akkari & Maleq, 2019). In a borderless, globalised world, the neoliberal global citizen is someone who participates in a global world economy irrespective of location: (s)he is able to move from one country to the next and increases the "transnational mobility of knowledge and skills with the goal of linking global citizenship directly to global economic participation" (Shultz, 2007, p. 252).

At the forefront of this worldview is the development of marketplace skills that make students eligible for employment in the globalised world economy. Neoliberal global citizen rhetoric is clear in models such as the Organisation for Economic Co-operation and Development, the World Bank and the World Economic Forum. These organisations are increasingly vocal in the discussion on education and are used as references in much 21st-century skills curriculum design.

Global citizenship and internationals schools

Since the whole idea of internationalism has become somewhat subsumed by globalisation, an increasing number of international schools today speak more of global citizenship than of internationalism. But which type of global citizenship is the one in question—critical, radical or neoliberal—and what are the implications for education and elitism?

Some international schools promote the concept of global citizenship explicitly with a focus on skills and some degree of criticality; for example, Yokohama International School (one of the world's first international schools) offers a "global citizen diploma" with an emphasis on "communications, global perspectives and community engagement" so as to provide students with "the academic and social skills that will enable them to fulfill their human potential as responsible global citizens" (Yokohama International School, 2020), while Sotogrande International School runs a "global citizenship programme" based on four pillars: "global mindedness; social entrepreneurship; service learning; environmental sustainability" (Sotogrande International School, 2020).

Many international schools are accredited by the Council of International Schools (CIS), an independent organisation that works with more than 1,300 institutions around the world, providing "services ... to inspire the development of global citizens" (CIS, 2020).

CIS puts global citizenship at the centre of an international education, stating that it has developed an understanding of global citizenship to denote the active development of ethics, diversity, global issues, communication, service (meaning service learning in school), leadership and sustainable lifestyles. These categories are detailed with descriptions that are broad and philosophical such as, under ethics, "research about, discussion of, and action related to issues of personal, local, and global importance", or under service, "the development of the understandings, skills and dispositions to serve the local and global community through engagement in meaningful service learning".

The aims of an international education tend to stress broad philosophical themes of intercultural unity and open-mindedness:

> [E]mphasis should be laid on a basic attitude of respect for all human beings as persons, understanding of those things which unite us and an appreciation of the positive values of those things which may seem to divide us, with the objective of thinking free from fear or prejudice.
>
> (Hill, 2006, p. 11)

The examples from CIS and Hill's definition lean towards a similar dedication to sustainability and human rights. Perhaps not surprisingly, the radical school of global citizenship does not make its way into these examples, as there is no mention of social justice in any of the abovementioned statements. Why is this?

International schools and plutocratic elitism

First, we need to consider the type of customer that the international schools market speaks to.

International schools have grown by 5% in the past few years with a spike in student numbers in the United Arab Emirates (UAE) (ICEF, 2018). Some reports speculate that there will be 16,000 international schools across the globe by 2028, grossing a combined sector revenue of US $95 billion. Other reports speculate that there will be 7 million international school students worldwide by 2023 (Civinini, 2019).

As mentioned earlier, although these are international schools, they are not necessarily designed for international (as in expatriate) students since the majority are local:

> [A]pproximately 20% of [international school] students are the children of expatriate families who are seeking a school offering the language of learning and curriculum from their home country. However, the vast majority of international school students today are the children of local families choosing, what they consider to be, the best possible education close to home to prepare their child for university overseas and global careers.
>
> (ICEF, 2018)

In other words, there has been a shift in function from the historical origins of international schools, which were built to provide expatriate children with a values-based education that would enable them to study in their home countries, to a model that provides an elitist education to local children whose parents see greater value added in sending their children to an international school than a local school.

Because international schools are so varied in their fee structures and because their fees will mean something different in every country once adjusted to the cost of living, it is difficult to discuss the average fees of an international school in comparison with other types of school, but on the whole they are far more expensive that state schools and often more expensive than UK public schools, American charter schools or private schools in general: analyses carried out by the International Schools Database in 2018 showed that the majority were charging between US $1,000 and $2,500 per month, while roughly one-third cost between 80% and 120% of the average price of a rental property. In the UAE, for example, top schools charge in excess of $25,000 per year, while the most expensive schools in the big Chinese metro markets top $40,000 annually, essentially the same as what parents might expect to pay in tuition fees at leading Western universities (Clark, 2014).

It is understandable that parents want to invest in an educational experience that gives their children some sort of advantage, especially in a highly competitive globalised economy. Most international schools are taught in English and this is clearly an important factor in parent choice given that English is seen as the language of today's globalised market (Clark, 2014).

Although this is never stated in their missions, clearly the reality of most international schools is that they are plutocratically elitist, leaving only a narrow opening for those that can afford the hefty fees. Bunnel goes so far as to describe international schools as "elite-class reproducing institutions growing in demand as the English language has been impinging ... on labour markets" (2014, p. 76). If this is true, then it is not surprising that the radical wing of global citizenship with its insistence on challenging the economic status quo and fighting for social justice does not make its way into the rhetoric of school mission statements. On the contrary, one could argue that international schools are seedbeds for future global elites. A number of well-established global leaders received this type of education, including Norman Schwarzkopf, Justin Trudeau, Willem-Alexander (the reigning King of the Netherlands), Dustin Aaron Moskovitz (the co-founder of Facebook) and Kim Jong Un. The fact that the ideological positioning and political behaviour of these public figures has been so different is in itself an admission of the conflict that runs through the concept of an international school graduate and, at the same time, a global citizen.

The value added of international schools

What exactly is it about international schools that interests parents to the point that they are prepared to pay substantial amounts of money to send their children to these institutions rather than to state schools? This leads to a discussion over whether it is the sociological advantage (children entering an elitist, networked class of cosmopolitans) or the curriculum argument (constructivist, values-based learning) that predominates.

The sociological argument

On average, international schools, like most independent schools, are better resourced than their state counterparts. There will often be more resources invested in the support of students with special needs (see, for example, the International School of Brussels or the International School of Geneva) with a greater investment made in university counselling and pastoral programmes.

More subtle and far-reaching is the social networking that international schools offer children: many will be part of a globalised elite in the future, meeting through international business opportunities later in life.

On the Study International website, advantages linked to the principles of neoliberal global citizenship are expressed:

> The emphasis on cultural exchange in international schools is phenomenal, and as world markets become increasingly interconnected, it is now more

desirable than ever to understand the dynamics of cultures different to your own. Many students of international schools have also shown their environment also provides early preparation for further study and work. A recent survey by ACS International Schools, which has a presence in London and Doha, Qatar, shows international schools students leave with a better range of "soft" skills such as time management, critical analysis and independent thinking.

(Patrick, 2017)

Scott Cherry, a reporter for ISC Research, commented on 2017 statistics on international school expansion in India thus: "There is a surge in demand from affluent, upwardly-mobile Indian families for an internationally oriented curriculum for their children with the necessary repertoire of skills to successfully pursue higher education and professional careers outside of India" (quoted in Marsh, 2017).

Indeed, the common perception is that an international education will prepare young people to thrive in a globalised economy better than had they attended state schools. This resonates with Torres's reflection that "Global citizenship education should play a major role in challenging neoliberalism, but as any other concept, it could become a sliding signifier, and hence it could be co-opted and implemented following a neoliberal rationality" (Torres, 2017).

The curriculum argument

Although there are different types of international school and they do not all follow the same curriculum structure, there are some central defining points that many international schools share, notably the adoption of international curricula such as the IB or Cambridge Assessment International Education courses.

The value added of the IB curriculum

The IB has a suite of programmes, K–12, that are connected by a learner profile, approaches to teaching and approaches to learning (International Baccalaureate Organization, 2020). The learner profile is a series of attitudes and skills that IB schools are expected to develop: students should leave school as citizens who are caring, principled, balanced, reflective, open-minded and knowledgeable while being risk-takers, thinkers, inquirers and communicators (International Baccalaureate Organization, 2013a). In these dispositions, one sees different elements of global citizenship predominate, mainly from the critical school. By focusing on these attributes, IB schools ensure a holistic education that is broader than the restrictive academic base that other types of school, such as state schools, might focus on.

Furthermore, IB schools drive a constructivist, student-centred pedagogy that is summarised as "approaches to learning" (thinking skills; communications skills; social skills; self-management skills; research skills) and "approaches to teaching" (based on "inquiry; focused on conceptual understanding; developed in local and global contexts; focused on effective teamwork and collaboration; differentiated to meet the needs of all learners informed by formative and summative assessment" (International Baccalaureate Organization, 2014).

It may be that this inquiry-based, constructivist and holistic approach of the IB differentiates IB international schools qualitatively from most non-IB state schools. Some studies suggest that IB students go further in their post-secondary studies than do their counterparts studying in national systems: "the IB Global Research department explored the university enrollment, retention and graduation rates of 2005 Diploma Programme [DP] graduates in the United States (n = 9,654). DP college graduation rates were consistently higher than institutional university rates" (Halic, 2013).

Studies in the UK have shown that "IB students were more likely to: enroll in a top 20 HEI; receive honours degrees or awards, in most subject areas; continue on to further studies; and be employed in graduate level positions and higher paid occupations" (HESA, 2011).

In the 1990s, 12 public schools in Chicago, USA, agreed to offer the DP to their students who were mostly "low income, racially diverse students with little or no history of college-going" (International Baccalaureate Organization, 2013b). A study sampling 18,075 graduates between 2003 and 2007 showed that "compared to similar non-DP graduates, DP graduates were more likely to enroll in college, to enroll in selective colleges, to stay enrolled and to perform better once there" (International Baccalaureate Organization, 2013b).

It is therefore understandable that schools offering the DP are chosen by parents since they wish to give their children an advantage in life.

Value added of Cambridge Assessment International Education programmes

Another provider of international education curricula is Cambridge Assessment, linked to the University of Cambridge and best known as the designer of the UK's A-level and GCSE qualifications but also for developing the IGCSE (International General Certificate in Secondary Education) and international A-levels. Cambridge courses are offered at over 10,000 international and state schools across the globe (Cambridge, 2020a).

The "Cambridge Pathway", for children aged between five and 19, involving a "Global Perspectives" course that emphasises critical thinking, not entirely unlike the IB, seeks to develop attitudes as well as skills. Students should be

> confident in working with information and ideas – their own and those of others; responsible for themselves, responsive to and respectful of others; reflective as learners, developing their ability to learn; innovative and equipped for new and future challenges and engaged.
>
> (Cambridge, 2015, p. 2)

The organisation's website elaborates further on the advantages of its educational offering:

> Cambridge programmes combine an emphasis on mastering subjects in depth with the development [of] skills for study and work in the future. We value deep subject knowledge as well as the conceptual understanding that helps students make links between different aspects of a subject. We also encourage students to develop higher order thinking skills – problem solving, critical thinking, independent research, collaboration and presenting arguments. These are transferable skills that will last a lifetime, preparing students for their future lives. They also make learning enjoyable and rewarding.
>
> (Cambridge, 2020a)

Like the IB, various so-called 21st-century skills are developed by Cambridge Assessment International Education programmes that correspond to critical strains of global citizenship such as "critical thinking", "independent research" and "presenting arguments".

Getting ahead

Ultimately, the value added in international education programmes lies in students' developing the so-called soft skills that are likely to be necessary in an unknown future where jobs will change frequently and many disruptions to society, mainly linked to the environment, will no doubt occur with increasing frequency. In an article on prominent international schools in Asia entitled "International schools that help students stand out in a global economy", schools are presented as standing out precisely because of this point: parents are told that their children will receive "an outstanding education that prepares your child for global citizenship … students … get a head start on what it's like to collaborate across borders" (Study International, 2019). Another school, where the faculty to student ratio is 1:7, is described as a place where "children from three to 18 years learn how to learn as well as how to continuously develop themselves in preparation for an uncertain future", while a third school, with "a 24 acre campus [that looks like] an oasis … has an impressive track record in educating future global leaders".

But just as getting ahead means experiencing a curriculum that will allow students to cope with a complex and unknown future, by declaring the types of skills and attitudes that will be needed for the future through mission and curriculum choices, renowned international schools are contributing to the likelihood that these skills will be necessary. In other words, if international schools continue to grow and to push for higher order thinking skills, interactions with high performing technology, STEM proficiency and business team-building skills, then there is a strong likelihood that these will be the skills that graduates expect to see in the workers they will employ in the future. Therefore, it becomes something of a circular argument, somewhat in the way that stock market giants dictate the morphology of economics by selling or buying shares, international school decisions will not just prepare for the future, they will shape the future.

And that future might very well be one where a small globalised elite, educated in international schools, holds an enormous amount of power and dictates an even more centralised global economy. International schools are seedbeds for the elite of the future because they are not just socioeconomically elitist, like public schools in the UK, they are globally elitist, forming a network of future leaders that will operate across natural boundaries.

Efforts to open access to international education

The United World Colleges

Not all international schools are plutocratically elite, however. The United World Colleges movement, founded in 1962 with the establishment of Atlantic College in Wales by Kurt Hahn, is a chain of 18 schools that works through a system of national committees whereby scholarships are given to "outstanding students who want to become change-makers for a better world, regardless of their socio-economic, religious, national, ethnic or cultural background" (UWC, 2020). The schools place significant emphasis on community service and enhance a number of "impact stories" that involve students working on social impact projects in local communities.

However, the United World Colleges are selective schools and only admit students who meet criteria related to values and mindset. Furthermore, not all students are on bursaries and the schools' financial models depend on fee-paying students who learn alongside bursary students. In a rather disparaging article entitled, paradoxically, "UWC Atlantic College: The elite school in a castle that's helping educate young refugees", journalist Etan Smallman writes:

> UWC Atlantic College's 350 pupils hail from 90 countries. The boarding school attracts wealthy teenagers whose parents pay fees of £58,000 for the two-year International Baccalaureate programme (alumni include the King of the Netherlands, two serving members of the Chinese Communist Central Committee and the offspring of Queen Noor of Jordan).
>
> (Smallman, 2017)

However, he goes on, "more than half of students receive some kind of scholarship – among them a contingent of refugees who have fled warzones in pursuit of a top-class education and sanctuary in the remote seaside castle". So it is that the United World College system represents a blend of the most wealthy and the poorest students in the world, not entirely unlike well-endowed American colleges that charge hefty fees but offer extensive bursary programmes too, thus allowing access to an elitist structure to those who normally would be deprived of such an opportunity.

Enko schools

Enko Education, the brainchild of the Cameroonian entrepreneur, Cyril Nkontchou, and the French businessman, Eric Pignot, aims to open up international education to the African middle class. Operating 15 schools in Côte d'Ivoire, Cameroon, South Africa, Senegal, Mali, Burkina Faso, Botswana, Zambia and Mozambique, this for-profit organisation has opened more IB schools on the African continent than any other group of schools.

The mission of the organisation is to offer "programmes [that] lead to globally recognized and sought-after qualifications ... at a fraction of the cost charged by other international schools in Africa" (Enko Education, 2020).

While Enko Education clearly aims to empower the youth of Africa with a relatively accessible pathway to the high standards of international education, its mission is clearly elitist as it states that its goal is for students to "access the world's elite universities and achieve success in extraordinary careers" (Enko Education, 2020). Various other references to the overarching goal of the organisation speak of accessing "the best universities in the world", "launchpads" and "top universities".

So, while the access base to international education is widened slightly by Enko Education's project, the eventual aim remains openly elitist, describing the function of schooling essentially as a pathway to highly selective universities. This is not an unusual phenomenon, as across the globe it is fair to assume that most parents see the primary function of secondary school as a pathway to university.

Scholarships

Most international schools, like many fee-paying UK public or independent schools, offer some form of scholarship, either through partial fee remission or through a developed programme with selection criteria.

This evokes a number of ethical questions related to education and elitism that will re-emerge in the closing chapter of this book as I suggest a model of educational provision that can address the dilemma in a sustainable fashion. The questions include the following:

- To what extent do scholarship programmes that give children access to otherwise elitist educational experiences address the problem of access to education in a sustainable fashion and at a macro level? More specifically, what are the risks that such programmes merely augment the social base of a future global elite?

- To what extent do scholarship programmes address the problem of the massification of demand for quality education given that some of the brightest students will leave national systems and enter private ones, thus further ghettoising state systems?

Like many ethical dilemmas, these involve a trade-off between what is best for the group and what is best for the individual: scholarships change lives and are a force for good but they do not necessarily address the wider collective problem whereby a few get ahead but the majority are left behind. If educational systems were free and of high quality, as they are in many Nordic models, there would be no need for scholarships.

International education in state systems

International curriculum frameworks are not only situated outside of national systems as an alternative offering but some are incorporated within state schools. This changes the dynamic of international education considerably and addresses the danger of international education being little more than an accelerator of elitism. On the contrary, there is an argument to be made that international education models are actually reducing elitism by widening access, especially when incorporated in national systems.

The International Baccalaureate

The IB has been supported, in different ways, by the governments of Canada, Ecuador, Japan, Germany, Malaysia, Armenia, Macedonia, Spain, the UAE and the United States (International Baccalaureate Organization, 2020a). These private-state partnerships are growing. In 2006, Hill stated that roughly half of all IB schools were actually state schools (2006, p. 31).

These partnerships involve different levels of support from governments:

> [T]he Ministry of Education [government of Ecuador] undertook an initiative beginning in 2006 to support the development of ... [the] DP in each of the country's 22 provinces (now 24 provinces). The efforts during this first phase resulted in 17 state schools offering the DP in the country.
>
> (Barnett, 2013, p. 1)

A number of states in Canada support the integration of IB programmes in the local systems, creating financial incentives for schools to implement the DP and substituting examination fees (International Baccalaureate Organization, 2014).

The majority of these state-private partnerships do not substitute the national curriculum with the IB and, rather, make allowances for the IB to run parallel to national systems, at an extra fee.

Some countries' governments subsidise the IB in their schools either partially or wholly. In the United States, 95% of all IB schools are state funded with 100% of fees paid by the state. It is important to note that in most cases, this involves schools offering some IB subjects but not necessarily the whole IB programme. All Scandinavian countries partially state fund IB programmes, most of them receiving 50% funding by the government. An example of a prominent international school that is 50% state funded is Copenhagen International School. All Dutch IB schools in the Netherlands except the International School of Amsterdam, the American School of The Hague, the British School Netherlands and the International School of Erde, receive 50% funding from the Dutch government.

This is not only the case in wealthy countries, for example, Machabeng College, International School of Lesotho, is mostly state funded.

However, the question has to be asked whether there is a distinct difference in outcome and attainment for students doing the IB in the national system as opposed to those doing the IB in private international schools. In Ecuador, students coming through private schools do better than those coming through state IB schools: "although, students in DP state schools seem to be benefiting from the programme in terms of academic and non-academic outcomes, students in Ecuador's DP private schools generally performed better in most subject areas" (Barnett, 2013).

In the UK, we have already seen how it is difficult to measure the precise academic value added of grammar schools and independent schools as compared to state schools because home advantages influence outcomes heavily. That said, some of the country's highest performing schools, such as Sevenoaks School, Godolphin and Latymer, and King's College School, are both independent and offer the IB.

In the United States, the schools that are ranked first in the US News & World Report (Academic Magnet High School, Maine School of Science and Mathematics, BASIS Scottsdale, Thomas Jefferson High School for Science and Technology, and Central Magnet School) do not offer the IB (Hess, 2019). However, a large section of the American press describes the IB as "prestigious" (Ramirez, 2008; Ayers et al., 2008, p. 280; Lipman, 2004, p. 64). A blog entitled "College Vine", advising students and parents on high school tracks in the United States, describes the IB thus:

> If you have an IB diploma, you'll be among a relatively small portion of the college applicant pool with this qualification. This distinction shows that you've not only taken on academic challenges, but done so through a program that's widely known to be reputable and rigorous and requires a good deal of independent work from its graduates. Not every student can present such a prestigious qualification when they fill out their college applications, and this relative uniqueness is an advantage.
>
> (Schuschu, 2017)

In other words, the advantage of doing the IB, outside of the intrinsic qualities of the programme (a holistic education, a balancing of breadth and depth), is that it stands out from other programmes and carries with it an ethos of elitism: students are part of a global network with a relatively scarce prestigious qualification.

This is not entirely fair on the IB, which has always been wedded to strong values above all else (Peterson, 1987) but has had to price itself out of the market somewhat due to the cost of its detailed assessment design involving hundreds of examiners and moderators throughout the world. Recent initiatives by the organisation have moved strongly in the direction of anti-pluto-cratic elitism, such as offering scholarships to teachers wishing to take degrees at the University of the People (International Baccalaureate Organization, 2020b) and the cancellation of examination registration fees. In 2019, the organisation posted the following on its website:

> As a responsible not-for-profit, the IB continues to seek out cost-effi-ciencies that can lower costs and open the door for more students to engage with the breadth of its world-class programmes. Other recent examples include:
>
> - No programme fee increases since 2015
> - Discounts for schools that offer three or more IB programmes beginning in 2018
> - Ongoing investment in more affordable professional development options.
> (International Baccalaureate Organization, 2020c)

As the IB continues to grow and to seek partnerships with nation states, one of its core missions is to widen access, so as to move its ethos away from its current select, elitist reputation to something more inclusive and less elitist.

Cambridge International programmes

Cambridge's IGCSE programme and International A levels were designed for international schools, essentially English medium schools outside of the UK wishing to offer GCSEs and A-levels. Cambridge International programmes are offered in 9,000 schools across 160 countries (Cambridge, 2020b) and are relatively cheap to implement and access. It is particularly prominent as an alternative to national systems on the Indian subcontinent and in Africa.

In Singapore, "Cambridge examinations are the state qualification for students in secondary school". The organisation also works closely with governments on education reform in Botswana, Namibia and Eswatini to "help to localise examinations by training officials, teachers, markers and examiners in curriculum development and assessment" (Cambridge, 2020b).

Cambridge works with a number of governments because its courses are designed to be flexible and can be tailored to suit the needs of local curricula and syllabi. At the time of writing, in North America, one state offers its qualifications; in Latin America, some Caribbean islands sponsor Cambridge examinations although none as national qualifications; in Sub-Saharan Africa, some countries use Cambridge qualifications to complement theirs while Cambridge works with countries to "localise" IGCSEs. One example is the Government of Bahamas' BGCSE (Bahamas General Certificate in Secondary Education), a programme that is "based on the United Kingdom General Certificate of Secondary Education (GCSE) and the International General Certificate of Secondary Education (IGCSE) models, but … has been tailored to meet the specific needs of the Bahamas" (Government of the Bahamas, 2011).

The organisation targets middle-class students looking to experience an international school experience at an affordable price. According to Peter Monteath, former regional director, UK and Ireland, Cambridge Assessment International Education:

> It's an exciting time to be in international education – the growth of the worldwide middle class and its desire to get children into top performing universities around the world means that, here at Cambridge International Examinations, we're expecting year on year growth both in numbers of schools and candidates for our International GCSEs and International A Levels.
>
> (Monteath, 2020)

Up until 2013, the IGCSE was offered by a number of state schools in the UK but following the reforms implemented by the then Secretary of State for Education, Michael Gove, the IGCSE is offered in private schools but in hardly any state schools.

The IGCSE is slightly different to its national counterpart, the GCSE, in that it is more flexible and contains more coursework, meaning that examinations are weighted less in the assessment model. Some view the IGCSE as an easier option, which has caused a number of heated debates in the UK. Verkaik writes:

> Today the average private-school pupil in the UK has three times more money spent on their education than a state-school pupil. The opportunity to sit an alternative qualification to the government-approved GCSE … surely only serves to compound that advantage.
>
> (Verkaik, 2020)

Although the Cambridge International programmes are relatively accessible financially speaking and, therefore, are offered in many schools, the kudos that the organisation offers is related to its brand name, Cambridge, which speaks to the highly selective and prestigious universe of Oxbridge and its associations with high standards, inner circles and social elitism.

That said, the Cambridge programmes speak to a larger, middle-class base, particularly in India, China and on the African continent.

Conclusion

International education's initial goal was resolutely idealistic: to bring children of different nationalities to learn together for a more peaceful world. The International School of Geneva's early and iconic director, Marie-Thérèse Maurette, told her students that it was a cardinal sin to mock another person because of their nationality and when Lord Mountbatten presented students with the very first IB diplomas in 1971, he later said of the moment, that it was his final contribution to the prevention of World War Three. This ideal, of education for peace through intercultural diversity, remains central to the ethos and mission of international schools.

However, while there was a clear emphasis on cultural and national diversity, there was never any clear mention of socioeconomic diversity, and from the outset international schools catered to fee-paying children whose parents worked for lavishly structured international organisations that could subsidise the fees. Over time, as the international schools movement grew and more and more parents enrolled their children in such schools, the bills for the relatively expensive fees were paid by globalised corporations or by parents who were independently well off, so these schools became increasingly the province of relatively wealthy families. With the exception of the United World College movement, most international schools became synonymous with plutocratic elitism. This is why the term that is commonly associated with international education is the word "prestige".

At the same time, the mission of international schools has evolved so that it focuses on global citizenship. Today, globalisation means that the way that we think about internationalism has changed: global citizenship education is not about several different nationalities and languages, it is about global problems of wealth disparity, social justice and environmental stability. As this chapter has shown, there are radically different ways of approaching these problems through the single umbrella term of global citizenship, which can come to represent different worldviews.

Hence, there is a rift that runs through international schools: that between critical global citizenship education, meaning citizenship education based on engagement with human rights, social justice and environmental sustainability; and neoliberal global citizenship education, meaning citizenship education that concentrates wealth and privilege in a tightly connected global elite that benefits from springboards to elitist universities and gainful employment. It is something of a dilemma that human rights lawyers, mega-wealthy CEOs and government dictators are all likely to have had an international education.

The future of international education will be marked by the extent to which it can bridge this tension and facilitate a broader base of access to its advantageous offering. This can be done in a number of ways: by lowering fees; by partnering with the state; or by offering more scholarships. If international education brings added value, the question is how to extend that value added to as many children as possible so as to work towards the fulfilment of SDG 4.

References

Akkari, A., & Maleq, K. (2019). *Global Citizenship: Buzzword or New Instrument for Educational Change?* https://ejop.psychopen.eu/index.php/ejop/article/download/1999/html?inline= 1#d2e153.

Aktas, F., Pitts, K., Richards, J.C., & Silova, I. (2017). Institutionalizing global citizenship: A critical analysis of higher education programs and curricula. *Journal of Studies in International Education*, 21(1), 65–80. https://doi.org/10.1177/1028315316669815.

Andreotti, V. (2006). Soft versus critical global citizenship education. *Policy & Practice: A Development Education Review*, 3, 40–51.

Ayers, W., Ladson-Billings, G., Michie, G., & Noguera, P.A. (eds.) (2008). *City Kids, City School: More Reports from the Front Row*. New York: The New Press, p. 280.

Barnett, E. (2013). *Research Summary Implementation of the Diploma Programme in Ecuador's State Schools*. International Baccalaureate Organization. https://www.ibo.org/globala ssets/publications/ib-research/ecuadorsummary_eng.pdf.

Boni, A., & Calabuig, C. (2015). Education for global citizenship at universities: Potentialities of formal and informal learning spaces to foster cosmopolitanism. *Journal of Studies in International Education*. https://doi.org/10.1177/1028315315602926.

Bunnell, T. (2014). *The Changing Landscape for International Schooling: Implications for Theory*. Oxford: Routledge.

Cambridge (2015). *Syllabus Guide: Global Perspectives*. Cambridge: Cambridge International Examinations. www.cambridgeinternational.org/Images/252230-2018-2020-syllabus.pdf.

Cambridge (2020a). *Cambridge Assessment International Education*. www.cambridgeinterna tional.org/.

Cambridge (2020b). *Assessment*. www.cambridgeassessment.org.uk/about-us/what-we-do/a ssessment/.

Civinini, H. (2019). International school student numbers forecast to reach 7 million by 2023. *Pie News*. https://thepienews.com/news/international-school-seven-million-2023/.

Clark, N. (2014). The Booming International Schools Sector. *WENR*. https://wenr. wes.org/2014/07/the-booming-international-schools-sector.

Council of International Schools (CIS) (2020). www.cois.org/.

Enko Education (2020). https://enkoeducation.com/.

Government of the Bahamas (2011). *Bahamas General Certificate of Secondary Education (BGCSE)*. www.bahamas.gov.bs/wps/portal/public/Education/Bahamas.

Halic, O. (2013). *Postsecondary Educational Attainment of IB Diploma Programme Candidates from US high schools*. Geneva: International Baccalaureate Organization.

Hayden, M., & Thompson, J. (2013). International Schools: Antecedents, Current Issues and Metaphors for the Future. In R. Pearce (ed.) *International Education and Schools: Moving Beyond the First 40 Years*. London: Bloomsbury, pp. 3–24.

Hess, A. (2019). The 20 Best High Schools in the US, According to US News & World Report. *CNBC*. www.cnbc.com/2019/05/01/us-news-world-report-the-20-best-high-schools-in-the-us.html.

Higher Education Statistics Agency (HESA) (2011). *International Baccalaureate Students Studying at UK Higher Education Institutions: How Do They Fare?* Cheltenham: HESA.

Hill, I. (2006) *International Baccalaureate Programmes and Educational Reform.* In P. Hughes (ed.) *Secondary Education at the Crossroads. Education in the Asia-Pacific Region: Issues, Concerns and Prospects,* Vol. 9. Dordrecht: Springer. https://doi.org/10.1007/1-4020-4668-5_2.

ICEF (2018). *Annual Survey Finds Continued Growth in International Schools.* https://monitor.icef.com/2018/09/annual-survey-finds-continued-growth-in-international-schools/#:~:text=The%202018%20Global%20Report%20on,over%20the%20last%20five%20years.

International Baccalaureate Organization (2014). *IB Related Policies in Canada.* www.ibo.org/globalassets/publications/university-admission/canada-policy-chart-june-30-2014.pdf.

International Baccalaureate Organization. (2013a). *IB Learner Profile.* www.ibo.org/contentassets/fd82f70643ef4086b7d3f292cc214962/learner-profile-en.pdf.

International Baccalaureate Organization (2013b). *Key Findings from Research on the Impact of the IB Diploma Programme.* www.ibo.org/globalassets/publications/recognition/finaldpone-pager-2.pdf.

International Baccalaureate Organization (2014). *Approaches to Teaching and Learning in the International Baccalaureate (IB) Diploma Programme.* www.isbasel.ch/uploaded/docs/IBO/approaches-to-teaching-learning-dp-en.pdf.

International Baccalaureate Organization (2020a). *Government Partnerships.* www.ibo.org/benefits/ib-as-a-district-or-national-curriculum/government-partnerships/.

International Baccalaureate Organization (2020b). *University of the People M.Ed. Scholarships.* www.ibo.org/professional-development/which-type-of-training-is-right-for-me/university-of-the-people/ib-scholarships.

International Baccalaureate Organization (2020c). *IB Announces Candidate Registration Fee Eliminated from November 2019.* https://www.ibo.org/news/news-about-ib-schools/ib-announces-candidate-registration-fee-eliminated-from-november-2019/.

International Schools Database (2018). *Comparing the Cost of International Schools Around the World: 2018 Edition.* www.international-schools-database.com/articles/comparing-the-cost-of-international-schools-2018.

ISC Research (2020). *About the International Schools Market.* www.iscresearch.com/about-us/the-market.

Knight, M., & Leach, R. (1964). International Secondary Schools. In G. Bereday, & J. Lauwerys (eds.) *The Yearbook of Education 1964: Education and International Education,* Vol. 5. London: Routledge, pp. 5–53.

Lipman, P. (2004). *High Stakes Education: Inequality, Globalization, and Urban School Reform.* New York: Routledge Falmer, p. 64.

Marsh, N. (2017). *India's international school enrolments surge 70%.* The Pie News. https://thepienews.com/news/india-international-school-enrolments-surge-70/.

Monteath, P. (2020). *Meeting the Needs of 160 Countries.* www.cambridgeassessment.org.uk/insights/meeting-the-needs-of-160-countries/.

Oxfam (2006). *Education for Global Citizenship: A Guide for Schools.* www.oxfam.org.uk/~/media/Files/Education/Global%20Citizenship/Global_Citizens hip_Schools_WEB.ashx?la=en.

Oxfam (2017). *Just 8 Men Own Same Wealth as Half the World.* www.oxfam.org/en/press-releases/just-8-men-own-same-wealth-half-world.

Patrick, H. (2017). *Benefits of Studying in an International School.* www.studyinternational. com/news/benefits-studying-international-school/.

Peterson, A.D.C. (1987). *Schools Across Frontiers: The Story of the International Baccalaureate and the United World Colleges.* La Salle, IL: Open Court Publishing.

Ramirez, E. (2008). American High Schools Try the International Baccalaureate Program. *US News.* www.usnews.com/education/articles/2008/12/11/american-high-schools-try-the-international-baccalaureate-program.

Reysen, S., & Katzarska-Miller, I. (2013). A model of global citizenship: antecedents and outcomes. *International Journal of Psychology*, 43, 858–870.

Rizvi, F. (2007). Internationalization of curriculum: A Critical Perspective. In M. Hayden, J. Levy, & J. Thompson (eds.) *Research in International Education.* London: SAGE, pp. 391–403.

Schuschu, M. (2017). What Are the Benefits of Earning an IB Diploma? *College Vine.* https://blog.collegevine.com/what-are-the-benefits-of-earning-an-ib-diploma/.

Shultz, L. (2007). Educating for global citizenship: Conflicting agendas and understandings. *Alberta Journal of Educational Research*, 53, 248–258.

Smallman, E. (2017). UWC Atlantic College: The elite school in a castle that's helping educate young refugees. *iNews.* https://inews.co.uk/news/education/they-capture-the-castle-the-refugees-receiving-a-top-flight-education-at-uwc-atlantic-college-526773.

Soros, G. (1998). *The Crisis of Global Capitalism.* London: Little, Brown and Company.

Sotogrande International School (2020). *Global Citizenship Programme.* www.sis.ac/global-citizenship-programme/.

Study International (2019). *International Schools That Help Students Stand Out in a Global Economy.* www.studyinternational.com/news/international-schools-that-help-students-stand-out-in-a-global-economy/.

Torres, C. A. (2009). Globalization, Education, and Citizenship: Solidarity vs Markets? *Globalizations and Education: Collected Essays on Class, Race, Gender, and the State.* New York: Teachers College Press, pp. 114–130.

Torres, C. A. (2017). *Education for Global Citizenship.* Oxford: Oxford Research Encyclopedia of Education. http://oxfordre.com/education/view/10.1093/acrefore/9780190264093.001.0001/acrefore-9780190264093-e-91.

United Nations Educational, Scientific and Cultural Organization (UNESCO) (2018). *What Is Global Citizenship Education?* https://en.unesco.org/themes/gced/definition.

Verkaik, T. (2020). The IGCSE isn't available in state schools, and many believe it benefits private-school pupils. *iNews.* https://inews.co.uk/news/education/igcse-private-school-benefits-education-reform-386152.

Walker, G. (2015). Review of Bunnell, T. The changing face of International Schooling: Implications for Theory and Practice. *Journal of Research in International Education*, 14(1), pp. 77–80.

Yokohama International School (2020). *Global Citizen Diploma.* www.yis.ac.jp/learning/high-school/global-citizen-diploma.

Zuboff, S. (2019). *The Age of Surveillance Capitalism.* London: Profile Books.

Chapter 7

Higher education and elitism

Zach and Anthony

The idea of going to university has never really occurred to Zach. None of his friends talk about university and even the older members of his family, like his cousin from Ougadougou, are not interested in the prospect. Just finishing school is not easy: many of Zach's classmates will drop out before graduating.

There are universities in the country that focus mainly on commerce and technical skills but they are expensive and, in any case, what is the point? How many years will be spent sitting in overcrowded lecture halls and where will this lead to? Zach's brother got where he did not by going to university but through an informal apprenticeship.

Anthony, on the other hand, has had his sights for some time on the prestigious top-tier university that his father and older brothers went to. He understands that he will be given preferential treatment because he is a legacy student but he has been told by his father not to concentrate on that too much or to be lulled into any sense of complacency. Hard work is one of his father's key principles and Anthony knows that nothing comes easy. Even if you belong to a privileged group, there will always be those who are more privileged than you. Anthony will be competing against students from all round the world and will have to be exceptional in every way to get noticed.

Anthony is too young to be working with the school US guidance counsellor but is ready to work hard with him to ensure that his grade average and preliminary standardised admissions tests (PSATs) are up to scratch, although fewer and fewer colleges are asking for SATs nowadays and they are not strictly necessary. Anthony wants to do them anyway, to have that in his file along with all the other items that are needed for his application which is still many years off but should never be far from sight. Anthony is not sure what he would like to do at college but in the long term he sees himself as a trader. If you take calculated risks, you can go far quickly. You can also get burned, but that's where he needs to build up the experience and confidence that his father has. Deep down inside Anthony does not actually believe that a university education is as important as it was in his father's day. He could get picked up on Google or

Facebook for an apprenticeship after school and skip college altogether. However, in order to keep all his options open, he will follow his father's wishes.

Introduction

The word university comes from the Latin *universitas*, meaning community. The concept is of a community of scholars who form a guild and offer qualifications. This notion, that a university is a community with its own terms of reference and certification, is in itself, to a certain extent, an admission of a type of sociological elitism. The university, from its origins, has always represented a group that is somehow set apart from the rest of society. The academic degrees and titles that universities bestow on graduates or employees create in-groups and out-groups.

The concept and purpose of the university has shifted over time: in the Middle Ages, the university was a religious centre of learning and there were relatively few in the world. With the acceleration of literacy in Europe from the 1500s onwards, universities were seen as centres of learning and specialisation. With the age of industrialisation and the massification of tertiary education in the 19th and 20th centuries, the perceived primary function of the university was—and still is to this day—as a degree-awarding institution that qualified scholars to enter the workplace. This shift has entailed different types of elitist practice and thinking, depending of course on the part of the world that is under analysis.

Broadly speaking, we can speak of two traditions: on the one hand, there is the continental European and Nordic model with examples from Switzerland, Norway, Denmark, Finland and Sweden, where universities are essentially free of charge and are perceived in a relatively non-hierarchical fashion; on the other, there is the Anglo-Saxon tradition, intensified in the United Kingdom and replicated in the United States, India, Australia and other parts of the world, where universities are expensive, ranked and perceived in a hierarchical fashion.

In the 21st century, the Anglo-Saxon model predominates as ranking systems are used to compare universities across the globe and students fight to gain entry into the small circle of 30 to 40 leading universities, most of them concentrated in the UK, the United States, Canada, the People's Republic of China and Singapore. Broadly speaking, these universities belong to the so-called top-tier category, meaning that they are ranked above most universities by ranking consortia such as QS World University Rankings or the Times Higher Education World University Rankings. The way in which universities are ranked is contentious, as the chapter will show.

As a result of the highly disruptive effect of the COVID-19 pandemic on educational systems across the globe, the structure and enrolment dynamics of universities is mutating. There is a strong likelihood that the world of universities will change radically in the next few decades and the dividing line between so-called top-tier universities and others will become more emphatic. The fact that so many universities are shifting to online learning forces a new discussion on the value of enrolment in expensive tertiary institutions with state of the art facilities that can no longer be accessed.

This chapter discusses the origins and development of universities across the globe with emphasis on the UK and the United States and case studies drawn from India, Australia, China and South Africa. The chapter will show how elitist discourses have dominated the world of universities in the UK and the United States very strongly, not only in setting certain universities apart from others but in setting certain in-groups within universities apart from others. An argument will be made that some of the social groups in the most selective universities, namely student societies and fraternities with their ritualistic initiation ceremonies and codes, are powerful symbolic sociological and psychological preparations for inner circles of political power and leadership.

A short history of universities

The world's first universities such as Taxila, in modern-day Pakistan (c. 500 BCE), Nalanda in India (c. 500 CE), Al- Karueein in Morocco (859 CE) or Al-Azhar in Egypt (970 CE) were all spiritual centres with a strong religious edict to propagate the faiths of Islam or Buddhism. However, they also offered studies in law, astronomy and various other formal abstract subjects. Education was offered to monks and scholars from around the Middle East and some sources suggest that it was free of charge:

> Before the Western influence, madrasahs imparted knowledge by a chain of transmission … Typically, a madrasah institution provided free education and library facilities; a wide range of subject expert teachers and students were provided with the necessary resources for their studies. A recognised early Sunni madrasah was Al-Azhar University, Cairo, one of the first Sunni centres of learning in the tenth century.
>
> (Hardaker & Sabki, 2019, pp. 8–9)

A second wave of the birth of institutions of higher learning in Europe saw the opening of Bologna in Italy (1088), Oxford in England (1096), Salamanca in Spain (1134) and Paris, France (1160). These were all essentially fee-paying universities. Bologna's origins are interesting to analyse as they contain many of the elements of arguments for private education.

Groups of students from different countries in Europe organised themselves collectively in the city of Bologna in order to hire renowned scholars to teach them specific subjects. As such, a type of bargaining system began where students paid scholars for tuition directly. Over time this evolved into a more institutionalised design called a *Studium* whereby the bargaining system became more structured and took place through a third party, which was essentially the university. If students were not satisfied with their tutors, they could have them removed or leave the university. Indeed, there was no doubt considerable pressure on instructors to perform although over time they unionised, as had the students, in order to protect themselves. Hence, Bologna grew into a modern university as we commonly understand the concept today, with fees, tenured faculty, unions and statutes.

There is evidence that the origins of the University of Paris are similar to those of Bologna's: students formed groups in order to hire renowned scholars and this process gradually became institutionalised. The emphasis was on religious studies and students were considered to be part of a monastic order. As such, they were part of a select group that swore allegiance to the church and were not considered to be subject to secular law (Sorbonne, 2020). Arguably, this independence gave Europe's first universities the type of intellectual freedom that came to characterise them so strongly throughout the Middle Ages and beyond, particularly at free-thinking establishments such as Oxford.

Universities grew quickly during the Renaissance: by the end of the Middle Ages there were only 29 universities in Europe (Grendler, 2004, p. 1), whereas by the end of the 18th century the number had risen to over 140 (Frijhoff, 1996, p. 75). Today, it is estimated that there are over 29,000 universities in the world (Webometrics, 2020).

MOOCs (Massive Online Open Courses) were first designed in 2008: "25 students attended the course on the campus of the University of Manitoba, and a further 2300 from around the world participated online" (MAUT, 2020). Stanford followed suit in 2011 with courses that attracted 160,000 students (20,000 completed the programme). The university set up the course provider Coursera in 2012 and soon after MIT and Harvard started to offer courses through their own platform, EdX. MOOCs are free, meaning that they totally deconstruct the idea of elitism and education. Today, EdX provides MOOCs through universities in Australia, the Netherlands, France, Hong Kong, Switzerland, Iceland, France, Canada, Japan and China. However, students do not receive full degrees upon completion of MOOCs but are awarded course completion certificates, the currency of which is debatable.

Some universities are called, informally, "mega-universities" since they use online subscriptions to boost their enrolments to gargantuan proportions: in 2019, Southern New Hampshire University was offering education to 130,000 students and Western Governors University had enrolment of over 110,000. In 2010, the University of Phoenix had more than 470,000 students (Salisbury & Horn, 2019).

As financial pressure mounts on universities, a number are seeking to merge. To give a few examples, in 2014 University College London merged with the Institute of Education (UCL, 2014); Corcoran College merged with George Washington University (Freed, 2014) and China has "more than 400 cases of mergers involving over 1000 higher education institutions" (Cai, 2019, p. 127).

Mergers can be viewed from several perspectives and are not always welcomed by all parties. Some complain that it is part of a globalised movement to corporatise universities which will lower academic standards (Hunt, 2016).

As the global economy witnesses a handful of powerful companies take the lead on the stock exchange (the so-called GAFA group notably), leading to globalised monopolies, some universities are expanding into global hubs with campuses across the world. After buying up the New College for the Humanities, Northeastern President Joseph E. Aoun is reported to have said:

> The whole idea is that this global system will allow the learners to access our education wherever they are and wherever they need it and also allows mobility so the students can start in Boston, move to Silicon Valley, go to Vancouver and London, and in each place they will have a different curriculum and a different experience.
>
> (Quoted in Redden, 2018)

The concept and purpose of a university

What exactly is the purpose of a university in the 21st century? Opinions differ and can essentially be grouped into three categories that intertwine. Each of these functions has a specific relationship with elitism:

- Guardians of critical thought (the gatekeeper image clearly resonates with notions of cultural elitism);
- Institutions that produce knowledge (this function can assume an elitist or anti-elitist stance depending on the angle taken with regard to knowledge and power);
- Degree-awarding educational institutions that create social transformation (at face value this prerogative works against elitism as degrees offer opportunity and access but arguments can be made that awarding degrees accentuates social division).

At a 2018 think tank held by the Centre for Industry Engagement at Pearson College London, a panel of academics declared that the purpose of a university was essentially two-fold: "to be the guardian of reason, inquiry and philosophical openness, preserving pure inquiry from dominant public opinions [and ... to allow] more people to transform their lives, if necessary, at the expense of some academic rigour" (Allan, 2018). This dichotomy holds within it the essence of the debate on the purpose of a university: on the one hand, the ivory tower, and on the other, the place of social transformation.

Different types of university

Whereas schools can be divided, roughly speaking, into two categories (non-selective, including comprehensive and state school, and selective, including grammar schools, independent schools, charter and magnet schools), tertiary education is far more complex and can be subdivided into at least six categories: vocational schools, community colleges, technical schools, professional schools, colleges and universities.

The prestige associated with universities depends on context and worldview, but in most systems, vocational and technical schools are not regarded as elitist as universities and colleges (St Esprit, 2019). This perception is changing rapidly as technical institutions such as the Massachusetts Institute of Technology (MIT), the Swiss Federal Institute of Technology Zurich (ETHZ) and the École polytechnique fédérale de Lausanne (EPFL) are ranked higher than most universities and the return on investment in terms of future employment prospects weighs heavily in favour of technical institutions.

Ranking

Today, the perceived prestige of universities is largely substantiated through ranking systems. There are many, which muddies the waters somewhat, and each one places different emphasis on the services of universities being evaluated, including teaching quality, faculty qualifications, faculty diversity, research indices and infrastructure. Some of the more popular ranking consortia include QR World University Rankings, the Times Higher Education World University Rankings, Shanghai Rankings and the Jiao Tong system.

These consortia tend to place the same universities in their list of the top five institutions, although not always in the same order. Generally, these include Harvard, Stanford, MIT, Oxford and Cambridge.

Criticisms of university ranking systems are based mainly on the validity of their criteria (Taylor & Braddock, 2007) and the fact that "differences between institutions are often statistically insignificant" (Hazelkorn, 2015, p. 52). Any ranking system in education is problematic, and university rankings have become a thorny issue since the top-ranked universities tend to be the wealthiest and a string of scandals over funding and playing the system in the United States in recent years has created significant cynicism about what is perceived by many as a scenario of privilege and extreme wealth more than pure academia and provision for learning (Stack, 2019).

Elite universities

The Unites States

There are over 4,000 degree-granting postsecondary institutions in the United States (Moody, 2019), which has the largest number of top-ranking and wealthiest universities in the world. "Tuition fees range from $5,000 to $50,000 per year. Most undergraduate degrees last four years, so, on average, students are graduating with $132,860 (£101,505) worth of debt" (THE, 2020b). The Bureau of Labor Statistics showed the median wage for workers in the first quarter of 2020 to be $49,764 per annum (Doyle, 2020).

In a globalised world, it has become something of a household dream for most young people, not just in the United States but throughout the world, to go to Harvard, Yale, Princeton or Stanford. Top US universities invest more money per student than do other countries: well over three times that which is invested per student at Oxford and Cambridge for example, and their broad-based undergraduate system is arguably something that attracts many prospective students. American universities tend to have impressive endowments, well-designed alumni associations and well-funded development offices.

Ivy League colleges and top tier

The traditional benchmark of elitism in North77 American universities is that which describes Ivy league colleges. A popular website states that these are

> the most sought-after institutions of higher learning in the country and around the world. These eight private Northeast schools are known for their highly selective admissions process, academic excellence and promising career opportunities for those who attend. The name recognition and social prestige don't hurt either.
>
> (US News, 2019)

These colleges, initially grouped as part of a sports conference, include the top-ranking universities Princeton, Harvard, Columbia, Yale and Pennsylvania. Less highly ranked but still considered prestigious for their Ivy League affiliation are Dartmouth, Brown and Cornell.

Interestingly, some of the highest-ranking so-called top-tier universities in the United States are not Ivy League (Stanford, MIT, California Institution of Technology). There is some debate regarding the precise advantage conferred by being a graduate from an Ivy League college: the college admissions guidance company Crimson states that "attending an Ivy League provides you with the potential of securing you an above average salary in the future. In fact, Harvard graduates make more money after college than graduates from any other college (with the exception of MIT)" (Crimson, 2019).

In his 2016 book *Where You Go Is Not Who You'll Be: An Antidote to the College Admissions Mania*, journalist Frank Bruni argues that attendance at an elite college does not guarantee success and, on the contrary, shows how leading CEOs are more likely to have graduated from state schools and universities than from private schools and Ivy League colleges. Bruni goes further to suggest that many elite colleges, particularly Ivy League colleges, run on reputation, prestige and historical assumptions. He also suggests that it is more plutocratic elitism that defines Ivy League colleges than strictly meritocratic elitism since these institutions have a strong tradition of legacy students (meaning that their parents attended the same college) who receive preferential treatment and essentially constitute a core group of privileged, wealthy individuals who make up the cultural engines of most Ivy League institutions.

A 2013 study at Harvard "found that legacy status conferred a 40-percentage point advantage of being accepted [albeit] mainly for students already in the most desirable applicant pool" (Larkin & Aina, 2018). Furthermore, a point made by Bruni and by others is that elite colleges in the United States encourage many students to apply so that their rejection statistics go up and entrance probability decreases. This is a classic structuring principle of elitism that we have encountered in previous chapters: scarcity.

Bruni (2018) argues that what is important, and often unexploited, is the type of social networking that students engage in while at university, the relationships they forge with their professors and the extent to which they are able to diversify their networks.

The value added of studying at a prestigious university in the United States

Using observational data from "587 courses across 9 institutions of higher education in the U.S", Campbell, Jimenez and Arrozal (2019) studied the correlation between instructional quality and reputation among prestigious and non-prestigious universities (p. 717). They came to the tentative conclusion that while their study "did not support the assertion that courses in higher prestige institutions have stronger teaching, there did seem to be a prestige pay-off in terms of the level of rigor" (p. 734). They found that "the highest level of cognitive complexity exhibited during the course was greater in courses at prestigious institutions when compared to those in less prestigious institutions" (p. 734).

Researchers from Stanford, on the other hand, after studying the relationship between the extent of a university's selectivity and the quality of the student experience, could find no significant relationship between a school's selectivity and student learning, future job satisfaction, or well-being. They found "a modest relationship between financial benefits and attending more selective colleges, and that these benefits apply more to first-generation and other underserved students" (Challenge Success, 2018, p. 2). The research team also found "that individual student characteristics (such as background, major, ambition) may make more of a difference in terms of post-college outcomes than the institutions themselves" (p. 2).

Scandals that have damaged the reputation of elite US colleges

In 2019, MIT Media Lab admitted to having accepted more than US $7 million in the form of anonymous donations from a convicted sex offender (Piper, 2019). In the same year, it was discovered that $20 million had been paid indirectly in the form of bribes to top-tier universities such as Yale and Stanford between 2011 and 2018. This became a nationwide scandal, popularly known as Varsity Blues, and eventually led to 50 people being accused of corruption by the US Justice Department. The media leaked allegations such as that parents paid $1.2 million to have their daughter, who did not play soccer, recruited as a soccer star, or that parents paid $200,000 to have their daughter appear listed as a rower for the US national team (Eckstein, 2019), and that an admissions officer organised false disability derogations for students written by psychologists for a fee (Harrison, 2019).

These incidents dented the moral reputation of many elite colleges in the United States, fuelling anti-elitist voices that see top-tier colleges as little more than ivory towers of wealth and privilege where amoral plutocratic elitism overrides meritocratic elitism.

Top-tier societies, fraternities and clubs

Elite colleges are often characterised by clubs and societies that constitute inner groups of elitism since only a select few are accepted and there tends to be a complex selection process to gain admission to a society. Members stay on after college, sometimes for life. These societies first came into existence in the 1700s at the College of William & Mary in Virginia and are characterised by initiation ceremonies called "hazing", secrecy and pledges of allegiance by members. Traditionally, behaviour at most of these clubs has been excessively decadent involving the heavy consumption of alcohol, dangerous social ceremonies and general boorishness. The rapport with wealth tends to be an important thread running through these clubs. Rumour has it that the Porcellian Club at Harvard requires members to earn at least US $ 1 million before the age of 40, although this may not be true. Similarly, aggressive rapports with wealth can be seen in other clubs. These behaviours function as codes of social cohesion. College societies were occupied by white men only until the early 1990s and some are still only open to men.

Some colleges, such as Princeton, have banned secret societies where practices and ethos have been deemed dangerous and over time many of the secrets of these societies have been leaked. The most prominent, Phi Delta Kappa, has now become a public academic institution in its own right but symbolises the idea of a circle that is exclusive and above others. Secret societies are closed and are modelled on fraternities. At Yale, for example, there are several societies, the three best known being the Scroll and Key, the Wolf's Head, and the Skull and Bones. The esoteric style of the names of these societies carry with it the mystical air of the occult and secrecy of 18th-century masonic societies which had an influence on the fraternities and their elitist structure. A symbol of this elitist structure is the fraternity ring that some college graduates wear, a clear distinction and reference to an inner circle.

In her 2002 book, *Secrets of the Tomb: Skull and Bones, the Ivy League, and the Hidden Paths of Power*, Alexandra Robbins discusses Yale's secret society, the Skull and Bones, to argue that powerful members of society such as presidents (George Bush senior and junior, for example) have been propelled into positions of power through their affiliation with the club.

Plutocratic and meritocratic elitism in the USA

Binder and Abel (2019) have shown that 70% of Harvard and Stanford students identify themselves as being of high socioeconomic status, whereas Kahlenberg (2010) has reported that three-quarters of students admitted to elite colleges have benefited from legacy preference. This makes it more difficult for non-legacy students to secure places. Shamash (2018) has argued that the US college admissions structure reproduces and even intensifies class hierarchy by admitting fewer lower income students.

Ornstein's article "Wealth, Legacy and College Admission" describes how Harvard and Yale in particular have become institutions "for educating the children of wealthy parents to preserve their privilege, rank and status in life" (2019, p. 335) and goes on to explain how their legacy "college admission policy can be construed as an affirmative-action policy for rich white students, and in turn help the rich and powerful exploit their position and ensure class domination for the next generation" (p. 335).

Top-tier colleges are extremely demanding in terms of admissions, often turning away students with full SAT scores (although more and more are seeking alternative entrance data to that of SATs). Su et al. (2012) describe how, between 1959 and 2008, relatively non-elite colleges witnessed an increase, of 525%, in their enrolment numbers, whereas in elite colleges the figure was closer to 250%. This reinforces the scarcity principle and meritocratic tightness of elitist admissions protocols (despite exceptions made for legacy enrolments). Despite the massification of higher education, elitist colleges have expanded at a much slower rate than others. It is the increasingly huge and worldwide demand for a university education that is making placements no longer a national but a global competition.

The United Kingdom

Oxford and Cambridge, founded in the 12th and 13th centuries, respectively, were the only British universities for over 200 years and were joined by a handful of Scottish universities in the 1400s and 1500s. It was only in the 1800s that three other English universities were founded (Durham, the University of London and Victoria University in Manchester). Civic universities (i.e. universities not requiring residency and focusing on medicine and engineering rather than on abstract knowledge) were set up from the 1900s. These were known as "red brick" universities in reference to Victoria University because many of them were affiliated with that institution.

Today there are over 130 universities in the UK. The majority of these were set up in the wake of the Further and Higher Education Act of 1992. Prior to that date, which signified the massification of tertiary education in the UK, there were only 46 universities in the UK (Writtle, 2017).

In 2020, English universities charged home students up to a maximum of £9,250, whereas in 1998 tuition fees amounted to £1,000. International students pay more than £30,000 per annuum, which is what the average Briton earns per year (Findcourses, 2019). More than one-quarter of university teaching income comes from international student fees, increasingly from China and the Middle East (Writtle, 2017). The cost of a university education is therefore considerable and, according to some studies, "two-thirds of UK students will never pay off their loan debt" (Burnett, 2018).

Universities in the UK follow a similar sociological trajectory to those of the United States in that there is a circle of universities considered to be better than others, somewhat like the Ivy League. This circle, called the Russell Group, "represents 24 leading UK universities" (Russell Group, 2020) including the most prestigious, namely Oxford and Cambridge. Oxford, famously, has produced 27 British prime ministers out of a total of 54 (Nimmo, 2016).

The 2019 Sutton Trust report entitled "Elitist Britain" describes "a country whose power structures remain dominated by a narrow section of the population: the 7% who attended independent schools, and the roughly 1% who graduated from just two universities, Oxford and Cambridge". The report goes on to explain how "52% of senior judges" came through a "pipeline from independent schools through Oxbridge and into top jobs" (Sutton Trust, 2019).

The legacy of elite universities remains strong in the UK, not just as a casual sociological distinguishing factor between people but in terms of employment opportunities in lucrative industries. For example, a survey of 600 investment bank trainees showed that "more than half the trainees hired by London's biggest investment banks come from just eight of the UK's top universities" (Clarke, 2019).

Not only is the university where one studied in the UK of importance, so too is the grade that one achieves in the final examinations, described either as a first, second or third-class pass. In 2018, the Institute of Student Employers claimed that a "2.1 [is] a minimum requirement [for] major corporate and public sector employers" (Coughlan, 2018). Furthermore, colleges are important, especially those that form the Universities of Oxford and Cambridge ("Oxbridge"), and they are all ranked. In 2019, *The Telegraph*, for example, ranked St John's College Oxford ahead of Trinity College Cambridge and Magdalen College Oxford (Kirk & Peck, 2019).

Therefore, if one is to be considered the "crème de la crème", or the elite of the elite, one should have studied at a renowned college at either Oxford or Cambridge and "come down" (i.e. graduate) with a first (although there is an argument that the true elite would disdain too high a pass as a sign of too much effort and would prefer a 2:1 to show that they were above such vulgarities as grading systems). This triple layer of elitism gives an idea of the complexity of class structure in the UK and the manner in which it is reflected in educational discourse.

Oxbridge clubs and societies

Universities in the UK tend to have numerous clubs and societies that are mainly academic. However, particularly at Oxbridge, a number of secret societies exist that are extremely exclusive and sociologically coded. They are not so much about academia but more about in-grouping. Some of these are called drinking societies and are made up of males only who usually have been to public schools. Heavy drinking, sexist behaviour and expensive dinners are ritualistic hallmarks of drinking societies.

The most famous is the Bullingdon Club at Oxford, previously attended by UK prime ministers Boris Johnson and David Cameron. This society is now less secret than it was before the press reported on it fulsomely, and a feature film, *The Riot Club* (2014), directed by Danish director Lone Scherfig, depicted it as a cruel, dissolute, misogynistic and even criminal group. The hedonistic rituals that formed a core part of the club represented disdain for any circle outside the aggressively protected and celebrated ambit of privilege that society members embodied: vandalism, for example, was a recurrent key behaviour. The club was criticised widely by the press for insisting that its members should wear tailcoats costing £3,500 apiece and for the act of burning money by way of an initiation ceremony. Although Cameron said he was "deeply embarrassed" by his involvement in the club, he went on to appoint three ministers who were members of the club with him while at Oxford (Cherwell, 2020).

The Bullingdon Club is apparently now very small as students are less keen to be associated with it than they were in previous years (Webb, 2018). However, there are other selective entry clubs that characterise the "hearty" ethos of Oxbridge, such as the Gridiron at Oxford (which was forced to admit women in 2016), or the Pitt in Cambridge. These clubs continue to propagate the quintessentially elitist ideas of class superiority, exclusivity and scarcity along with marked symbolic behaviours that explicitly tear away from middle-class decency and order. This recklessness can be associated with patterns of behaviour in leadership caucuses historically: Suetonius reminds us of the immoral behaviour of Roman emperors, and stories are still told about sexual licentiousness in the gardens of the Borgias.

Polytechnics

At the other end of the spectrum, far from the world of drinking societies and ranked university colleges, are the polytechnics. These started with the Industrial Revolution in the early 1800s and provided an education primarily in STEM subjects. Many were established in the 1960s and became independent degree-awarding institutions following the passage of the 1992 Further and Higher Education Act. Known rather disparagingly as "new universities", polytechnics often have lower entry requirements than universities and are viewed, therefore, as second-class institutions, which is not the case in other parts of the world: "in Britain, only 32 percent of youngsters between 14 and 18 have experienced any vocational training, whereas in Austria, Finland, Denmark, the figure receiving vocational skills is more like 65 to 70 per cent", said former Secretary of State for Education Lord Baker (Warrell, 2013).

The prestige that is associated with more formal academic courses of study has remained a strong bias based on assumptions, historical legacy and shared narratives, especially in the UK (McInerney, 2014). When describing the situation in the UK former Secretary of State for Education, Damien Hinds, said that the national attitude to education was that of "technical education snobs" and that vocational courses were "OPC courses: for other people's children" (Kernohan, 2018). This is less the case in continental Europe where good technical courses in Switzerland and Germany, for example, are not viewed this way. In fact, the École Polytechnique in France is considered to be one of the most prestigious tertiary institutions in the country.

There have been some attempts to change perceptions of polytechnics but this is not viewed as particularly sincere:

> The desire for parity between vocational and academic streams has been a mantra of politicians over the decades. Prime ministers, mainly Oxbridge graduates, have stood in front of the cameras and said that they will no longer tolerate the notion that a vocational education is inferior. But none have developed a proper strategy to counter this, and parity of esteem has not followed.
>
> (University Business, 2020)

It could be argued that polytechnics have done much to open access to education and reduce plutocratic and social elitism. From the 1960s,

> [p]olytechnics also expanded access to new kinds of students. They were particularly successful in increasing numbers of women, students from ethnic minorities, mature students and, to some extent, students from working-class backgrounds. More than half of degree entrants had non-traditional qualifications. A higher proportion of their graduates than those from universities entered employment, particularly in engineering and manufacturing.
>
> (University Business, 2020)

Plutocratic and meritocratic elitism in the UK

The British university educational model is meritocratically elitist in that students are admitted according to final high school grades and, for Oxbridge, after supplementary entry tests and interviews. UK universities are plutocratically elitist in that the overwhelming majority of Oxbridge students come from socioeconomically privileged backgrounds, but they are arguably less plutocratically elitist than American universities that charge fees of up to US $50,000 per annum and give preference to legacy students.

In terms of the philosophy and sociology of elitism, the British approach to vocational education is part of a broader system of cultural elitism that opposes, hierarchically, what Basil Bernstein called the vertical (abstract, knowledge-based) and horizontal (practical, common sense, technical) discourses of education (Bernstein, 1999). In short, his thesis was that the upper class protects itself from other groups through the use of esoteric, canonical and self-referentially coded discourses leading to white-collar positions that can be differentiated from practical knowledge that might typically be associated with blue-collar employment.

It would take a long analysis to explore the full depths of this thesis as it reposes on centuries of class division and might have stemmed from the 19th-century Industrial Revolution's creation of a *nouveau riche* who competed with the landed aristocracy and whose pragmatic ethos would, therefore, be looked down upon by members of the so-called upper class, creating a rift between them and the creation of protective discourses and institutions. Indeed, idioms to describe different classes of higher education institutions are still in use in the UK today, namely "Oxbridge" (the Universities of Oxford and Cambridge), "red brick" (the Russell Group universities) and "plate glass" (the former polytechnics).

This informal distinction between different levels of knowledge and education is not uniquely British. The American sociologist Michael Apple, in his famous *Ideology and Curriculum* (1990), argues that schools and universities can effectively be defined by the extent to which they practice either middle-class, theoretical discourses which lead to executive positions or practical, proletariat discourses which lead to working-class positions.

India

There are 884 higher education institutions in India, categorised as state, central, private and "deemed" (UniRank, 2020). The most prestigious tertiary institutes in India are Institutes of Technology (IITs) and indeed universities that confer qualifications in engineering, business or medicine are generally seen as being of a higher status than other universities (although there are exceptions such as the Maharaja Sayajirao University of Baroda). Some of the most prestigious institutions include Indian Institute of Management Ahmedabad (known as IIM Ahmedabad), the National Institute of Technology, Trichy, and SRM Institute of Science and Technology, Chennai. Fees for these institutions are, roughly speaking, between 100,000 and 150,000 rupees (or US $1,300–$2,000) per annum for a BTech (Kumar, 2020).

With the massification of demand and India's colossal population of 1.3 billion, the 23 IITs in the country are insufficient to cater for the million-plus applicants each year. Entrance examinations to gain entry to IITs are exceptionally difficult, so much so that prior to taking the entrance test, students enrol in coaching colleges that are specifically designed to prepare them for entrance examinations. The city of Kota has become well known as a testing "epicentre": "for months, even years, teens who've barely left their parental homes before live alone, in austere hostel rooms, cramming morning, noon and night in the hope of a secure, financially lucrative future" (Kale, 2018). The pressure on students to secure a place at one of these prestigious colleges is so great that it can lead to severe mental health problems and even suicide: between 2011 and 2014, 45 students committed suicide in the city of Kota (Kale, 2018).

Many Indian students study abroad: in 2016 for example, over three million students attended universities outside of India with 45% studying in the United States. Most were particularly attracted by STEM programmes (Choudaha, 2019). That percentage is decreasing, however, as immigration laws are tightened (20 years ago, almost 60% of all Indian students studied at US universities). The drift is currently towards Australian universities (Choudaha, 2019).

The Indian government is keen to see Indian institutions climb up the global league tables. In 2016, the Indian government pledged to spend 10 billion rupees to "support 20 institutions [ten public and ten private] to compete on the world stage" (Padma, 2018), but this initiative did not reach its goal for a number of political and administrative reasons.

Plutocratic and meritocratic elitism in India

Some argue that recently there has been a wave of purely plutocratic elitism sweeping over India that is more concerned with material wealth than levels of education or university references. *Times of India* blogger Keva Shirali argues that "today, it doesn't matter that you might have a Harvard Law degree, or that you read extensively, or that without the two of those, you might be capable of making intelligent decisions for yourself ... it's a question of maintaining appearances" (Shirali, 2019).

Essentially, the university market in India is geared towards plutocratic elitism since degrees leading to high-paying professions are in over demand, and towards meritocratic elitism since acceptance rates to study at India's' most prestigious colleges are extremely low, requiring extraordinary academic preparation and, therefore, societal pressure on young people to gain admission places.

South Africa

There are 26 public universities in South Africa distributed across the county's nine provinces (USAf, 2020). The highest ranking universities are the University of Cape Town, the University of the Witwatersrand, Stellenbosch University, and the University of Kwazulu-Natal (THE, 2020a). In 2019, data showed that annual university fees, on average, were approximately 64,000 rand (approximately US $3,800) for the first year but these were expected to increase to over 160,000 rand by 2030 (*BusinessTech*, 2019). The average South African worker earns 270,000 rand per year (*BusinessTech*, 2020).

Under apartheid, quality university education was primarily reserved for white students. For example, in 1959, the Extension of University Education Act closed English-language universities to black students (Morris, 2012, p. 65). Many years later, there is still much to be done to undo the elitist structures of the past that were based on race. In 2013, the South African Department of Higher Education and Training published a White Paper that pointed out that "communities have learning needs that have not been catered for by the current public education and training centres" (DHET, 2013, p. 20), and that post-secondary education opportunities have been "insufficient" and of "poor" quality (p. 21).

Rhodes Must Fall

Perceptions of elitism are inextricably linked to racial and political issues in South Africa. Matters came to a head in 2015 when students began a series of protests across South Africa known as Rhodes Must Fall in reference to Cecil John Rhodes, the British colonist whose statues were defiled in Cape Town (with human excrement)—some were removed later. A series of statues of colonists were then defiled and/or removed in other parts of South Africa. Rhodes is seen as a symbol of a lack of political, cultural and economic transformation.

The movement's genesis was particularly focused on the University of Cape Town where protesters view department structure and curriculum as neo-colonial. This anti-elitist movement spiralled into a #FeesMustFall movement, demanding the freezing of university fee increases and increased government funding of universities. The Rhodes Must Fall movement spread to Oxford and Harvard and became intertwined in the global Black Lives Matter movement and broader movements on decolonising the curriculum. This will be investigated in some detail in Chapter 8 in this volume.

Jonathan Jansen's *As by Fire: The End of the South African University* (2018) gives a critical, pragmatic and somewhat conservative account of the Rhodes Must Fall `movement from the perspective of a university chancellor. At the other end of the spectrum of analysis is *Rhodes Must Fall: The Struggle to Decolonise the Racist Heart of Empire* (Chantiluke, Kwoba & Nkopo, 2018). The titles of these two books alone speak volumes on the extent to which discussion around race and privilege in South African academia is polarised.

Plutocratic and meritocratic elitism in South Africa

South African universities are not particularly elitist meritocratically since a pass in the local examination board ("matric") generally makes local students eligible for a place. International students will need a certain grade average on their high school certificates to be admitted. However, given the demographics and economics of South Africa, the university system is plutocratically elitist, making it nearly impossible for millions of low-income nationals to access a university education.

Australia

There are 43 universities in Australia and a number of vocational institutions (Government of Australia, 2020). The average fees are over A$30,000 per annum with local students receiving a substantial subsidy from the government that they pay back through taxes (Australian Universities, 2020). The average salary in Australia is around A$84,000 per annum (Carey, 2020) and "the average Australian student graduates with over 21 000 dollars in debt with a substantial portion holding twice that amount" (Pallardy, 2019).

Australia's top-ranking universities are Melbourne, Queensland, Monash, the Australian National University, and Sydney (THE, 2020a). The so-called Go8 (Group of Eight), which constitute these five universities plus Adelaide, New South Wales and the University of Western Australia, is considered to be Australia's Ivy League (Go8, 2020).

The first peoples of Australia, sometimes—depending on context—referred to as indigenous or Aboriginal peoples, along with the Torres Strait Islanders, do not receive special grants or free entry to university. In 2012, statistics showed that university enrolments comprised less than 1.5% of this group and an even smaller proportion was found among the academic staff (Carlson, 2020).

The university business represents the third largest industry in the country. The financial model of Australian universities has been widely criticised as it represents a form of internal plutocratic elitism: vice-chancellors can earn over A$1.5 million per annum, while low-level academic staff, who hold precarious temporary positions, earn some of the lowest salaries in the world, at least compared to similar posts in other tertiary systems (Singhal, 2019; Kunkler, 2020).

Australian universities depend on international students financially. Union activist Ben Kunkler (2020) claims that Australian universities were "sick before the pandemic": "more than thirty years of bipartisan deregulation and funding cuts to higher education, as well as the introduction of ever-growing fees, have made Australian universities deeply dependent on the lucrative international market, in the form of overseas student enrollments".

He explains that "in 1990, there were just 24,990 international students studying in Australia. By 2018, that number had risen to 876,400, a growth sustained by double-digit increases year after year" (Kunkler (2020). The vast majority of these students, from China and India, have sustained the growing university industry. With COVID-19-related travel restrictions affecting international student enrolment, there is fear and doubt over the financial future of Australian universities: in July 2020 it was forecast that "Australian universities expect to lose Aus$3 billion to $5 billion (US$2 billion to $3 billion), mainly in fees from international students" (Witze, 2020).

Plutocratic elitism and Australian universities

Entrance requirements to Australian universities vary by college but generally speaking are that of a high school diploma. While Australian universities are, therefore, not known to be as exigent as American or British universities at the level of admissions, they are relatively expensive: the higher hurdle is financial, especially for international students who need to buy health insurance and will pay higher fees than locals.

Switzerland

It is worth considering the Swiss model as it differs substantially from the Anglo-Saxon model in a number of ways, especially with regard to the construct of elitism.

There are 12 public universities in Switzerland. Of these, ten are cantonal, meaning that they are funded by their local jurisdictions, and two are federal, meaning that they are nationwide institutions and are funded by the government. Four of these feature in the top 100 global rankings (THE, 2020a), with the two federal institutions, both polytechnic colleges (ETHZ and EPFL), ranking in the top 20 universities in the world, according to QS World University Rankings (QS, 2020).

Although a number of universities in Europe are free for EU citizens but not for non-EU citizens, the majority of universities in Switzerland are extremely inexpensive for all students (charging between 400 and 3,700 euros per annum for undergraduate studies and even less for postgraduate studies) (Vioreanu, 2020). This is essentially because most Swiss universities are state funded.

Students with local high school leaving certificates can gain access to any Swiss university. International students have to meet a grade threshold that is demanding. There are, of course, some problems with this system: many local students drop out of the first year of the more demanding university courses since the level is extremely high and students gain access relatively easily.

In order to be eligible for admission to Swiss universities, local students must have gained access to the *matura/maturité/maturità* programme (the Swiss equivalent of the British A-levels or the US and Canadian Advanced Placement examinations), and this can only be done after the successful completion of an entrance test taken at the end of middle school. Clearly, there is some screening that takes place quite early during a student's educational journey.

All things considered, Swiss universities are meritocratically selective for international students, extremely accessible financially for all students and do not rank institutions according to their technical, vocational or academic offerings. The system is therefore neither meritocratically or plutocratically elitist and yet universities in Switzerland are considered to be of a very high standard.

Industries bypassing university qualifications

As universities in most countries are increasingly massified and expensive, the extent to which the tertiary sector can continue to grow and remain a viable option for young people, leading to employment, is contested.

A number of leading employers such as Google, Apple, Hilton and Costco are publicising the fact that they are prepared to employ young people without university degrees (Glassdoor, 2020). This dents the elitist aspirations of universities that have historically provided young people with a palpable boost in the employment market.

Although it is still commonly perceived as an advantage to have attended an elite university, students will have to think hard about the return on investment given the debt that university enrolment typically incurs ($1.5 trillion), comprising 42% of all consumer debt in the United States (Ow Ca, 2018), and moreover a changing job market that is no longer as strictly correlated with tertiary qualifications as it was 40 odd years ago.

The Swiss model of vocational training, whereby students who have not qualified for an academic route specialise in technical skills through an apprenticeship from a relatively early stage, leads to a high percentage of employment and a high average income. More than two-thirds of all Swiss students qualify for a vocational route (Swissinfo, 2019). There is an argument to be made for future tertiary systems allowing for a more inclusive, pluralistic approach to different types of qualification.

Voices in favour of university elitism

The pro-elitist perspective on universities is that they have become too massified and are losing their inherent selective identity.

New Statesman journalist Harry Lambert, for instance, complains that the massification of universities in the UK has led to low standards; universities are guilty of grade inflation: "for every student who got a First in the early 1990s, nearly 20 do now" (Lambert, 2019). He quotes professors who bemoan low standards from students who have been through feeder-schools that have "'spoon-fed' them … not taught [them] to read, quickly and critically [or] to communicate their ideas". For Lambert, universities have lost their soul—students are more interested in passing exams than really learning.

The elitist solution would be to make universities even more elitist, as this—in theory—would restrict entry, drive up standards and further diversify the activities of youth: "with fewer young people in higher education, more could freely enter employment, where they are increasingly needed" (Writtle, 2017).

The ivory tower should be protected, therefore, not only to keep the standards of university at a meaningful level but to distract too many young people from trying to enter it as this merely saturates the entire system, ultimately making it meaningless. "University education needs once again to be an elite option. And 'elite' should not be a dirty word: selection is at the heart of undergraduate admissions, graduate research and academic employment, just as it determines all job applications" (Writtle, 2017).

There is also a cultural elitist position to consider: the "dreaming spires" of Oxford should preserve a caucus of intellectuals ensconced in high culture as they will ultimately become responsible for "the self-consciousness of a society … the shared reference among educated people" (Scruton, 2012).

Voices against university elitism

The American idealist and founder of the University of Chicago, William Rainey Harper, declared passionately, at the turn of the 20th century, that "it is the university that … comfort[s] and give[s] help to those who are downcast, taking up its dwelling in the very midst of squalor and distress" (quoted in Benson & Harkavy, 2000, p. 179). Indeed, the pragmatist approach to education in general, championed by John Dewey, sees a university education as a cornerstone of democracy not just because it reinforces the critical thinking and knowledge necessary for a well-functioning civic society but also because it provides opportunity and access, thereby minimising rather than increasing inequalities. More radical voices suggest that the ivory tower of the university should be toppled entirely and grassroots, free universities should be considered instead.

Various initiatives to democratise universities have been attempted; for example, the French philosopher and public intellectual Michel Onfray founded the "Université Populaire de Caen" in 2002, at which lectures and seminars were offered to the broad public free of charge (although he left the university in 2018 after the French radio station France Culture stopped broadcasting his lectures). Israeli entrepreneur Shai Reshef founded the University of the People in 2009, an online university that is tuition-free, charging only US $500 for examinations (UoPeople, 2020).

Reducing elitism in universities is not just about opening access, it also involves a rethinking of the role of the academic, with a view to the active public intellectual as opposed to the bookish scholar removed from society:

> When academics recognise and engage with the knowledge embedded in communities, the inbreeding and exclusionary nature of scholarship, that is, scholars citing, exploring and refuting other scholars' views will change. The circle of scholarship will expand. Academic voices will co-exist with non-academic voices, creating an engaged scholarship that is respectful and appreciative of the unique and perceptive contributions of non-academics.
> (James, 2018)

In describing the outcomes of his open-access Summer Schools, based on Fanonian and Freirean principles of community-based learning, James states the following essential factors for universities to consider in order to be more socially active and accessible:

- Liberating education from its elitist captivity, creating access and widening participation in higher education and training.
- Mobilising university research and teaching for the public good.
- Developing academic activists.
- Developing socially responsive curricula. (James, 2018)

Conclusion

On the one hand, universities can be considered bastions of elitism, in some cases to the extent of moral decadence and corruption. On the other, the relevance and currency of university degrees along with the extent to which they are worth the expense and debts incurred by students can be called into question.

As demand becomes ever more massified, is it important that top-ranking universities remain extremely exclusive so as to protect the currency of their degrees, vouching for high quality, or should the industry of tertiary education be made more accessible financially and academically so as to educate as many people as possible?

Whichever view is espoused, elitist or anti-elitist, the future of universities needs to be recalibrated as the world heads towards an increasingly complex future, which the next chapter describes.

References

Apple, M. (1979). *Ideology and Curriculum*. New York: Routledge & Kegan Paul.

Australian Universities (2020). *Tuition Fees for International Students*. https://australianuniversities.click/tuition-fees-international-students/#:~:text=Tuition%20fees%20for%20international%20students%20in%20Australia%20start%20at%20around,time%20study%20(8%20Ounits).

Benson, L., & Harkavy, L. (2000). Integrating the American System of Higher, Secondary and Primary Education to Develop Civic Responsibility. In T. Ehrlich (ed.) *Civic Responsibility and Higher Education*. Phoenix, AZ: Oryx Press, pp. 174–196.

Bernstein, B. (1999). Vertical and horizontal discourse: An essay. *British Journal of Sociology of Education*, 20(2), 157–173.

Binder, A.J., & Abel, A.R. (2019). Symbolically maintained inequality: How Harvard and Stanford students construct boundaries among elite universities. *Sociology of Education*, 92 (1), 41–58. http://dx.doi.org/10.1177/0038040718821073.

Bruni, F. (2016). *Where You Go Is Not Who You'll Be: An Antidote to the College Admissions Mania*. New York: Grand Central Publishing.

Bruni, F. (2018). How to get the most out of college. *New York Times*. www.nytimes.com/2018/08/17/opinion/college-students.html.

Burnett, K. (2018). UK universities face a crisis of over-ambitious expansion. *Financial Times*. www.ft.com/content/6f0d7502-90f5-11e8-9609-3d3b945e78cf.

BusinessTech (2019). How much it will cost to send your kids to school and university over the next 18 years in South Africa. *BusinessTech*. https://businesstech.co.za/news/finance/293330/how-much-it-will-cost-to-send-your-kids-to-school-and-university-over-the-next-18-years-in-south-africa-2/.

BusinessTech (2020). This is the average salary in South Africa right now. *BusinessTech*. https://businesstech.co.za/news/finance/386327/this-is-the-average-salary-in-south-africa-right-now-4/.

Cai, Y. (2019). University Mergers in China. In L. Cremonini, S. Paivandi & K.M. Joshi (eds.) *Mergers in Higher Education: Practices and Policies*. New Delhi: Studera Press, pp. 127–146.

Campbell, C., Jimenez, M., & Arrozal, C. (2019). Prestige or education: college teaching and rigor of courses in prestigious and non-prestigious institutions in the U.S. *Higher Education*, 77, 716–738. doi:doi:10.1007/s10734–10018–0297–0293.

Carey, A. (2020). Survey reveals scores of high income learners think they need more money to be "comfortable". news.com.au. www.news.com.au/finance/money/costs/survey-reveals-scores-of-high-income-earners-think-they-need-more-money-to-be-comfortable/news-story/caa1b7824144c2be213165c3cb6e168f.

Carlson, B. (2020). Here's the truth about the "free ride" that some Australians think Indigenous peoples get. SBS. www.sbs.com.au/topics/voices/culture/article/2016/12/07/heres-truth-about-free-ride-some-australians-think-indigenous-peoples-get.

Challenge Success (2018). *A "Fit" Over Rankings: Why College Engagement Matters More Than Selectivity*. https://ed.stanford.edu/sites/default/files/challenge_success_white_paper_on_college_admissions_10.1.2018-reduced.pdf.

Chantiluke, R., Kwoba, B., & Nkopo, A. (eds.) (2018). *Rhodes Must Fall: The Struggle to Decolonise the Racist Heart of Empire*. London: Zed Books.

Cherwell (2020) Beyond the Bullingdon: A closer look into Oxford's secret societies. *Cherwell*. https://cherwell.org/2020/03/12/beyond-the-bullingdon-a-closer-look-into-oxfords-secret-societies/.

Choudaha, R. (2019). A new wave of Indian students now studying abroad. CNBC. www.cnbctv18.com/economy/a-new-wave-of-indian-students-now-studying-abroad-2096281.htm#:~:text=The%20total%20number%20of%20Indian,from%20UNESCO%20Institute%20of%20Statistics.

Clarke, P. (2019). Big banks lean on eight elite universities for new recruits. *Financial News*. www.fnlondon.com/articles/big-banks-lean-on-elite-universities-for-new-recruits-20190902.

Coughlan, S. (2018). Does it matter what degree grade you get?BBC. www.bbc.com/news/education-45939993.

Crimson (2019). *The Benefits of the Ivy League*. www.crimsoneducation.org/ca/blog/campus-life-more/benefits-of-Ivy-League/.

Department of Higher Education and Training (DHET) (2013). *White Paper in Post School Education and Training*. Pretoria: DHET.

Doyle, A. (2020). Average salary information for U.S. workers. *The Balance Careers*. www.thebalancecareers.com/average-salary-information-for-us-workers-2060808.

Eckstein, R. (2019). College admission scandal grew out of a system that was ripe for corruption. *The Conversation*. https://theconversation.com/college-admission-scandal-grew-out-of-a-system-that-was-ripe-for-corruption-113439.

Findcourses (2019). *Average UK Earnings by Job.* https://14105#:~:text=Their%20yearly %20survey%20showed%20that,for%20those%20in%20part%2Dtime.

Freed, B. (2014). Corcoran students say they do not feel welcome at George Washington University. *Washingtonian.* www.washingtonian.com/2014/12/10/cor coran-students-say-they-do-not-feel-welcome-at-george-washington-university/.

Frijhoff, W. (1996). Patterns. In H.D. Ridder-Symoens (ed.) *Universities in Early Modern Europe, 1500–1800, A History of the University in Europe.* Cambridge: Cambridge University Press, p. 75.

Glassdoor (2020). *15 More Companies That No Longer Require a Degree—Apply Now.* www.glassdoor.com/blog/no-degree-required/.

Government of Australia (2020). *Universities and Higher Education.* https://www.studyina ustralia.gov.au/English/Australian-Education/Universities-and-Higher-Education.

Grendler, P.F. (2004). The universities of the Renaissance and Reformation. *Renaissance Quarterly,* 57, 1–3.

Group of Eight (Go8) (2020). www.go8.edu.au.

Hardaker, G., & Sabki, A.A. (2019). *Pedagogy in Islamic Education: The Madrasah Context.* Bingley: Emerald Group Publishing, pp. 8–9.

Harrison, A.G. (2019). U.S. college admissions scandal means more scepticism of genuine invisible disabilities. *The Conversation.* https://theconversation.com/u-s-college-adm issions-scandal-means-more-skepticism-of-genuine-invisible-disabilities-115502#:~:text= The%20U.S.%20College%20admissions%20scandal,accommodation%20was%20supposed %20to%20do.

Hazelkorn, E. (2015). *Rankings and the Reshaping of Higher Education: The Battle for World-Class Excellence.* 2nd edn. London: Palgrave Macmillan.

Hunt, E. (2016). University of Sydney calls off merger of art college amid protests. *The Guardian.* www.theguardian.com/australia-news/2016/jul/28/university-of-sydney-calls-off-m erger-of-art-college-amid-protests.

James, G. (2018). Releasing Higher Education from its elitist captivity: The change agency of Unisa's Chance 2 Advance programme. *HTS Teologiese Studies/Theological Studies,* 74(3), a5045. https://doi.org/10.4102/hts.v74i3.5045.

Jansen, J. (2018). *As by Fire: The End of the South African University.* Cape Town: Tafelberg.

Kahlenberg, R.D. (2010). *Affirmative Action for the Rich: Legacy Preferences in College Admissions.* New York: The Century Foundation Press.

Kale, S. (2018). In India, high-pressured exams are creating a student suicide crisis. *Wired.* www.wired.co.uk/article/india-kota-student-suicide-exams-institutes-of-technology.

Kernohan, D. (2018). Other people's children: Hinds on technical education. *WONKHE.* https://wonkhe.com/bolgs/other-peoples-children/.

Kirk, A., & Peck, S. (2019). Why St John's, Oxford, is the best Oxbridge College, according to our league table. *The Telegraph.* www.telegraph.co.uk/education-and-ca reers/2019/09/30/st-johns-oxford-best-oxbridge-college-according-league-table/.

Kumar, S. (2020). IIT B.Tech Fee Structure: Check IIT Fees for BTech in 2020. *CollegeDekho.* www.collegedekho.com/articles/iit-btech-fee-structure/.

Kunklet, B. (2020). Australian universities were sick before the pandemic. *Jacobin.* https:// jacobinmag.com/2020/04/australian-universities-coronavirus-austerity-funding-privatiz ation.

Lambert, H. (2019). The great university con: How the British degree lost its value. *New Statesman*. www.newstatesman.com/politics/education/2019/08/great-university-con-how-british-degree-lost-its-value.

Larkin, M., & Aina, M. (2018). *Legacy admissions offer an advantage—and not just at schools like Harvard*. NPR. www.npr.org/2018/11/04/663629750/legacy-admissions-offer-an-advantage-and-not-just-at-schools-like-harvard.

Lorbeer, E. (2020). Contemporary elitism in higher education in the United States: An issue scan, *SSRN*, January 1. https://ssrn.com/abstract=3512115.

McGill Association of University Teachers (MAUT) (2020). A Brief History of MOOCs. MAUT. www.mcgill.ca/maut/current-issues/moocs/history.

McInerney, L. (2014). Snobbery about vocational education is denying our children opportunities. *The Guardian*. www.theguardian.com/education/2014/jan/21/snobbery-vocational-academic-education-opportunities-children.

Moody, J. (2019). A guide to the changing number of U.S. universities. US News. www.usnews.com/education/best-colleges/articles/2019-02-15/how-many-universities-are-in-the-us-and-why-that-number-is-changing.

Morris, M. (2012). *Apartheid: An Illustrated Story*. Cape Town: Jonathan Ball.

Nimmo, J. (2016). Why have so many prime ministers gone to Oxford University? BBC. www.bbc.com/news/uk-england-37500542.

Ornstein, A. (2019). Wealth, legacy and college admission. *Society*, 56, 335–339.

Ow Ca, P. (2018). Will university degrees become less relevant in the future? *Medium*. https://medium.com/@patrickow/will-university-degrees-become-less-relevant-in-the-future-9e5794896850.

Padma, T.V. (2018). India struggles to select 20 elite universities. *Nature India*. www.natureasia.com/en/nindia/article/10.1038/nindia.2018.86.

Pallardy, R. (2019). Student loans in Australia. Savingforcollege.com. www.savingforcollege.com/article/student-loans-in-australia.

Piper, K. (2019). Why MIT Media Lab thought it was doing right by secretly accepting Jeffrey Epstein's money. *Vox*. www.vox.com/future-perfect/2019/9/11/20860717/mit-media-lab-joi-ito-epstein.

QS World University Rankings (2020). *Top Universities*. www.topuniversities.com/university-rankings/world-university-rankings/2020.

Redden, E. (2018). Northeastern to acquire London College. *Inside Higher Ed*. www.insidehighered.com/news/2018/11/14/northeastern-plans-acquire-humanities-college-london.

Russell Group (2020). www.russellgroup.ac.uk.

St Esprit, M. (2019). The stigma of choosing trade school over college. *The Atlantic*. www.theatlantic.com/education/archive/2019/03/choosing-trade-school-over-college/584275/.

Salisbury, A.D., & Horn, M. (2019). Why mega universities should lead the way on quality assurance. *EdSurge*. www.edsurge.com/news/2019-07-22-why-mega-universities-should-lead-the-way-on-quality-assurance.

Scherfig, L. (2014). *The Riot Club*. BluePrint Pictures.

Shirali, K. (2019). A new wave of elitism that plagues modern India. *Times of India*. https://timesofindia.indiatimes.com/blogs/the-blogging-beatnik/a-new-wave-of-elitism-that-plagues-modern-india/.

Singhal, P. (2019). *University vice-chancellor salaries soaring past $1.5 million—and set to keep going*. www.smh.com.au/education/university-vice-chancellor-salaries-soaring-past-1-5-million-and-set-to-keep-going-20190620-p51zq3.html.

Su, X., Kaganovich, M., & Schiopu, I. (2012). *College expansion and curriculum choice.* Working paper no. 2012–2025, University of Alberta.

SwissInfo (2019). *Apprenticeship System.* www.swissinfo.ch/eng/apprenticeship-system/43796482.

Scruton, R. (2012). High culture is being corrupted by a culture of fakes. *The Guardian.* www.theguardian.com/commentisfree/2012/dec/19/high-culture-fake.

Shamash, R. (2018). (Re)production of the contemporary elite through higher education: a review of critical scholarship. *Berkeley Review of Education,* 8(1), 5–21. http://dx.doi.org/10.5070/B88134482.

Sorbonne (2020). *The Sorbonne in the Middle Ages.* www.sorbonne.fr/en/the-sorbonne/history-of-the-sorbonne/la-fondation-de-la-sorbonne-au-moyen-age-par-le-theologien-robert-de-sorbon/.

Stack, M. (2019). Ignore university rankings, but make education an election issue. *The Conversation.* https://theconversation.com/ignore-university-rankings-but-make-higher-education-an-election-issue-118434.

Sutton Trust (2019). *Elitist Britain.* www.suttontrust.com/wp-content/uploads/2019/12/Elitist-Britain-2019.pdf.

Taylor, P., & Braddock, R. (2007). International university ranking systems and the idea of university excellence. *Journal of Higher Education Policy and Management,* 29(3), 245–260.

Times Higher Education World University Rankings (THE) (2020a). *World University Rankings 2020.* www.timeshighereducation.com/world-university-rankings/2020/world-ranking#!/page/0/length/25/sort_by/rank/sort_order/asc/cols/stats.

Times Higher Education World University Rankings (THE) (2020b). *The Cost of Studying at a University in the United States.* www.timeshighereducation.com/student/advice/cost-studying-university-united-states.

UniRank (2020). *Top Universities in India.* www.4icu.org/in/.

University Business (2020). The post-1992 universities: overseas, overstretched? *University Business.* https://universitybusiness.co.uk/Article/post-1992-universities-overseas-overstretched/.

University College London (UCL) (2014). *UCL and the Institute of Education Confirm Merger.* www.ucl.ac.uk/news/2014/nov/ucl-and-institute-education-confirm-merger.

University of the People (UoPeople) (2020). www.uopeople.edu/.

Universities South Africa (USAf) (2020). www.usaf.ac.za.

US News (2019). *Ivy League Schools.* www.usnews.com/education/best-colleges/ivy-league-schools.

Vioreanu, D. (2020). Tuition fees and living costs in Switzerland. *Studyportals.* www.mastersportal.com/articles/1831/tuition-fees-and-living-costs-in-switzerland.html.

Warrell, H. (2013). Call to revive old-style polytechnics to fill UK skills deficit gap. *Financial Times.* www.ft.com/content/79bd7ad6-cf8c-11e2-a050-00144feab7de.

Webb, S. (2018). Posh Posse. *The Sun.* www.thesun.co.uk/news/2833129/bullingdon-club-oxford-why-burn-50-notes/.

Webometrics (2020). www.webometrics.info/en/node/54.

Witze, A. (2020). Universities will never be the same after the coronavirus crisis. *Nature,* 582, 162–164. www.nature.com/articles/d41586-020-01518-y.

Writtle, A. (2017). Varsity Blues. *The Spectator.* www.spectator.co.uk/article/varsity-blues.

Chapter 8

The lessons of 2020
A turning point for education and elitism

Zach and Anthony

When the government closed Zach's school in March 2020, lessons continued on the radio. A crackling voice over the ether could barely be picked up from his mother's transistor. He tried to take notes but could not hear what was being said. With no books at home, Zach has spent most of his time sweeping the compound, helping the community on various building and farming projects, and washing clothes.

It is not the first time that Zach's school has been closed: repeated attacks by Islamist groups on schools in the region have meant multiple closures (Mednick, 2020). Schooling for Zach is often disrupted and often children do not come to class because they have been threatened by extremists who do not want them to receive a "haram" education.

Zach has been lucky because he has not been stopped on the road to school as some of his friends have. Now everybody is at home and there is less danger. Zach's mother, like his teacher Mama Estelle, has told him that he must wash his hands much more frequently because of COVID-19. It is not clear when he will be able to get back to school.

For Anthony, the onset of the COVID-19 pandemic meant that he had to shift to online learning. Lessons carried on in more or less the same way but through the medium of Google Classroom, which made them slightly shorter, and with what his teachers called "adapted learning objectives". Anthony managed to fly home quickly after the announcement of the impending lockdown and quite enjoyed going to school from his bedroom although after a few weeks the experience became somewhat monotonous. His teachers were creative in the ways that they taught online: some made short films, others used an interactive whiteboard or devised special projects.

As part of his online learning, Anthony did a research project on bitcoin and economies of the future. He received a distinction for it. His teacher told him that it was a "fabulous" piece of work showing great "entrepreneurial thinking".

During the first lockdown, the school ran some assemblies on racism. This was after the death of George Floyd. Students were invited to post their feelings on Padlet and they heard from special guest speakers about the Black Lives Matter protest. Anthony does not feel racist in any way: his school's values are about respecting differences and there are many different student nationalities in the school. In one discussion group, a black girl said that she thought it was strange that all the teachers and leadership at the school were white. Anthony had not thought about that before. He feels that focusing on the colour of someone's skin is not right and does not see colour as important.

Introduction

The year 2020 was particularly important for questions about education and elitism. Two major historical events unearthed tensions relating to access to education, costs and curricula.

The COVID-19 pandemic forced school and university closures, a shift to online learning and online/face-to-face hybrid models of instruction. This had deep consequences for the sociology of education at the individual, collective and public level. The pandemic exacerbated learning gaps between students within institutions, between institutions in districts, and between countries. The concept of elitism, be it meritocratic, plutocratic or cultural, assumed renewed significance during a period of lockdown and remote schooling, as the chapter shows.

The death of George Floyd in May 2020 in Minneapolis, USA, led to public outcry. The Black Lives Matter protests that took place in numerous cities around the world called for a critical response to institutional racism in schools and universities, and a series of cultural battles took place between pro- and anti-elitist voices. These were polarised around two movements: one, the Rhodes Must Fall movement, which focused on debates about the pulling down of statues and the decolonisation of the curriculum, the other being the argument by proponents of "cancel culture" that a public hard line should be taken against prejudicial discourses. Both of these movements are inextricably linked to notions of elitism and education.

What lessons has the year 2020 taught educational institutions and what will this entail for future models of education?

COVID-19

First identified in December 2019 in the Wuhan province of China, the coronavirus disease (COVID-19) pandemic spread across the globe during 2020 and, at the time of writing, had infected close to 13 million people, and killed more than half a million (WHO, 2020).

As educational institutions are places where much social interaction takes place and disease prevention involves social distancing, schools and universities were shut down in most parts of the world: in April 2020, at least 1.5 billion learners had been affected (91.3% of total enrolled students in schools) across

188 countries (UNESCO, 2020a) and 109 country-wide closures of schools were reported as of July (UNESCO, 2020b).

It is likely that phenomena similar to COVID-19 will reoccur as industrialised human activity and the hunting of endangered species increase the likelihood of future health hazards. In 2015, scientists discovered 28 new viral groups frozen for centuries 50 metres beneath the Guliya ice cap in Tibet (Perez Ortega, 2020). As icecaps continue to melt due to human behaviour, there is a likelihood that they will release new viruses and this could cause a series of future pandemics. This means that disruptions of educational structures are to be envisaged that could well lead to future lockdowns, hybrid teaching and online instruction.

Whether schools go 100% online or opt for hybrid models with reduced class sizes and physical distancing between students, the social dynamic of schools and universities is seriously disrupted: "campus life" and the "college experience" are removed and important distinguishing features of elite institutions (sports facilities, cultural centres, etc) no longer come into the equation. Societies—secret or open—and clubs also disintegrate. This weakens the power of the symbolism of elitism. Furthermore, in the long term, disrupted learning whereby lessons take place online or in configurations that do not allow students to appreciate the culture and physical identity of the institution will, at some point, lead to a lowering of cost: it is highly unlikely that institutions will be able to charge expensive fees for online learning for very long, especially in a climate of economic recession. How easy will it be for schools and universities to remain elite if enrolment becomes entirely electronic in the future?

However, even if fees drop and a number of elite institutions are forced to reposition themselves, the consensus among commentators and analysts is that the COVID-19 pandemic will widen social gaps (Lewin, 2020; Goldstein, 2020): a number of studies have shown that the disruption caused by COVID-19 has exacerbated social differences between institutions through a widening of the digital divide (meaning different levels of access to technology).

Schools

Widening gaps

The closure of schools has widened gaps in learning and future disruption to schools caused by pandemics or other environmental or social turbulence will probably boost elite circles to even more advantaged positions. The so-called Matthew effect (Rigney, 2010) means that students who are already at an advantage move further ahead, whereas disadvantaged students tend to fall further behind. The notion is used to describe situations whereby children who have consolidated the first steps in learning are able to build on that knowledge relatively quickly and easily, whereas those who have not yet consolidated the basics will fall behind. Children from socioeconomically privileged backgrounds who have been exposed to elaborate codes, intellectually stimulating reading material and sophisticated dinnertime conversation tend to access new information in the classroom more easily than those from comparatively less educationally privileged households who have to work much harder in order to access new information and often fall further behind rather than advance.

This point is important as it explains why there is a positive and direct corollary between plutocratic and meritocratic elitism; why it is, on the whole, socioeconomically comfortable students who gain entry to grammar schools and why institutions that are highly selective meritocratically but socioeconomically need-blind still finish with a majority of wealthy students. Wealth begets wealth but it also begets levels of literacy, general knowledge and social codes. The general reading of the COVID-19 pandemic is that it will intensify this situation (Di Pietro et al., 2020).

In the case of a lockdown or school closure, children from affluent backgrounds will have better technological resources to access learning and will most likely have already been educated in a digitally enhanced classroom environment, whereas children from poor neighbourhoods will not be able to access learning and, if they do, will have more obstacles and novelties to navigate since a digitised classroom will be less familiar to them. Generally, teachers in the former category will have been trained in new technologies to a greater extent than teachers in the latter category. Studies run across the United States showed that during a lockdown, "schools with higher concentrations of students from low-income households have been less likely to expect teachers to provide real-time lessons, track students' attendance, or grade their assignments" (Lake & Makori, 2020). In the United Kingdom, a survey of more than 6,000 teachers by the Teacher Tapp app showed that only 40% of those in state schools were able to broadcast a video lesson, compared with 69% of teachers at independent schools (*The Economist*, 2020a).

In a number of countries, it is girls who are falling behind the most. In Mali, Niger and South Sudan, lockdowns have forced more than four million girls out of school (Giannini & Albrectsen, 2020). Bangalore Centre for Budget and Policy Studies researchers Jyotsna Jha and Neha Ghatak surveyed "700-odd students studying in ten government schools in Patna and Muzaffarpur districts in Bihar" (Jha & Ghatak, 2020) and could only reach half of the students because so many did not have phones or could not be reached and those that did have phones were in families where girls did not have access to them.

The World Food Programme's "Global Monitoring of School Meals during COVID-19 School Closures" showed that more than 360 million children were no longer receiving school meals, which were a major source of sustenance for them, often compensating for a lack of adequate nutrition at home (WFP, 2020).

An April 2020 Pew Research Center survey showed that "overall, roughly one-in-five parents with homebound schoolchildren say it is very or somewhat likely their children will not be able to complete their schoolwork because they do not have access to a computer at home" (Vogels et al., 2020). However, at the other end of the spectrum, students at elite schools not only navigated the lockdown with much greater ease: they were able to make considerable progress in their learning due to small class sizes and therefore more flexibility (Dickler, 2020), access to high performing technology, sophisticated and flexible programmes of study (Goldstein, 2020) and high levels of training in academic staff.

Private schools

There are different schools of thought concerning the future of private schools in the light of the socially disruptive phenomena that pandemics and environmental catastrophes will bring. On the one hand, the economic fallout will result in less spending power and therefore private schools may well suffer the loss of clientele and closure. On the other hand, since such schools are more likely to navigate exceptionally disruptive situations much better than state schools, some parents will be willing to make a supplementary investment to ensure that their children are not left even further behind because of the "Matthew effect".

In May 2020, the Cato Institute in the United States reported that over 40 private schools, mostly Catholic, were closing permanently due to the COVID-19 "economic downturn" (McClusky, 2020). In the UK, as of June 2020, at least 30 private schools had been threatened with closure because parents were no longer able to afford the fees as a result of the COVID-19-related economic fallout (Turner & Stephens, 2020) According to the Director of the Cato Institute's Centre for Educational Freedom,

> many private schools perennially get by on shoestring budgets as they try to compete with "free" public schools. That means they are often in precarious financial situations. And, of course, some private schools are not all that good, have been rocked by clergy scandals, are facing demographic changes—many things affect any given school. In other words, the COVID-19 recession may just be the final nail in a school's coffin.
>
> (McClusky, 2020)

Lindsey Burke, director of the Heritage Foundation's Center for Education Policy, argues that private schools are good for American society in that they express diversity and freedom of parental choice. She says:

> the biggest concern is the loss of family access to the school they had chosen as the right fit for their child. A permanent loss of these critical institutions, a private schooling sector whose history precedes modern-day government schooling, would be an incalculable loss to American society.
>
> (Burke, 2020)

Following this logic, the COVID-19 economic fallout could mean less diversity in the landscapes of schools and, therefore, an impoverishment of the world of schooling in general. US and UK governments provided aid to private schools in mid-2020 because many were either closing or threatening to close.

However, many parents have expressed dissatisfaction with the reaction of state schools to the crisis. The monolithic, standardised approach of entire districts or ministries is not necessarily as nimble, responsive and creative as that of many private schools. In Ottawa, Canada, for example, when in late June 2020 the public authorities announced possible future directions that state schools might take, there were "three possible scenarios for September, including continuing at-home learning and a hybrid option [and] many parents of children in the public school system were unimpressed with the choices" (Cotnam, 2020) and started to express interest in expensive private schools as an alternative.

Implications and possible outcomes

The COVID-19 pandemic and future disruptions that are likely to occur, will have a lasting effect on education and elitism in schools. The learning gap between students operating in under-resourced schools and those learning in privileged ecosystems will widen and create even more select, elite pockets of opportunity for the few that will be out of reach for the many. The economic fallout of such crises tends to hit the poorest hardest and favour the wealthy.

Lewin (2020) outlines the main socio-educational asymmetries due to COVID-19 as "the loss of opportunities to attend school, extreme variations in the capacity of households to homeschool children, and uneven disruptions to teacher deployment and absenteeism". Meanwhile, *The Economist* makes the argument that the long-term effect of children being out of school for extended periods is egregious and that reopening schools, with all the risks that this entails, is a far better option than letting "millions of minds go to waste". However, reopening schools in a time of crisis is expensive and complex. Therefore, stronger economies should help weaker ones for the sake of the common good (*The Economist*, 2020b).

The help of governments and inter-governmental agencies will be needed to narrow this divide. Impactful work can also be done by technology company consortia that agree to partner for the public good, such as those working with UNESCO's ITU Broadband Commission that work towards "broadband connectivity [being] made available to all schools, free of charge [with] the costs of coverage for schools [being] slashed to enable universal coverage" (Iyengar, 2020).

Some wealthy schools have pledged support for their underprivileged counterparts in the light of the COVID-19 economic fallout. For instance, Eton College is reported to have committed to "invest 100 million pounds ($125 million) over five years to help disadvantaged children in East Anglia, the Midlands and the north. The money will come from Eton's charitable endowment and fundraising" (Faulconbridge, 2020).

Universities

The economic implications of COVID-19

The relationship between elitism and education in the tertiary sector has been disrupted even more radically than it has in schools. The main challenge concerns international students whose enrolment has decreased because of COVID-19, thus denting the finances of universities across the globe:

> Wealthy private US universities, such as Johns Hopkins University in Baltimore, Maryland, expect to lose hundreds of millions of dollars in the next fiscal year. UK universities collectively face a shortfall of at least £2.5 billion (US$3 billion) in the next year because of projected drops in student enrolment, according to the UK consulting firm London Economics. And Australian universities could shed up to 21,000 full-time jobs this year, including 7,000 in research.
>
> (Witze, 2020)

Economic challenges mean that universities will have to rethink their modus operandi. There are a number of possible outcomes: some universities might decide to operate off lower enrolment figures, meaning that they will reduce their staff and possibly push tuition fees even higher, while others will look to offer more courses online at a lower cost and possibly for a greater number of students.

In an article entitled "The coming disruption", *New York Magazine* columnist James Walsh points out that the pandemic has disrupted university education in fundamental ways:

> The value, the price, the product [of education] has fundamentally shifted. The value of education has been substantially degraded. There's the education certification and then there's the experience part of college. The experience part of it is down to zero, and the education part has been dramatically reduced. You get a degree that, over time, will be reduced in value as we realize it's not the same to be a graduate of a liberal arts college if you never went to campus.
>
> (Walsh, 2020)

It is difficult to imagine that in the future students at top-tier universities in the United States will be prepared to pay $50,000 to attend online lectures and not to experience the social bonding, lavish infrastructure and general "college experience" that create many of the subtle codes and insider references that distinguish top-tier graduates from others. The sociological codification of elitism will be difficult to maintain without the culture of the campus life experience.

Increased elitism or increased egalitarianism

Post-COVID-19, universities will no doubt follow one of three trajectories:

1   A return to normal (or perhaps a "new normal" to put it more accurately) whereby fees, enrolment patterns and the general operational structure of universities remains intact.
2   A dramatic reduction in physically enrolled students, meaning a necessary shift to online learning.
3   A hybrid model whereby some students are on campus some of the time.

Options 2 and 3 mean that fees will have to be adapted. This could lead to a flattening effect whereby universities are no longer as sharply differentiated by their costs or it could mean that elitist universities will find ways to keep their offer expensive.

In an analysis of the effect of COVID-19 on universities, Witze states:

> The coronavirus crisis is forcing universities to confront long-standing challenges in higher education, such as skyrocketing tuition costs and perceptions of elitism—and some of the resulting changes could be permanent. Over the long term, universities might shift many classes online (a trend already under way), have fewer international students and even refashion themselves to be more relevant to local and national communities—both to solve pressing problems and to prove their worth at a time when experts and public institutions are coming under increased criticism.
>
> (Witze, 2020)

Therefore, one pathway that COVID-19 could open is that leading to a more inclusive, distributed and less elitist tertiary education sector whereby access is broadened and made more affordable. This would reduce elitism greatly and reposition universities as actors of social renewal rather than the bulwark of class hierarchy.

New synergies

Entrepreneur and thought leader Scott Galloway predicts a post-pandemic elitist university enrolment expansion that will be enabled through "partnerships between the largest tech companies in the world and elite universities … offering hybrid online-offline degrees" (Walsh, 2020). Such ideas as MIT@Google, iStanford and HarvardxFacebook are entertained. He believes that most brick and mortar establishments will cease to exist and that the only ones that do survive will be extremely elitist, catering for just 1% of the population.

Indeed, a societal crisis such as COVID-19, when public institutions are strained and resource distribution is threatened, human beings tend to drift to references that inspire confidence and involve less perceived risk. Trauma reinforces habits. In a globalised tertiary education sector, this could well mean that Oxbridge and top-tier universities will be even more heavily in demand. Because these institutions are well endowed in terms of human resources and funding, and are at the cutting edge of much research and scientific development, they will also be in a better position to offer students learning solutions that are forward-looking and fit for purpose.

Online learning

Most universities have shifted learning online, a necessary measure to achieve the physical distancing of students from one another and from their lecturers. "Online learning platform Coursera, founded by two Stanford professors, has seen more than 25 million enrolments [in June 2020] since mid-March, a 520% increase from the same period last year" (Sheng, 2020).

Online learning reduces elitism not only because it removes the physical structure of the university from the learning experience but because it can increase enrolment dramatically and offer more places. However, online learning is not entirely free from elitism, especially in parts of the world where access to broadband connection is by no means a given. In response to Great Zimbabwe University asking its students to use Google Classroom and Midlands State University making use of WhatsApp for tutorials, Everton Mutsauri from the Economic Freedom Fighters-Zimbabwe said that such a move was elitist:

> It is important for policy-makers and the universities to look at the very high data tariffs. Only the elite will be able to attend all online lectures. This is an example of policies being enacted by the elite for the elites.
>
> (Cited in Mukeredzi et al. 2020)

At present, top-tier and Oxbridge universities offering tuition online have not reduced their fees, banking on the brand and status of their name and the overall quality of the educational experience, albeit online, as being sufficient to maintain fees (Isaeva, 2020). However, universities in the second and third tier, so to speak, if we are to apply a ranking criterion to these institutions, are expected to freeze tuition fees, make budget cuts and possibly even reduce fees (Seltzer, 2020).

Protests against racism, Rhodes Must Fall and cultural wars around racism and elitism

Another significant disruption to the world of education that took place in 2020 was the outbreak of protest movements against racism that swept across the globe following the death of George Floyd while in police custody in Minneapolis, USA, on May 25.

Floyd's death was a catalyst for protest but the deaths of a number of black Americans at the hands of the police had been recorded prior to this incident (Trayvon Martin in 2013; Eric Garner, Michael Brown and Tamir Rice in 2014; Walter Scott in 2015; Alton Sterling and Philando Castile in 2016; Stephon Clark in 2018; and Breonna Taylor in 2020) (BBC, 2020).

However, the protests that raged through the United States and other countries in the world during May and June 2020 went deeper than addressing police brutality and evoked questions of systematic, cultural and structural racism. Various articles in the press and on social media as well as public debates about race have underpinned broader questions concerning elitism and education. These evoke the following central questions:

- How accessible are the top rungs of educational leadership to ethnic out-groups?
- Whose culture and history are taught in schools and why?
- What is the historical legacy of racism in education and how should it be treated?

The symbolism of statues: racial elitism and education

The relationship between elitism and race is not new (Filkins, 1988; Anderson, 1988; Tyler, 2001) in that racism, being a system of supremacy, privilege and discrimination, is an extreme form of elitism. Of course, this is not to say that all forms of elitism are racist or grossly discriminatory, but it can be said that racism is built on notions of ethnic and cultural elitism.

The death of George Floyd ignited a strong groundswell of frustration in many parts of the world on the theme of racism. People took to the streets to denounce what they saw as a lack of justice in social institutions, more specifically situations of white privilege.

The death of George Floyd also reignited the Rhodes Must Fall movement that began in 2015, calling for the removal of statues of past colonists and slave owners including a statue of Cecil John Rhodes at Oriel College, Oxford, which the Oxford authorities eventually agreed to remove. Widespread protests across the United States called for the removal of more than 1,700 Confederate monuments and memorials located all over the country (Walsh, 2020), while protesters in the UK and in Europe desecrated or removed statues of historical figures responsible for slavery or colonisation, such as Leopold the Second of Belgium and slave-trading Royal African Company director Edward Colston—whose statue was thrown into Bristol harbour, a gateway to the Atlantic Ocean (Lander, 2020).

Arguments for the removal of statues

Statues of colonisers and slave owners are seen as symbols of the elite, privileged and white narrative of history, told by the victors that has come to dominate the majority of culture and history in the Western world. The act of desecrating or pulling down these statues is a symbolic dethroning of key figures of racist power and authority. The arguments for removing their statues, and therefore their symbolic prominence, is that they represent a worldview and political activity that is exclusivist, elitist, discriminatory or, in extreme cases, genocidal.

These historical figures are the heroes of history textbooks and occupy a privileged place in the curriculum. Postcolonial protestors refute the celebration of their historical significance through nationwide iconography and request that their historical roles be reviewed. Harvard Law School historian, Annette Gordon-Reed, says that the "Confederacy stood for open and unrepentant white supremacy" (Walsh, 2020) and that it is understandable that protesters should want to see it removed.

Edinburgh City Council leader Adam McVey, in speaking about the statue of Henry Dundas, whose parliamentary act allowed slavery to continue for 15 more years, said: "we need to tell our story and make sure people understand Edinburgh's role in the world historically—not just the bits that we're proud of but frankly the bits we're ashamed of as well" (BBC, 2020).

The case of Winston Churchill in particular is worth some emphasis: on the one hand, Churchill is regarded as a British national hero who steered Britain through the victorious Second World War. On the other hand, he was responsible for extremely racist, elitist views as documented by the British historian Richard Toye: Churchill is quoted to have said "why be apologetic about Anglo-Saxon superiority?" (Toye, 2020).

Toye goes further to suggest that removing statues is not simply an act of purifying history, it is a movement against "great man theory", which is a cult of individual elitism:

> Portraying Churchill as the root of all wickedness, as some of the more extreme social media comments appear to do, is as problematic as viewing him as the single-handed saviour of freedom and democracy. By elevating him to a place of supreme importance—albeit by presenting him as uniquely wicked rather than splendidly virtuous—it reinforces Churchill's own theory of history as driven by great white men. That is a vision from which, surely, we urgently need to break free.
>
> (Toye, 2020)

Arguments against the removal of statues

The arguments against the removal of statues essentially point to the importance of retaining the legacy of history, warts and all, for the sake of the truthful transmission of the past. There is also a discourse that it becomes difficult to judge actors from previous periods of history using the moral compass of the 21st century along with the "slippery slope" argument, suggesting that such removals will pave the way for future acts of censorship.

In response to the desecration of the statues of Winston Churchill, UK Prime Minister Boris Johnson said that "we cannot try to edit or censor our past" (Walker, 2020). Meanwhile, in President Donald Trump, in the wake of the attacks on numerous statues in the United States, including, paradoxically, that of General Ulysses Grant, issued an "Executive Order on Protecting American Monuments, Memorials, and Statues and Combating Recent Criminal Violence" which decreed that "My Administration will not allow violent mobs incited by a radical fringe to become the arbiters of the aspects of our history that can be celebrated in public spaces" (The White House, 2020).

Professor Louise Richardson, vice-chancellor of Oxford University, in discussing the removal of Cecil John Rhodes' statue from Oriel College, said that

> My own view on this is that hiding our history is not the route to enlightenment … We need to understand this history and understand the context in which it was made and why it was that people believed then as they did … This university has been around for 900 years. For 800 of those years the people who ran the university didn't think women were worthy of an education. Should we denounce those people? Personally, no—I think they were wrong, but they have to be judged by the context of their time.
>
> (Cited in Coughlan, 2020)

The debate about statues elicits an important discussion about the nature of elitism: to what extent should public institutions reflect the broadest constituency possible in an egalitarian sense so that no one feels offended or excluded by its symbols and messages of power? And to what extent should public iconography and symbolism speak to power groups and inner circles, at the expense of the many and in favour of the few but nonetheless be representative of historical accuracy?

Racism in elite educational institutions

Elite institutions tend to be conservative by nature in that they represent bastions of power and tradition. It stands to reason, therefore, that they are often particularly resistant to change. Furthermore, elite institutions tend to reflect privilege in their enrolment and employment patterns, thus reinforcing the narrative of racism and inequality.

London School of Economics academic Clive Nwonka claims that less elite universities such as Birmingham University or Goldsmiths have made substantive efforts to reduce prejudice in their ranks:

But world-class institutions founded and sustained on social and economic elitism, like universities, struggle to change precisely because they
want to maintain the cachet and traditionalism that makes them distinct.
Much of their prestigious appeal has been built in part on historical social
exclusivity as well as the economic dividends of colonialism, empire and
slavery. The rigidness, traditionalism and protectionism at the heart of
elite universities, the need to defend the historic high canons of teaching,
and the very small presence of BAME students and staff continue to
restrict efforts to dismantle monolithic curriculums.

(Nwonka, 2020)

This is the case "especially among Russell Group universities, where the proportion of undergraduate black students was less than 4% in 2017–18"
(Nwonka, 2020).

King's College London student Mariya Hussain points out that

BAME students find themselves unrepresented, their histories and cultures
completely ignored in the academic field because for many years white
writing and history has been given a higher standing, and universities continue to perpetuate this idea of certain sources holding academic privilege.

(Hussain, 2020)

A number of articles were released on social media in 2020 describing experiences of racism in international schools.

In an open letter to a recruitment company working in international education, African international school teacher Safaa Abdelmagid (2020) stated that
"You have consistently failed to use your privilege to advocate for teachers of
colour and leadership of colour in the international school circuit. You have
acted as gatekeepers, preserving a majority white institutional world". She goes
on to describe the international school circuit as an elitist, self-protecting
enclosure of white privilege:

[F]or thirty years you have helped white male administrators bounce around
the world exchanging headships, uninterrupted, some with heinous scandals
trailing behind. You stood by watching white privileged teachers getting
hired for being in the same fanbase of a football or hockey team as the head
of the school, or the familiarity of shared white cultures, hometowns and
cities. You have witnessed schools operate as mid-twentieth century colonial
schools in order to keep their local expatriate populations happy.

(Abdelmagid, 2020)

International school consultant Proserpina Dlamini-Fisher states that "Schools
rationalize the terrible practice of excluding teachers and leaders of color by
citing parent expectations [and] visa laws" (Dlamini-Fisher, 2020).

This is paradoxical because international schools' normative values are centred on global citizenship and intercultural competences. However, as Council of International School administrator Nunana Nyomi (2020) points out, "International education is so financially dependent on the elite players in a western-dominant global financial system grounded in slavery, (neo)colonialism and hegemony, that we should not be surprised that our institutional stances on diversity have fallen short in achieving racial equity." He also points out that "93% of the leaders in American international schools [are] white" (Nyomi 2020).

The perception of racism in international schools, therefore, at least on the part of vocal bloggers working in international schools, is that it is a major problem that occurs at the level of recruitment. This goes back to the central tension in international schools that exists between an overarching mission statement based on normative values and an operational structure that is largely pragmatic, as outlined in Chapter 6 in this volume. The accusations made against the administrators of international schools is that they are not sufficiently inclusive in their recruitment practices, and therefore are continuing a system of elitism that privileges one group over others and operates in closed circuits of power.

Solutions to addressing this perception include more concerted efforts to recruit diversely and more explicit, open discussions about colour-blindness, privilege and racism in international schools.

A counter-voice to the charge that international schools are racist would be the just-world hypothesis, stating that unequal positions of leadership in schools are not due to deliberately exclusivist practices but are an honest reflection of the competences and qualifications on the ground that are not necessarily distributed harmoniously across different social groups. This is not to say that a naturally unequal playing field is the result of biological and phenotypical differences but could be for a whole host of reasons including politico-historical legacy. Efforts to diversify staffing lead to positive discrimination, a new type of elitism and other systems of inequality.

Nicholas Tate points out that there is a new type of elite which he calls the "metro-elite", which is a type of social media-driven politically correct force. According to Tate, this includes

Politicians, the BBC, academics, artists, 'luvvies', celebrities, public pontificators and verbalists of all kinds – which set the limits of debate and thrust their own vision of the world on the rest of society at every opportunity: on immigration, diversity, health, Europe, Islam, matters of personal morals and habits, and on what can and cannot be thought and said. The sense of power of this elite has been enhanced by the spread of 'social media' and the way in which these can permit vocal minorities supporting 'elite opinions' to bully into submission those with alternative points of view.

(2018, p. 56)

Cancel culture

As the Black Lives Matter and Rhodes Must Fall movements became stronger and more vocal during 2020, various celebrities posted their views related to identity politics on social media. Some of these postings received strong reactions and even a calling to "cancel" them.

Defined as "a social climate in which a person, organization, etc is likely to be ostracized in response to a perceived wrongdoing" (Collins, 2020), cancel culture, according to the American academic Lisa Nakamura, is a form of "cultural boycott … an agreement not to amplify, signal boost, give money" (cited in Bromwich, 2018). When a public figure, usually in the entertainment industry, is "called out" for posting or saying something polemical and perceived as discriminatory (such as the American rapper Kanye West claiming that slavery was a choice or British author JK Rowling tweeting her views on transgenderism), active groups on social media can proclaim them "cancelled", which means that the general public is called upon to ignore their views and statements. Media studies specialist Meredith Clark calls this "an act of withdrawing from someone whose expression—whether political, artistic or otherwise—was once welcome or at least tolerated, but no longer is" (cited in Bromwich, 2018).

In relation to the debate about elitism and education, cancel culture is a strongly anti-elitist phenomenon that is changing the dynamic of who has the power to express views and how it is done. Since online communities act against public voices, they are creating a deinstitutionalised and decentralised culture of communal accountability. The old order meant that voices of authority would be broadcast by a third party—usually a publisher or producer—and the public would receive this information somewhat passively. Social media facilitates a dynamic interaction between spokespeople and recipients, so that everyone, technically speaking, has a voice, at least in countries where social media is allowed, thereby flattening the traditional hierarchy of information dissemination and reception. For anti-elitists, this is a more egalitarian situation, allowing communal views to be shared and forcing levels of accountability onto the elite who face a live, active and worldwide audience. For elitists, it is something of a mob rule climate where necessary protocol and hierarchy are disrupted by a type of kangaroo court.

There is a clear link between cancel culture and the Rhodes Must Fall/Black Lives Matter attacks on statues in that, in both cases, citizens act directly without the intercession of public authorities. Statesmen like Boris Johnson and Donald Trump are not in favour of this as it indicates, from their perspective of organised leadership, a type of anarchy. In 2020 there was an upswell in this particular tension and it suggests that future relationships between power and discourse will escape at least some of the elitist trappings of the past. Of course, we should not forget Nicholas Tate's warning that a power group, even if it appears to be anti-elitist and grassroots, can come to represent a new elite.

The implications for schools and universities are substantial as "calling out", "no platforming" and "cancellation" tend to be direct expressions of students without the endorsement of the institution's administration. Often, it is the students themselves who impose a cancellation on a public speaker in direct confrontation with the administration.

Culture wars

University of Chicago President Robert Zimmer, after allowing the polemical and—according to many—openly racist political advisor Steve Bannon to be invited to speak at the university, stated in 2018 that "the ideas of different members of the university community will often and quite naturally conflict. But it is not the proper role of the university to attempt to shield individuals from ideas and opinions they find unwelcome, disagreeable, or even deeply offensive" (cited in Marek, 2018). A group representing the Chicago University School of Social Service Administration issued a public statement in response which explained that, while believing in academic freedom, it was "essential that we acknowledge that some members of our community are uniquely at risk of being harmed by expressions that question their intellect, culture, humanity and whether they belong in this country" (SSA, 2020). This is an example of a cultural battle between absolute freedom of speech on the one hand, allowing offensive statements to be made in public, and protecting victims of discrimination and what are perceived as dehumanising ideologies on the other.

The debate goes beyond the core principle of freedom of speech, however, as politically it represents a conflict between the university administration and the larger community that essentially comprises active students. This signifies an erosion of classic elitism in that unilateral decisions taken by executive powers are no longer as simple for academics or even the vice-chancellor to make. Cancel culture is a counterpoint to elite authority.

On July 7, 2020 a group of 153 public intellectuals published an open letter in *Harper's Magazine* in which they expressed concern about cancel culture:

> Censoriousness is also spreading more widely in our culture: an intolerance of opposing views, a vogue for public shaming and ostracism, and the tendency to dissolve complex policy issues in a blinding moral certainty. We uphold the value of robust and even caustic counter-speech from all quarters. But it is now all too common to hear calls for swift and severe retribution in response to perceived transgressions of speech and thought.
> (Ackerman et al., 2020)

In the letter the authors mention, without giving precise details or palpable examples, cases of people losing their jobs because they have made statements or taken positions that were not perceived to be politically correct. The letter argues that freedom of speech, a cornerstone of Western democracy, is threatened.

Journalist Rachel John responded to the letter by saying that

> a look at the signatories of the letter indicates that certain parameters needed to be considered—a large following, prominence, wealth. In a nutshell, they are all privileged. Thus, when people who already have a massive platform lament the lack of one, forgive me for being uncomfortable.
>
> (John, 2020)

She goes on to point out that many of the members of the elite who have been "cancelled" (which essentially means that they had been lambasted on social media) were not particularly perturbed professionally by this:

> After [JK Rowling's] anti-trans tweet, where she basically erased the lived experiences of trans women, she did face massive backlash. But other than perhaps hurting her feelings, she is still pretty much the same. Still powerful, still rich and still very much making her anti-trans stance public.
>
> (John, 2020)

She discusses the MeToo movement of 2017 and 2018 when a number of cases of violence against women, misogyny and sexism were "called out" only to leave powerful men in elitist circles free of any lasting damage:

> Looking back, three years later, several of these men who were allegedly 'cancelled' then have found their way back to their professional spheres. People like former Hollywood producer Harvey Weinstein, despite being convicted, still hold enough sway—when a female comedian criticised him, she was the one lambasted.
>
> (John, 2020)

The *Harper's Magazine* open letter caused a strong response in the form of another open letter signed by a large group of journalists who took issue with its positioning, claiming that the real concern behind the letter was that "in truth, Black, brown, and LGBTQ+ people—particularly Black and trans people—can now critique elites publicly and hold them accountable socially; this seems to be the letter's greatest concern" (Binowski et al., 2020). The second open letter also explains that the authors of the *Harper's Magazine* open letter

> are afforded the type of cultural capital from social media that institutions like Harper's have traditionally conferred to mostly white, cisgender people. Their words reflect a stubbornness to let go of the elitism that still pervades the media industry, an unwillingness to dismantle systems that keep people like them in and the rest of us out.
>
> (Binowski et al., 2020)

Therefore, the fundamental debate underpinning the *Harper's Magazine* letter and its rebuttal is about elitism. Although the stage for the debate is on what, on one side of the fence, some would call excessive, unbridled discriminatory speech and, on the other side of the fence, others would call politically correct coercion and closed mindedness, the actual structural dynamic of the debate is a culture war involving an in-group that historically has had a privileged voice and a larger out-group of traditionally silenced figures who have not been able to position themselves with the same authority.

It is the use of Twitter and social media that undergirds this conflict since privileged platforms are no longer exclusive and have to co-exist alongside grassroots level platforms that involve millions of common people. There is also a generational divide in the discussion, with the defenders of classical freedom of speech (which could be deconstructed as elitist, privileged access to discourse) as "baby boomers", whereas the younger social media-savvy counter-voices are Generation X and Z voices, speaking from a contemporary perspective where notions of the ivory tower, appeal to authority and elitism do not function in the same manner.

The cultural war centred on cancel culture is more subtle and deep-running than it may appear as it is creating a reality whereby, like many new technology-driven processes such as blockchain economics, everyone is watching everyone else, generating new levels of accountability and disrupting older systems of privilege. Future elites will have to find ways of surviving in this environment that could be seen as a healthy democracy or the tyranny of the masses, depending, of course, on whether the view taken is elitist or anti-elitist.

This has broad ideological and philosophical ramifications for the world of education:

- Where does trustworthy knowledge come from? Who is vetting it?
- To what extent does elitist privilege and power influence the choice, perspective and character of distributed information?
- How do we analyse past sources of information in the light of the new paradigm of crowd wisdom?

And at the concrete on-the-ground level, the following questions might be evoked in schools and universities:

- How executive and top-down is the decision making on what goes into the curriculum?
- What role do students play in defining the moral parameters by which public and political figures can be judged?
- What is the role of social media in defining contemporary meaning-making narratives?

How the events of 2020 might reduce elitism

Open education resources

UNESCO responded to the COVID-19 pandemic by making available a number of open education resources through a global partnership with non-governmental organisations and the private and civil sectors of the economy (UNESCO, 2020c), and other initiatives such as #OER4Covid and the EdTEch hub have done this too. Governments have shared resources for home-schooling (Gov.UK, 2020).

The degree of partnership, sharing of resources and collaboration that the COVID-19 pandemic has created, has broken down some of the walls that traditionally separate elite institutions from non-elite institutions. The spirit of partnership that has prevailed has changed relationships and perspectives, possibly in permanent ways. It could be that greater access to quality and degree-awarding educational experiences will be enabled by post-COVID-19 synergies.

Some elite tertiary institutions have expanded their provision through free online platforms. These include Carnegie Mellon University's "Open Learning Initiative", Duke's classes through Coursera and Harvard's through edX, MIT's "OpenCourseWare" and Stanford's MOOCs (Ladders, 2019). However, it should be noted that these are non-credit courses and most often do not involve interaction with instructors or graded assignments so one might argue that while the principle is a good one, in practice it is a largely symbolic offering.

Social media

From the killing of George Floyd to the open denunciation of various authorities, both past and present, in the world of politics, entertainment and public affairs, social media has democratised information, created new levels of accountability and may well continue to do so in the future: "Twitter has in a way democratised the business of opinions. Now, instead of a one-way spoon feeding, people can actively engage with what they deem as problematic" (John, 2020). This means that cultural elitism, whereby canons of knowledge are given value by gatekeepers such as critics and academics, is being recalibrated. Elite knowledge, which is rare and arcane by nature, and has characterised the make-up of selectiveness and exclusivity for centuries, is imploding, losing relevance and is being superseded by common knowledge. Furthermore, opinions are no longer scripted by authorities but are developed in an ongoing thread of public views that interact.

Most importantly in terms of the sociology of elitism, the figures that are frequently "called out" or "cancelled" on social media can no longer enjoy the summit of power that they would in an institutional ivory tower; instead, they are at the mercy of the crowd. This democratises the process of curriculum design—curriculum in the largest informal sense here—and forces a review of culturally elitist prerogatives.

Black Lives Matter and Rhodes Must Fall

The protests and debates of 2020 have led to the accelerated circulation of curriculum materials that reposition the narrative of history from a less elitist viewpoint. These include the Zinn Education Project, a series of resources that started to be developed in 2008 in the vein of the thinking of the late political scientist Howard Zinn (1922–2010). Its website states that:

> A people's history flips the script. When we look at history from the standpoint of the workers and not just the owners, the soldiers and not just the generals, the invaded and not just the invaders, we can begin to see society more fully, more accurately. The more clearly we see the past, the more clearly we'll see the present—and be equipped to improve it.
>
> (Zinn Education Project, 2020)

Books such as Jill Lepore's *These Truths* (2018), a race-conscious political history of the United States or David Olusoga's *The Kaiser's Holocaust: Germany's Forgotten Genocide and the Colonial Roots of Nazism* (2010), a history of the genocide against the Herero and Nama peoples in Namibia, or his *Black and British: A Forgotten History* (2017), a recounting of black people's historical experience in Britain, inform a postcolonial reading of history in schools and universities. Furthermore, a number of publishers and resource distributors have made available texts that teach anti-racism, inclusivity and egalitarianism (see Reeve, 2020; Harvard Kennedy School, 2020). *Understanding Prejudice and Education: The Challenge for Future Generations* (2017) by the author of this chapter offers schools a framework to reduce inequalities and elitism based on race, gender and identity.

How the events of 2020 might exacerbate elitism

The COVID-19 pandemic, with the changes in the structure and offer of schools and universities that it brings, might erode the dream of equality and instead exacerbate elitism and the gap between the privileged and those lacking sufficient learning resources.

Private schools and universities racing ahead

As pandemics such as COVID-19 create uncertainty and require a nimble institutional response, state systems can appear unwieldy in comparison to the private sector. As a head of an independent school in Canada says:

> [I]t's an opportunity for independent schools to showcase what makes us unique and special—to be nimble, to pivot, to respond to changing

conditions … I think independent school teachers are a special breed, and right now, they are perhaps uniquely well-positioned.

(Our Kids, 2020)

Schools will be judged by their responses to disruption as well as the extent to which they can prepare young people to navigate complexity and uncertainty. Private schools can move quickly and are in a better position to respond to the needs of parents than are state schools:

> While public schools must practice 6-feet social distancing, limit class sizes, and require face coverings, hundreds of North Carolina private schools have the autonomy to decide how to resume lessons during the coronavirus. No single approach categorizes all private schools, but many—like Grace Christian—plan for more aggressive reopenings as school leaders say families and staff are ready to reenter classrooms.
>
> (Gordon, 2020)

It may well be that parents are prepared to pay more to ensure that their children are in private school environments that absorb disruption better than the somewhat clunky, massive state system. Elitism in this case becomes a case of avoiding potentially serious gaps in learning.

With regard to universities, there is something of a consensus that online learning is not at the same level of quality as face-to-face learning and there have been numerous lawsuits against universities in the United States with students demanding tuition and fee refunds (Keshner, 2020). However, elite universities are confident that their value proposition is still worth the cost and will not budge (Berman, 2020). This confidence shows that the very top-tier institutions realise that disruption intensifies elitism and does not dilute it: the reputation of an Oxbridge or Ivy League degree will become even more important as the socioeconomic climate becomes more turbulent, somewhat in the manner that the value of gold renews its stability in times of economic turmoil.

Blurring the waters of meritocratic elitism

When highly disruptive factors interfere with admissions protocols, it becomes less clear how students will be selected for entry into elite institutions. Hence, departments of education and admissions boards have had to rethink entry criteria since test scores, attendance rates and examinations are no longer always available (Brody, 2020). Increasing numbers of top-tier universities in the United States are moving away from standardised tests and are seeking other metrics.

However, issues of rater bias, unfairness and increased social inequality come to the fore when a standardised instrument is no longer used (Nadworny, 2020): if candidates are no longer assessed through the prism of reliable test scores and examination results, it may well intensify in-grouping, corruption and meritocratic elitism, since SATs were actually designed to protect ethnic minorities that were disfavoured by interviews and more qualitative admissions measures (Riley, 2020).

Superficial approaches to diversity allowing the continuation of discriminatory practice

Although the Black Lives Matter and Rhodes Must Fall movements evoked strong reactions in the media and seem to pave the way for much reform and rethinking of social hierarchy in educational institutions and in the way educational narratives paint reality for students, there is a risk that these movements will merely follow a hype cycle and, after a superficial buzz, die out, leaving iniquitous systems in place.

University of Boston sociologist Saida Grandy suggests that institutional responses involving guest speakers, professional development or reading lists, create an excuse not to take any meaningful, structural action:

> When offered in lieu of actionable policies regarding equity, consciousness raising can actually undermine Black progress by presenting increased knowledge as the balm for centuries of abuse. Executives at major corporations such as Amazon, for instance, have invited race scholars and writers to "help [them] unpack" such topics as the American justice system and how to be an anti-racist ally. Yet Black employees at many of these companies have pointed to the hypocrisy of in-house dialogues about race while practices like labor exploitation continue. In the form of hollow public statements and company-sponsored conversations, consciousness raising is often toothless.
>
> (Grundy, 2020)

By paying lip service to this form of social and cultural elitism, little will be done to truly address it, meaning that it will continue in covert forms against a rhetoric pointing in the opposite directions. This scenario, from an anti-elitist perspective, would make matters worse.

Conclusion

Thus, 2020 is a watershed year because of the massive disruption it has caused to society, physically, structurally and symbolically. The constant has been change. The French philosopher Edger Morin argues that the "new normal" is the unexcepted:

> All the 20th-century futurologies that predicted the future by carrying currents through the present into the future have collapsed. Yet we

continue to predict 2025 and 2050 while we are unable to understand 2020. The experience of the eruption of the unexpected in history has barely penetrated consciousness. The arrival of the unpredictable was foreseeable, but not its nature. Hence my permanent maxim: "Expect the unexpected".

(Morin, 2020, p. 3)

The big question is whether elitism intensifies with uncertainty, or whether it is reduced. One argument, following what history has shown us, is that elitist structures are strengthened by uncertainty: the English and French revolutions created new, secular forms of monarchy; the Bolshevik Revolution gave way to an elitist inner circle of leadership; and independence movements across Africa heralded the ascendancy of elitist dictatorships. Another opposing viewpoint is that a more egalitarian state of affairs comes about in the wake of great turmoil: access to wealth was more open after the First and Second World Wars, and the Black Death essentially destroyed the feudal system.

This book has argued that educational elitism tends to follow broader socio-economic and technological developments. It stands to reason, therefore, that access to education and questions about elitism and education will follow the broader social trajectory of life after the events of 2020. What exactly that trajectory will be remains to be seen.

References

Abdelmagid, S. (2020). Black lives should have always mattered: An open letter to search associates. *Medium.* https://medium.com/@mabrouka/black-lives-should-have-always-mattered-an-open-letter-to-search-associates-ad8e688f1cd1.

Ackerman, E. *et al.* (2020). A letter on justice and open debate. *Harper's Magazine.* https://harpers.org/a-letter-on-justice-and-open-debate/.

Anderson, T. (1988). Black encounter of racism and elitism in white academe: A critique of the system. *Journal of Black Studies,* 18(3), 259–272. https://doi.org/10.1177/002193478801800301.

Berman, J. (2020). Harvard and other elite schools say classes will be mostly remote this fall. *MarketWatch.* www.marketwatch.com/story/as-pandemic-rages-prominent-colleges-announce-online-semesters-11594130062.

Binowski, B. *et al.* (2020). A more specific letter on justice and open debate. *The Objective.* https://theobjective.substack.com/p/a-more-specific-letter-on-justice.

British Broadcasting Corporation (BBC) (2020). George Floyd: Timeline of black deaths caused by police. BBC News. www.bbc.com/news/world-us-canada-52905408.

Brody, L. (2020). Coronavirus forces New York City to rethink admissions to elite schools. *Wall Street Journal.* www.wsj.com/articles/coronavirus-forces-new-york-city-to-rethink-admissions-to-elite-schools-11589485405.

Bromwich, J. E. (2018). Everyone is canceled. *New York Times.* www.nytimes.com/2018/06/28/style/is-it-canceled.html.

Burke, L. (2020). The coronavirus will crush the private school industry. *National Interest.* http s://nationalinterest.org/feature/coronavirus-will-crush-private-school-industry-162673.

Collins English Dictionary (2020). Cancel culture. *Collins English Dictionary.* www.col linsdictionary.com.

Cotnam, H. (2020). `Fed up families exploring private school options. CBC. www.cbc. ca/news/canada/ottawa/covid-19-school-return-private-schools-increased-interest-1. 5623540.

Coughlan, S. (2020). Don't hide history, says Oxford head in statue row. BBC News. www.bbc.com/news/education-52999319.

Di Pietro, G., Biagi, F., Costa, P., Karpiński Z., and Mazza, J. (2020). *The Likely Impact of COVID-19 on Education: Reflections Based on the Existing Literature and International Datasets.* Luxembourg: Publications Office of the European Union. doi:doi:10.2760/126686.

Dickler, J. (2020). When it comes to public vs. private schools, some families may choose based on reopening plans. CNBC. www.cnbc.com/2020/07/14/public-vs-p rivate-school-it-could-come-down-to-the-reopening-plan.html.

Dlamini-Fisher, P. (2020). Racism in Recruiting: The elephant in our international education room. *The International Educator.* www.tieonline.com/article/2725/racism -in-recruiting-the-elephant-in-our-international-education-room.

The Economist (2020a). How covid-19 is interrupting children's education. *The Economist,* March 18. www.economist.com/international/2020/03/19/how-covid-19-is-interrup ting-childrens-education.

The Economist (2020b). The risks of keeping schools closed far outweigh the benefits. *The Economist.* www.economist.com/leaders/2020/07/18/the-risks-of-keeping-schools-closed -far-outweigh-the-benefits?fsrc=newsletter&utm_campaign=the-economist-today&utm_ medium=newsletter&utm_source=salesforce-marketing-cloud&utm_term=2020-07-17& utm_content=article-link-1.

EdTech Hub (2020). *Open Educational Resources.* https://edtechhub.org/coronavirus/oer/.

Faulconbridge, G. (2020). COVID-19 shines a light on inequality, Britain's elite Eton College says. Reuters. www.reuters.com/article/us-health-coronavirus-britain-eton-idU SKBN22E0E9.

Filkins, K.M. (1998). Revisiting the bell curve: Refuting classism, racism, and elitism measured lies: The bell curve examined. *Educational Forum,* 62(2), 188–189. doi: doi:10.1080/00131729808983806.

Giannini, S., & Albrectsen, A.B. (2020). Covid-19 school closures around the world will hit girls hardest. UNESCO. https://en.unesco.org/news/covid-19-school-closures-a round-world-will-hit-girls-hardest.

Goldstein, D. (2020). The class divide: Remote learning at 2 schools, private and public. *New York Times.* www.nytimes.com/2020/05/09/us/coronavirus-public-private-school. html.

Gordon, B. (2020). With more autonomy, N.C. private schools plan more aggressive reopenings. *Citizen Times.* https://eu.citizen-times.com/story/news/local/2020/07/26/ nc-private-schools-reopen-full-classrooms-students-during-covid-19/5477899002/.

Gov.UK (2020). *Online Education Resources for Home Learning.* www.gov.uk/governm ent/publications/coronavirus-covid-19-online-education-resources.

Grundy, S. (2020). The false promise of anti-racism books. *The Atlantic.* www.theatlantic. com/culture/archive/2020/07/your-anti-racism-books-are-means-not-end/614281/.

Harvard Kennedy School (2020). *Racial Justice, Racial Equity, and Anti-Racism Reading List*. www.hks.harvard.edu/faculty-research/library-knowledge-services/collections/diversity-inclusion-belonging/anti-racist.

Hughes, C. (2017). *Understanding Prejudice and Education: The Challenge for Future Generations*. Oxford: Routledge.

Hussain, M. (2020). Why is my curriculum white?National Union of Students. www.nus.org.uk/en/news/why-is-my-curriculum-white/.

Isaeva, L. (2020). Opinion: Face-to-face lectures in Cambridge have been cut, so why haven't tuition fees? *The Tab*. https://thetab.com/uk/cambridge/2020/05/23/opinion-face-to-face-lectures-in-cambridge-have-been-cut-so-why-havent-tuition-fees-138011.

Iyengar, R. (2020). Education as the path to a sustainable recovery from COVID-19. *Prospects*. https://doi.org/10.1007/s11125-020-09488-9.

Jha, J., & Ghatak, N. (2020). What a survey of children in Bihar revealed about online schooling. *The Wire*. https://thewire.in/education/online-school-education.

John, R. (2020). Obama, Chomsky called out the cancel culture. Are they baiting us to yell "OK, boomer"? *The Print*. https://theprint.in/opinion/pov/obama-chomsky-called-out-the-cancel-culture-are-they-baiting-us-to-yell-ok-boomer/463398/.

Keshner, A. (2020). At least 100 lawsuits have been filed by students seeking college refunds—and they open some thorny questions. *MarketWatch*. www.marketwatch.com/story/unprecedented-lawsuits-from-students-suing-colleges-amid-the-coronavirus-outbreak-raise-3-thorny-questions-for-higher-education-2020-05-21?mod=article_inline.

Ladders (2019) *7 elite universities offering free online classes*. www.theladders.com/career-advice/7-elite-universities-offering-free-online-online-classes.

Lake, R., & Makori, A. (2020). The digital divide among students during COVID-19: Who has access? who doesn't? *The Lens*. https://www.crpe.org/thelens/digital-divide-among-students-during-covid-19-who-has-access-who-doesnt.

Lander, M. (2020). In an English city, an early benefactor is now "a toxic brand". *New York Times*. www.nytimes.com/2020/06/14/world/europe/Bristol-Colston-statue-slavery.html.

Lepore, J. (2018). *These Truths: A History of the United States*. New York: Norton.

Lewin, K.M. (2020). Contingent reflections on coronavirus and priorities for educational planning and development. *Prospects*. https://doi.org/10.1007/s11125-020-09480-3.

McClusky, N. (2020). Private school COVID-19 permanent closure tracker. Cato at Liberty. www.cato.org/blog/private-school-covid-19-permanent-closure-tracker.

Marek, L. (2018). U of C stakes its claim as the anti-Berkeley. *Crain's Chicago Business*. www.chicagobusiness.com/article/20180202/ISSUE01/180209960/university-of-chicago-s-zimmer-as-free-speech-protector.

Mednick, S. (2020). In Burkina Faso, violence and COVID-19 push children out of school and into harm's way. *New Humanitarian*. www.thenewhumanitarian.org/news-feature/2020/07/07/Burkina-Faso-children-coronavirus-jihadists-Sahel.

Morin, E. (2020). *Un festival d'incertitudes. Tracts de crise: Un virus et des hommes*. Paris: Gallimard, pp. 404–419.

Mukeredzi, T., Kokutse, F., & Dell, S. (2020). Student bodies say e-learning is unaffordable and elitist. *University World News*. www.universityworldnews.com/post.php?story=20200422075107312.

Nadworny, E. (2020). Colleges are backing off SAT, ACT scores: But the exams will be hard to shake. NPR. https://www.npr.org/2020/06/12/875367144/colleges-are-backing-off-sat-act-scores-but-the-exams-will-be-hard-to-shake?t=1596016268642.

Nwonka, C. (2020). Elite universities are too obsessed with tradition to tackle racism effectively. *The Guardian*. www.theguardian.com/education/2019/oct/10/elite-universities-are-too-obsessed-with-tradition-to-tackle-racism-effectively.

Nyomi, N. (2020). International education perpetuates structural racism and anti-racism is the solution. *CIS Persepctives*. www.cois.org/about-cis/perspectives-blog/blog-post/~board/perspectives-blog/post/international-education-perpetuates-structural-racism-and-anti-racism-is-the-solution.

OER4Covid (2020). *OER support group for educators during covid19*. https://oer4covid.oeru.org/.

Olusoga, D., & Erichsen, C.W. (2011). *The Kaiser's Holocaust: Germany's Forgotten Genocide and the Colonial Roots of Nazism*. London: Faber & Faber.

Olusoga, D. (2017). *Black and British: A Forgotten History*. London: Pan Books.

Our Kids (2020). *Private schools' response to COVID-19*. www.ourkids.net/school/responding-to-covid-19.

Perez Ortega, R. (2020). Ancient viruses found in Tibetan glacier. *Science*. www.sciencemag.org/news/2020/01/ancient-viruses-found-tibetan-glacier.

Reeve, J. (2020). 14 antiracist books for kids and teens recommended by BIPOC teachers and librarians. *New York Times Wirecutter*. www.nytimes.com/wirecutter/reviews/antiracist-books-for-kids-and-teens/.

Rigney, D. (2010). *The Matthew Effect: How Advantage Begets Further Advantage*. New York: Columbia University Press. doi:doi:10.7312/rign14948.

Riley, J. (2020). Scrapping the SAT won't help black and Latino students. *WSJ Opinion*. www.wsj.com/articles/scrapping-the-sat-wont-help-black-and-latino-students-11590532734.

School of Social Service Administration (SSA) (2020). *SSA Statement on Steve Bannon Invitation*. www.ssa.uchicago.edu/ssa-statement-steve-bannon-invitation.

Seltzer, R. (2020). Pricing pressures escalate. *Inside Higher Ed*. www.insidehighered.com/news/2020/04/27/tuition-freezes-and-cuts-show-colleges-and-universities-are-face-downward-price.

Sheng, E. (2020). The threat unleashed by the coronavirus that could make traditional college degrees obsolete. CNBC. www.cnbc.com/2020/06/17/threat-unleashed-by-covid-that-could-sink-high-priced-college-degrees.html.

Tate, N. (2018). *The Conservative Case for Education: Against the Current*. Abingdon: Routledge.

Toye, R. (2020). Yes, Churchill was a racist. It's time to break free of his "great white men" view of history. CNN. https://edition.cnn.com/2020/06/10/opinions/churchill-racist-great-white-men-view-toye-opinion/index.html.

Turner, C., & Stephens, M. (2020). 30 private schools preparing to close due to Covid-19. *The Telegraph*. www.telegraph.co.uk/news/2020/06/06/30-private-schools-preparing-close-due-covid-19/.

Tyler, F.B. (2001). Elitism, Racism, and Professionalism. *Cultures, Communities, Competence, and Change*. The Springer Series in Social/Clinical Psychology. Boston, MA: Springer.

United Nations Educational, Scientific and Cultural Organization (UNESCO) (2020a). *COVID-19 Educational Disruption and Response*. https://en.unesco.org/covid19/educationresponse.

United Nations Educational, Scientific and Cultural Organization (UNESCO) (2020b). *COVID-19 Impact on Education*. https://en.unesco.org/covid19/educationresponse.

United Nations Educational, Scientific and Cultural Organization (UNESCO) (2020c). *Global Education Coalition.* https://en.unesco.org/covid19/educationresponse/globa lcoalition.

Vogels, E.A., Perrin, A., Rainie, L., & Anderson, M. (2020). 53% of Americans say the internet has been essential during the COVID-19 outbreak. Pew Research Center. www.pewresearch.org/internet/2020/04/30/53-of-americans-say-the-internet-has-bee n-essential-during-the-covid-19-outbreak/.

Walker, P. (2020). "We cannot edit our past": Boris Johnson's statue tweets explained. *The Guardian.* www.theguardian.com/politics/2020/jun/12/we-cannot-edit-our-pa st-boris-johnsons-statue-tweets-explained.

Walsh, C. (2020). Must we allow symbols of racism on public land? *Harvard Gazette.* https:// news.harvard.edu/gazette/story/2020/06/historian-puts-the-push-to-remove-confedera te-statues-in-context/.

The White House (2020). *Executive Order on Protecting American Monuments, Memorials, and Statues and Combating Recent Criminal Violence.* www.whitehouse.gov/presidentia l-actions/executive-order-protecting-american-monuments-memorials-statues-comba ting-recent-criminal-violence/.

Witze, A. (2020). Universities will never be the same after the coronavirus crisis. *Nature,* 582, 162–164. www.nature.com/articles/d41586-020-01518-y.

World Food Programme (WFP) (2020). *New digital map shows terrible impact of COVID-19 on school meals around the world.* www.wfp.org/news/new-digital-map-shows-terri ble-impact-covid-19-school-meals-around-world.

World Health Organization (WHO) (2020). *Coronavirus disease (COVID-19) pandemic.* www.who.int/emergencies/diseases/novel-coronavirus-2019.

Zinn Education Project (2020). *Zinn Education Project.* www.zinnedproject.org/.

Part III

Solutions

Chapter 9

Reconciling education and elitism

Zach and Anthony

Zach's great-grandfather never went to school. However, this does not mean that this great-grandfather did not receive an education. He knew the customs of his people; he knew how to build a traditional house; and he understood the ancient oral tradition that was passed down to him by his father and grandfather. He came from a generation when every child knew these traditions. Education was something that happened informally through the oral tradition, and through community meetings when the elders spoke, and the transmission of farming methods was a living thread that ran from generation to generation.

The most mesmerising instances of this oral tradition of education took place when stories, myths and fables were related by the elders around a fire late at night. This was when the youth of the village would learn about the sacred spirits in the world of the unborn, the secret power of certain animals, and how ancient traditions, such as the sharing of food and the obligatory welcome one should give a stranger, came from rites and customs.

From the colonial perspective, education only started with the arrival of the missionaries, but in reality it had always been there, whispered by mothers to their children, acted out dramatically by storytellers, sung through the piercing narrative of the village griots and inscribed in the traditions of village life. Access to this type of education was lost during the colonial period: the children of Burkina Faso were "given" a compulsory education that taught them about France, gave them the French language but disrupted and essentially destroyed the traditional education they had been receiving for generations.

From his great-grandfather down to his father and finally to Zach himself, the transmission of culture and heritage had been disrupted, while education had become less and less relevant, and more of an empty exercise done under poor conditions. Hopefully it would allow Zach to progress in life, for despite his experiences, this is what he had been told and what he believed. His dream of becoming a great football player remained hidden in his heart, carefully wrapped in secrets and hopes. That was the ticket to a higher plain, away from the dead end where he found himself and, increasingly, could sense was all around him.

Anthony's great-grandfather had not been to school either. He had lived through the terrible trials and tribulations of serfdom when there was little to eat and it was bitterly cold during the winter months. But the transmission of culture was strong, and the stories of Baba Yaga and the Orthodox faith were passed down carefully. The Soviet regime undid much of that culture but brought another, more academic education to the people of Russia, which had been of benefit to Anthony's father and grandfathers.

However, it was Anthony's father who broke free of the gridlock of poverty that had gripped the family. It was because of him that the gilded path opened up for Anthony. Although Anthony has easy access to free education in Switzerland, a high-performing education system belonging to one of the best human capital development hubs in the world, his father chose to send him to a private boarding school. His parents briefly discussed the merits of him attending a state school and quickly came to the conclusion that it would not be good for either his social codes or network. At the state schools, Anthony's mother complained one night over dinner, children swear and smoke, they speak with rough accents and, perhaps most importantly, they come out of school with a poor grasp of English. English is the language of global trade, the language of success, and with the kind of money Anthony's father was making, it was just not on the agenda to even consider that Anthony might leave school without being proficient in that language. Besides, the plan for him to go to a top-tier university after school would become complicated if his English was not at native speaker level. And the plan was not just to have Anthony get by in English with basic interpersonal skills for transactional and functional use, the idea was to have him master the idioms and subtleties of the Anglophone world, to speak with the smooth confidence of the native speaker who would rub shoulders with Oxbridge and Ivy League graduates, with their polished accents and air of calm self-assurance.

Anthony's father felt self-conscious about his strong accent; he wanted his son to mix and mingle with Wall Street traders, Silicone Valley CEOs and venture capitalists with ease, laughing at the same jokes, speaking with the sophisticated elision, imagery and in-house references that American and British businessmen share in locker rooms and over lunch. Anthony's father had had to bear the brunt of subtle frowns, bemused smiles and chuckles along with the occasional sarcastic comment as he built up his business empire, working with Anglo-Americans who, he always felt deep down inside, did not respect him because he was at a loss to respond to their cryptic stories about rowing, university clubs, political correctness movements or good French and Californian wines.

Anthony's father did not want Anthony to have to go through the same humiliating experiences as him. The boarding school option made sense, not only because the language of instruction was English, but because the staff were all from the United Kingdom, the United States, Canada or Australia. Even more reassuring was the fact that the headmaster had studied at Eton and Oxford: he told the students which books to read and ensured that they were acquiring the right manners. The irony was that most of the students at Anthony's boarding school came from the People's Republic of China, the Russian Federation and the Middle East, and they all spoke with an accent. But over time, their accents diffused into a mildly American, somewhat British third culture lilt that sounded like it belonged to someone who travelled the world, traded stocks and read several books a month.

How is it that Zach and Anthony live in such diametrically opposed circumstances: the vicious cycle of poverty on the one hand and the virtuous cycle of wealth on the other? What does it come down to? Is it luck? Fate? Hard work? Structural unfairness? Are the cards played in such a way that the game is unfair from the start, with the only available deal conferring the rights to propagate and to continue inequality?

And, as difficult and unfair as it might appear, could it be that inequality is a necessity? Could it be that the only way that a good education is to be experienced is for that education to be for the few and not for the many?

The divide

There is a spectrum that runs from Plato to Marx: from strong leadership, hierarchy and selection, to egalitarianism, equality and access. Discussions about elitism, whether they are in the realm of politics, economics, culture or education, tend to be polarised. It seems difficult to reconcile two positions that are so fundamentally opposed ontologically and socially.

On one side of the fence, those who protect the ivory tower warn of populism, of political correctness, inverse discrimination, a dropping of standards and, ultimately, mediocrity. Human political and social structures follow the laws of nature, so deeply embedded in the animal kingdom, whereby some are meant to rule and others are meant to follow. If this is understood and respected, society will be harmonious and productive as Plato predicted in his *Republic*.

On the other side of the fence, there are those who look at the ivory tower with dismay. For them, human society should strive for a world that gives equal opportunity, where there is compassion and continual efforts to help those who are falling behind, those who have been handicapped by the unfairness of social injustice. Just as the binding political texts of the Enlightenment such as the Bill of Rights and the Declaration of Independence decree, along with the 1947 United Nations Universal Declaration of Human Rights, human beings have unalienable rights, are born free and equal and, therefore, social structures should enable the greatest degree of equality and even equity. The resources of the world should be shared fairly and equally, much in the vein of the idealistic writings of Marx and Engels, or the less radical egalitarianists such as Jean-Jacques Rousseau or John Rawls.

And yet, for the future of education, a well-functioning society and that elusive goal of living together peacefully, it is essential to discuss the issue with an open mind, to fully understand both sides of the story. That is what this book has set out to do.

As we approach the second quarter of the 21st century, the world is threatened by multiple destructive forces: the annihilation of the environment, multiple economic recessions, health pandemics, extremism, xenophobia and an increasingly untenable divide between the haves and the have-nots globally. At the same time, new markets and economies, the rise of artificial intelligence, extraordinary scientific advances in fields such as medicine and communications mean that there are unprecedented opportunities that humanity has never had before. Therefore, reconciling a position of education and elitism is necessary, so as to bring to a halt the cultural wars, political disagreements and institutional tensions that are preventing a more fluid, mindful collaboration across the planet.

This chapter presents three major principles that seek to address the question of education and elitism in a sustainable fashion across different contexts and sectors of education. Before presenting these principles, it is helpful to summarise the positions for and against elitism in education.

Arguments for and against elitism in education

For cultural elitism

Following the theories of cultural critics, academics and theoreticians such as Matthew Arnold, TS Eliot, Harold Bloom, Roger Scruton and Christopher Hitchens—to mention just a few—cultural elitism essentially argues the following.

High culture is intellectually stimulating, refined and symbolically rich. It is superior to low culture, which is mass culture that entertains rather than probes, lulls into mindless and vegetative acceptance and carries little symbolic wealth. Schools and universities must transmit, defend and embellish high culture in order to empower young people with its virtues, which allow for an appreciation of the aesthetic, historical and even spiritual. If educational institutions do not vigorously promote high culture, young people will not access it elsewhere and those from less culturally developed families will fall even further behind. The central premise of cultural elitism is that knowledge is power, and that knowledge of the classics is vital.

Against cultural elitism

In line with the thinking of philosophers such as Raymond Williams, Michel Foucault and Ngũgĩ Wa Thiong'o, anti-cultural elitists argue that schooling tends to reproduce systems of cultural hegemony that colonise the mind and prevent the flourishing of free thought that might liberate students from mainly neoliberal ideology. Contemporary movements like Black Lives Matter and Rhodes Must Fall also criticise current cultural elitism as being skewed to represent white, Anglo-European power structures and argue that educational curricula and staffing in the 21st century should represent more cultural and ethnic diversity than they currently do.

For meritocratic elitism

In line with the thinking of JS Mill, ED Hirsch and many others, meritocratic elitism is based on the premise that education should allow the brightest students to flourish and progress. A meritocratic system, such as the grammar school, is academically selective and values the virtues of industry, acumen and intellect. A meritocratic system is fair in that it does not seek to bolster the socially advantaged or pull down the academically gifted but rewards talent. Meritocratic schools and universities stimulate cultural and intellectual production, creating healthy knowledge economies based on respect for knowledge and skill.

Against meritocratic elitism

Positions against meritocracy are nuanced, ranging from that of TS Eliot, who argued that meritocracies would create classes of technically adept but culturally indisposed individuals, incapable of quality cultural transmission; Michael Young, who warned of the dangers of a society that would become dehumanised in its value system by rewarding talent in a mechanical, excessively functional manner; Lampert (2013) who points out that meritocracies leave some behind, carrying feelings of worthlessness and despondency; and Jo Littler (2017) who, like many other commentators, has observed the socio-economic dynamics at work in meritocratic systems which, despite their good intentions, actually exacerbate class differences.

Arguments for plutocratic elitism

Although it is difficult to find public figures who openly put their names to the belief system of educational plutocracy, it is a strong and influential force. Following neoliberal concepts of a free market and quality driven by open competition, plutocratic elitists understand educational experience as an opportunity to design social networking opportunities where children's future successes will be enhanced by the class and station of their peers. Extremely expensive schools and universities force a social selectivity that ensures that a small, empowered elite experiences the full gamut of its social advantages. Plutocratic elitism sees education as access and opportunity and, therefore, it should be used pragmatically, politically and socially. If some have the means to access the most selective experience, then that phenomenon should be enhanced and encouraged, not destroyed in the name of egalitarianism.

Arguments against plutocratic elitism

The main argument against plutocratic elitism is based on Marxist principles of equality and class struggle. If educational institutions are ranked by cost and the most venerated and respected are out of reach to many children because of their financial means, it is morally unfair since education is supposed to be a right. Critics of plutocratic elitism, such as Paolo Freire, Peter McLaren and Michael Apple point out that schools reproduce class elitism by indoctrinating children into accepting neoliberal practices and discourses, often in unconscious and subtle ways.

A contemporary anti-plutocratic elitism stance is that which argues that educational institutions, particularly universities, have been hijacked by business models that are more focused on profit and enrolment dynamics than on educating students well and producing knowledge. Ultimately, the pressures of finance distort and damage the mission of education in its roles to enhance critical thinking and create social impact.

Disruption

From the first agricultural revolutions to the present day, human beings have codified and organised education according to the pressures of context. Surges in technology, economics, politics and demographics have all left their imprint on educational policy from the highly elitistist and exclusivist approach to the egalitarian, inclusive approach. Historic milestones have included the invention of writing, the printing press, the Industrial Revolution, two world wars and the internet. Twenty-first-century developments in the fields of artificial intelligence and block chain technologies will affect the dynamic of education and elitism further.

The year 2020 was a turning point for two reasons. First, the COVID-19 pandemic, causing the closure of schools and universities and heralding the introduction of online learning as a substitute for physically present learning, widened gaps educationally and socially, further enclaving elite groups and institutions and under-resourced groups and institutions. Second, the Black Lives Matter protests and ensuing debate about racism and representation intensified cultural battles over the privileged narratives, staffing and curriculum structure that have been in place in most educational and social institutions historically. Arguments about cancel culture, affirmative action, decolonising the curriculum and rethinking the past came to a head, opposing, among others, elitist and anti-elitist schools of thought.

Thus, 2020 was an ambivalent year because both of these social phenomena (COVID-19 and Black Lives Matter) have created, simultaneously, opposite consequences, intensifying and lessening elitism at the same time. There is a strong likelihood that the sustained aftermath of 2020 will be greater cultural egalitarianism (reforms in the representation and social status of ethnicity) but greater economic elitism (top-tier structures peeling away from the second and third tier even more rapidly). Therefore, the future will be at once more and less elitist in education.

Solutions

How to bridge the situation? Which principles should be emphasised in the policy decisions that governments, districts and boards will take and what might teachers, parents and every citizen do to strive for a world where the best of both the elitist and egalitarianist principles meet harmoniously?

Six essential steps might be considered. The first three work off the premise that elite institutions are still in operation and that the status quo has not been severely disrupted. The second three are more complex and seek to reduce the prominence of elite discourses and institutions by reviewing the underlying structure altogether to create a new approach.

State–private mergers

As state systems become increasingly massified and struggle to cope with demand and the private sector peels away from the mainstream ever more rapidly, every private institution should partner up with at least one state system in order to share best practice, ideas and even classes where possible. Many public schools in the UK are already committed to this course of action (such as Eton and Westminster) and if more institutions were to do the same, gaps between elite institutions and others would be reduced. Such initiatives could involve private schools running education centres directly for under-resourced communities, such as the work done by Wesley College Australia for first peoples in the Northern Territories. Remote learning opportunities enhanced by technology mean that state-private synergies can take place relatively easily. If private companies that sponsor social impact initiatives are serious about enhancing opportunities for children in less developed environments, they could sponsor such partnerships (teacher training programmes, merged or extra classes, teacher and student exchanges, etc).

Scholarship programmes

Students showing talent, competence and a positive attitude should be given opportunities to learn at top-ranking institutions. Therefore, private schools and universities should ensure that a quota of their annual enrolment is made up of full bursary students. Such schemes can be funded by a number of sources whether private, governmental or corporate. Scholarship admissions testing should be fair, done blind and based on criteria that not only reflect skills and knowledge enhanced by middle-class sociology (such as literacy, cultural and scientific references) but also on baseline psychometrics and raw ability. One way of ensuring that scholarships do not merely feed on the cycle of class and education is to restrict entry to lower-income brackets. Much of this is done already, of course, but not enough since studies show, overwhelmingly, that the current system favours middle-class children and not those, one might argue, most in need of access. However, scholarships do evoke an important question: if a possible solution to the problem of lack of access to educational quality is to select disadvantaged students and give them a well-provisioned experience, to what extent does this run the risk of merely converting that group into a future elitist class?

Cheaper private education

In an article in the *Spectator*, journalist James Tooley reports on the growth of low-cost international schools across Africa and South Asia:

> In Lagos State, Nigeria, alone, there are an estimated 14,000 low-cost private schools, serving two million children. In the slums of Monrovia, Liberia, enrolment in low-cost private schools is over 70 per cent—the same level that is common across urban sub-Saharan Africa and South Asia. In India, there are an estimated 400,000 low-cost private schools, serving 30 per cent of the rural population as well as the 70 per cent in urban areas.
>
> (Tooley, 2018)

He goes on to explain that

> testing random samples of children, controlling for background variables, shows children in low-cost private schools doing significantly better than those in government schools. Moreover, private schools are affordable even to those on the poverty line: typically, poor parents can find schools that won't require them to spend more than 10 per cent of their income on fees for all their children.
>
> (Tooley, 2018)

According to Tooley, this is something of an uncomfortable truth in that it flies in the face of development research in education that has long advocated for greater impact on social good coming from investment in state systems. His article, and an earlier one published in the *Spectator* in 2015 (see Tooley, 2015) argue that low-cost private schools are the answer to the massification of education and will effectively get us closer to achieving Sustainable Development Goal 4 than will improvements to the state system.

More robust state systems

At present, there is not enough investment in education to ensure high quality across the board.

> UNESCO's (2015) costing models estimate an annual total cost of $340 billion to achieve universal pre-primary, primary, and secondary education

in low- and lower-middle-income countries by 2030. The average annual per-student spending for quality primary education in a low-income country is predicted to be $197 in 2030, creating an estimated annual gap of $39 billion between 2015 and 2030. Financing this gap calls for action from private sector donors, philanthropists, and international financial institutions.

(Iyengard, 2020)

Lewin points out that "low and Low Middle Income countries (LICs and LMICs) will need to spend 6% of GDP [gross domestic product] and to collect more than 25% of GDP in revenue to achieve and sustain universal enrolment in schools of minimal quality" (Lewin, 2020). If standards are to be raised across the board so that highly selective elite institutions—usually private—do not overshadow and outstrip mainstream educational infrastructure, more work needs to be done on the ground to reinforce the state sector. This is not only a question of resource allocation though, it is equally a question of philosophy of education and choice of pedagogy: Hirsch (2006) has argued that stronger literacy programmes in all schools lessen the "Matthew effect" and has advocated for some time that a more knowledge-centred approach to schooling will create more fairness across all systems, socio-economically, in the long term (pp. 80–90).

However, it should be stated that this approach will not address the lure of sociological in-grouping that causes many to opt for elite private institutions. Much research has shown that such educational experiences do not actually add academic value so much as networking possibilities and that parents send their children to such schools for socio-economic rather than academic reasons. Nonetheless, greater human and resource investment in state education by governments will lessen the divide and distance between state and private.

More varied and multiple competences for higher education and employment admission

So long as universities and employers continue to use traditional metrics, references pegged on elite systems and performances on established standardised tests, it will be difficult to break the circuit that favours, for the large part, candidates who are middle class, socially and ethnically privileged. For example,

Research has consistently shown that ACT and SAT scores are strongly linked to family income, mother's education level and race. The College Board and ACT Inc., which owns the ACT, say their tests are predictive of college success, but (as with many education issues) there is also research showing otherwise.

The National Center for Fair and Open Testing, a nonprofit known as FairTest, just analyzed SAT scores for the high school class of 2019. It reported that the gaps between demographic groups grew larger from a year earlier, with the average scores of students from historically disenfranchised groups falling further behind students from more privileged families.

(Strauss, 2019)

This, in turn, is used to filter job applicants:

> The intuition underlying the relationship between elitism and inequality lies in the fact that duality in higher education permits [institutions] to separate the individuals according to their ability. Indeed, since universities are divided into elite and standard universities, we can get a signalling equilibrium so that high ability individuals are graduating from elite universities, and low ability individuals from standard ones. This separating equilibrium explains some of the difference in labor productivity leading to wage inequality.
>
> (Brezis, 2018, p. 202)

Metrics on a range of competences such as character, social interaction, the ability to adapt and curiosity would allow a greater variety of applicants to succeed in post-secondary school fields based on strengths in less socially influenced skills than logical thinking or literacy. Competence-based metrics such as those developed by the International School of Geneva's Universal Learning Programme (Hughes, 2020a, 2020b), the Organisation for Economic Co-operation and Development's learning compass (OECD, 2020) and the Mastery Transcript (Mastery Transcript Consortium, 2020) are examples of criteria that seek qualities other than those that are measured and enhanced by current administrative systems. The more diverse and widespread the criteria for selection, the less narrow becomes the range of students' choices.

Online learning

Although online learning has not yet fully replaced the complex sociology of education, it could very well do so in the near future. As the world of education experienced something of a near institutional collapse during the first wave of the COVID-19 pandemic, causing schools and universities to close, learning shifted online. This could very well be a trend in the future, constituting a "new normal". This will make it extremely difficult for a number of elite institutions to justify their exorbitant fees. Although, as this study has argued earlier, the top tier is likely to weather the storm and may gain even higher levels of confidence as crises ensue (because human beings tend to flock to assured values in times of instability), sub-top-tier elitist institutions will suffer and many will fold. This will result in fewer elitist educational institutions. On the one hand, this will mean an even greater concentration of power and privilege for fewer establishments, but on the other, it will mean that hundreds of elitist institutions and their students will have to reconvert to a new socio-educational structure.

Conclusion

Pro-elitist views on the tension between education and elitism might be that standards have suffered from years of poorly implemented egalitarian reform and that future solutions must include higher fees and more rigorous admissions restrictions. Anti-elitists will argue that for the access and opportunity that might achieve more social mobility, it is necessary to have greater state funding and the curbing of lavishly elitist educational institutions.

If the core aim of an education is to improve learners' skills, knowledge, attitudes and dispositions in order to improve their cultural, spiritual, physical and intellectual prospects, and if this is to be done for the benefit of as many students as possible, every effort should be made for every individual at every level. Education is not only what happens at school and university, however, it is what happens at home, among friends, through culture and the rich, mysterious tapestry of life in general. Perhaps the final word remains with the student, no matter how adverse or privileged the circumstances are. As the ancient Chinese philosopher Lao-Tzu said: "when the student is ready, the teacher appears".

For some, the gilded path opens up from birth, for others, there are barriers and mountains to climb. Given the disruption, complexity and ambiguity created by the phenomena of the 21st century, every student will need resolve, determination and fortitude. It will be the responsibility of educators and policymakers to ensure that the opportunities that they receive are as fair, balanced and humane as possible.

References

Brezis, E.S. (2018). Elitism in higher education and inequality: Why are the Nordic countries so special? *Intereconomics*, 53(4), 201–208.

Hirsch, E.D. (2006). *The Knowledge Deficit: Closing the Shocking Education Gap for American Children*. New York: Houghton Mifflin.

Hughes, C. (2020a). *The Universal Learning Programme: Transforming Education for Individual, Collective and Public Good*. Washington, DC: Center for Strategic Intelligence.

Hughes, C. (2020b). *The Universal Learning Programme: Educating Future-ready Citizens*. In-Progress Reflection no. 34. on Current Issues in Curriculum, Learning and Assessment. Paris: UNESCO-IBE.

Iyengar, R. (2020). Education as the path to a sustainable recovery from COVID-19. *Prospects*, 49, 77–80. https://doi.org/10.1007/s11125-020-09488-9.

Lampert, K. (2013). *Meritocratic Education and Social Worthlessness*. Basingstoke: Palgrave Macmillan.

Lewin, K.M. (2020). Contingent reflections on coronavirus and priorities for educational planning and development. *Prospects*. https://doi.org/10.1007/s11125-020-09480-3.

Littler, J. (2017). *Against Meritocracy: Culture, Power and Myths of Mobility*. Oxford: Routledge.

Mastery Transcript Consortium (2020). https://mastery.org/.

Organisation for Economic Co-operation and Development (OECD) (2020). *Learning Compass 2030*. www.oecd.org/education/2030-project/teaching-and-learning/learning/learning-compass-2030/.

Strauss, V. (2019). A record number of colleges drop SAT/ACT admissions requirement amid growing disenchantment with standardized tests. *Washington Post*. www.washingtonpost.com/education/2019/10/18/record-number-colleges-drop-satact-admissions-requirement-amid-growing-disenchantment-with-standardized-tests/.

Tooley, J. (2015). A lesson in bias on private schools: The "rigorous review" for DFID of private education in poor countries is anything but. *The Spectator*. www.spectator.co.uk/article/a-lesson-in-bias-on-private-schools.

Tooley, J. (2018). We're not talking Eton across Africa and Asia, cheap private schools are often better than state-run alternatives. *The Spectator*. www.spectator.co.uk/article/we-re-not-talking-eton.

Index

Page numbers followed by 'n' refer to notes.